The Double Eagle Guide to

CAMPING *in*

WESTERN

PARKS *and* FORESTS

VOLUME V
NORTHERN PLAINS

NORTH DAKOTA
SOUTH DAKOTA
NEBRASKA
KANSAS

A DOUBLE EAGLE GUIDE™

DISCOVERY PUBLISHING
BILLINGS, YELLOWSTONE COUNTY, MONTANA USA

The Double Eagle Guide to Camping in Western Parks and Forests
Volume V Northern Plains

PUBLISHED BY
Discovery Publishing
Editorial Offices
Post Office Box 50545
Billings, Montana 59105 USA

Discovery Publishing is an independent, private enterprise. The information contained herein should not be construed as reflecting the publisher's approval of the policies or practices of the public agencies listed.

Information in this book is subject to change without notice.

Cover Photos (clockwise from the top):
      Humboldt National Forest, Nevada
      Lake Owyhee State Park, Oregon
      Memphis Lake State Recreation Area, Nebraska
      Big Bend National Park, Texas

Frontispiece: Shawnee Lake County Park, Kansas

10 9 8 7 6 5 4 3 2 1

September 22, 1994   11:05 AM Mountain Time

Produced, printed, and bound in the United States of America.

ISBN 0-929760-25-5

TABLE OF CONTENTS

INTRODUCTION TO THE *Double Eagle*™ SERIES

Whether you're a veteran of many Western camps or are planning your first visit, this series is for you.

In the six volumes of *The Double Eagle Guide to Camping in Western Parks and Forests*, we've described most public campgrounds along or conveniently near the highways and byways of the 17 contiguous Western United States. Also included is basic information about jackcamping and backpacking on the millions of acres of undeveloped public lands in the West. Our goal is to provide you with accurate, detailed, and yet concise, *first-hand* information about literally thousands of camping areas you're most likely to want to know about.

The volumes which comprise the *Double Eagle*™ series constitute a significant departure from the sketchy, plain vanilla approach to campground information provided by other guidebooks. Here, for the first time, is the most *useful* information about the West's most *useable* public camping areas. We've included a broad assortment of campgrounds from which you can choose: From simple, free camps, to sites in deluxe, landscaped surroundings.

The name for this critically acclaimed series was suggested by the celebrated United States twenty-dollar gold piece--most often called the "*Double Eagle*"--the largest and finest denomination of coinage ever issued by the U.S. Mint. The *Double Eagle* has long been associated with the history of the West, as a symbol of traditional Western values, prosperity, and excellence.

So, too, the *Double Eagle*™ series seeks to provide you with information about what are perhaps the finest of all the West's treasures--its public recreational lands owned, operated, and overseen by the citizens of the Western United States.

We hope you'll enjoy reading these pages, and come to use the information in the volumes to enhance your own appreciation for the outstanding camping opportunities available in the West.

Live long and prosper.

Thomas and *Elizabeth Preston*
Publishers

CONVENTIONS USED IN THIS SERIES

The following conventions or standards are used throughout the *Double Eagle*™ series as a means of providing a sense of continuity between one park or forest and other public lands, and between one campground and the next.

State Identifier: The state name and number combination in the upper left corner of each campground description provides an easy means of cross-referencing the written information to the numbered locations on the maps in the Appendix.

Whenever possible, the campgrounds have been arranged in what we have determined to be a reasonable progression, and based on *typical travel patterns* within a region. Generally speaking, a north to south, west to east pattern has been followed. In certain cases, particularly those involving one-way-in, same-way-out roads, we have arranged the camps in the order in which they would be encountered on the way into the area, so the standard plan occasionally may be reversed.

Campground Name: The officially designated name for the campground is listed, followed by the park, forest, or other public recreation area in which it is located.

Location: This section allows you to obtain a quick approximation of a campground's location in relation to nearby major communities.

Access: Our *Accurate Access* system makes extensive use of highway mileposts in order to pinpoint the location of access roads, intersections, and other major terminal points. (Mileposts are about 98 percent reliable--but occasionally they are mowed by a snowplow or an errant motorist, and may be missing; or, worse yet, the mileposts were replaced in the wrong spot!) In some instances, locations are noted primarily utilizing mileages between two or more nearby locations--usually communities, but occasionally key junctions or prominent structures or landmarks.

Since everyone won't be approaching a campground from the same direction, we've provided access information from two, sometimes three, points. In all cases, we've chosen the access points for their likelihood of use. Distances from communities are listed from the approximate **midtown** point, unless otherwise specified. Mileages from Interstate highways and other freeway exits are usually given from the approximate center of the interchange. Mileages from access points have been rounded to the nearest mile, unless the exact mileage is critical. All instructions are given using the current official highway map available free from each state.

Directions are given using a combination of compass and hand headings, i.e., "turn north (left)" or "swing west (right)". This isn't a bonehead navigation system, by any means. When the sun is shining or you're in a region where moss grows on tree trunks, it's easy enough to figure out which way is north. But anyone can become temporarily disoriented on an overcast day or a moonless night while looking for an inconspicuous campground turnoff, or while being buzzed by heavy traffic at a key intersection, so we built this redundancy into the system.

Facilities: The items in this section have been listed in the approximate order in which a visitor might observe them during a typical swing through a campground. Following the total number of individual camp units, items pertinent to the campsites themselves are listed, then information related to 'community' facilities. It has been assumed that each campsite has a picnic table.

Site types: (1) Standard--no hookup; (2) Partial hookup--water, electricity; (3) Full hookup--water, electricity, sewer.

We have extensively employed the use of *general* and *relative* terms in describing the size, separation, and levelness of the campsites ("medium to large", "fairly well separated", "basically level", etc.). Please note that "separation" is a measure of relative privacy and is a composite of both natural visual screens and spacing between campsites. The information is presented as an *estimate* by highly experienced observers. Please allow for variations in perception between yourself and the reporters.

Parking Pads: (1) Straight-ins, (sometimes called "back-ins")-- the most common type, are just that--straight strips angled off the driveway; (2) Pull-throughs--usually the most convenient type for large rv's, they provide an in-one-end-and-out-the-other parking space; pull-throughs may be either arc-shaped and separated from the main driveway by some sort of barrier or 'island' (usually vegetation), or arranged in parallel rows; (3) Pull-offs--essentially just wide spots adjacent to the driveway. Pad lengths have been categorized as: (1) Short-- a single, large vehicle up to about the size of a standard pickup truck; (2) Medium--a single vehicle or combination up to the length of a pickup towing a single-axle trailer; Long--a single vehicle or combo as long as a crew cab pickup towing a double-axle trailer. Normally, any overhang out the back of the pad has been ignored in the estimate, so it might be possible to slip a crew cab pickup hauling a fifth-wheel trailer in tandem with a ski boat into some pads, but we'll leave that to your discretion.

Fire appliances have been categorized in three basic forms: (1) Fireplaces--angular, steel or concrete, ground-level; (2) Fire rings--circular, steel or concrete, ground-level or below ground-level; (3) Barbecue grills--angular steel box, supported by a steel post about 36 inches high. (The trend is toward installing steel fire rings, since they're durable, relatively inexpensive--50 to 80 dollars apiece--and easy to install and maintain. Barbecue grills are often used in areas where ground fires are a problem, as when charcoal-only fires are permitted.)

Toilet facilities have been listed thusly: (1) Restrooms--"modern", i.e., flush toilets and usually a wash basin; (2) Vault facilities--"simple", i.e., outhouses, pit toilets, call them what you like, (a rose by any other name.....).

Campers' supply points have been described at five levels: (1) Camper Supplies--buns, beans and beverages; (2) Gas and Groceries--a 'convenience' stop; (3) Limited--at least one store which approximates a small supermarket, more than one fuel station, a general merchandise store, hardware store, and other basic services; (4) Adequate--more than one supermarket, (including something that resembles an IGA or a Safeway), a choice of fuel brands, and several general and specialty stores and services; (5) Complete--they have a major discount store.

Campground managers, attendants and hosts are not specifically listed since their presence can be expected during the regular camping season in more than 85 percent of the campgrounds listed in this volume.

Activities & Attractions: As is mentioned a number of times throughout this series, the local scenery may be the principal attraction of the campground (and, indeed, may be the *only* one you'll need). Other nearby attractions/activities have been listed if they are low-cost or free, and are available to the general public. An important item: *Swimming and boating areas usually do not have lifeguards.*

Natural Features: Here we've drawn a word picture of the natural environment in and around each campground. Please remember that seasonal, even daily, conditions will affect the appearance of the area. A normally "sparkling stream" can be a muddy torrent for a couple of weeks in late spring; a "deep blue lake" might be a nearly empty hole in a drought year; "lush vegetation" may have lost all its greenery by the time you arrive in late October. Elevations above 500' are rounded to the nearest 100'; lower elevations are rounded to the nearest 50'. (Some elevations are estimated, but no one should develop a nosebleed or a headache because of a 100' difference in altitude.)

Season, Fees & Phone: Seasons listed are approximate, since weather conditions, particularly in mountainous/hilly regions, may require adjustments in opening/closing dates. Campground gates are usually unlocked from 6:00 a.m. to 10:00 p.m. Fee information listed here was obtained directly from the responsible agencies just a few hours before press time. Fees should be considered **minimum** fees *per camping vehicle*, since they are always subject to adjustment by agencies or legislatures. Discounts and special passes are usually available for seniors and disabled persons. The listed telephone number can be called to obtain information about current conditions in or near that campground.

Camp Notes: Consider this section to be somewhat more subjective in nature than the others. In order to provide our readers with a well-rounded report, we have listed personal comments related to our field observations. (Our enthusiasm for the West is, at times, unabashedly proclaimed. So if the prose sometimes sounds like a tourist promotion booklet, please bear with us--there's a lot to be enthusiastic about!)

Editorial remarks (Ed.) occasionally have been included.

A Word About Style...

Throughout the *Double Eagle*™ series, we've utilized a free-form writing concept which we call "Notation Format". Complete sentences, phrases, and single words have been incorporated into the camp descriptions as appropriate under the circumstances. We've adopted this style in order to provide our readers with detailed information about each item, while maintaining conciseness, clarity, and conversationality.

A Word About Print...

Another departure from the norm is our use of print sizes which are 20 percent larger (or more) than ordinary guides. (We also use narrower margins for less paper waste.) It's one thing to read a guidebook in the convenience and comfort of your well-lit living room. It's another matter to peruse the pages while you're bounding and bouncing along in your car or camper as the sun is setting; or by a flickering flashlight inside a breeze-buffeted dome tent. We hope *this* works for you, too.

A Word About Maps...

After extensive tests of the state maps by seasoned campers, both at home and in the field, we decided to localize all of the maps in one place in the book. Campers felt that, since pages must be flipped regardless of where the maps are located, it would be more desirable to have them all in one place. We're confident that you'll also find this to be a convenient feature.

A Word About 'Regs'...

Although this series is about public campgrounds, you'll find comparatively few mentions of rules, regulations, policies, ordinances, statutes, decrees or dictates. Our editorial policy is this: (1) It's the duty of a citizen or a visitor to know his legal responsibilities (and, of course, his corresponding *rights*); (2) Virtually every campground has the appropriate regulations publicly posted for all to study; and (3) If you're reading this *Double Eagle*™ Guide, chances are you're in the upper ten percent of the conscientious citizens of the United States or some other civilized country and you probably don't need to be constantly reminded of these matters.

And a Final Word...

We've tried very, very hard to provide you with accurate information about the West's great camping opportunities But occasionally, things aren't as they're supposed to be .....

If a campground's access, facilities or fees have been recently changed, please let us know. We'll try to pass along the news to other campers.

If the persons in the next campsite keep their generator poppety-popping past midnight so they can cook a turkey in the microwave, blame the bozos, not the book.

If the beasties are a bit bothersome in that beautiful spot down by the bog, note the day's delights and not the difficulties.

Thank you for buying our book. We hope that you'll have many terrific camping trips!

North Dakota

Public Campgrounds

The North Dakota map is located in the Appendix on page 151.

Northwest Plains

Please refer to the North Dakota map in the Appendix

North Dakota 1

LEWIS AND CLARK
Lewis and Clark State Park

Location: Northwest North Dakota east of Williston.

Access: From North Dakota State Highway 1804 at milepost 300 +.9 (17 miles east of Williston, 53 miles west of New Town), turn south onto Williams County Road 15; proceed 3 miles to the park entrance station; turn east (left) into the entrance, then almost immediately turn north (left); continue north then east for 1 mile to the campground. (Note: if westbound on U.S. Highway 2 from Minot, easiest access is from U.S. 2 milepost 63 +.2 south of Tioga; turn south onto County Road 21 (paved) for 10.5 miles to North Dakota Highway 1804; travel west on ND 1804 for 18 miles to County Road 15; continue as above.)

Facilities: 70 campsites, approximately half of them with electrical hookups, plus a tent camping only section; sites are generally small, fairly level and closely spaced; parking pads are small, gravel pull-offs/straight-ins; adequate space for a large tent in most sites; fire rings in some units; b-y-o firewood; water at several faucets; restrooms with showers; holding tank disposal station; paved driveways; complete supplies and services are available in Williston.

Activities & Attractions: Fishing (especially for walleye and northern pike); boating; marina; swimming beach; amphitheater; Prairie Nature Trail; hiking trails; cross-country ski trails.

Natural Features: Located on the gently sloping north shore of Lake Sakakawea on the Missouri River; campground vegetation consists of light to medium-dense hardwoods and acres of grass; grassy hills and high, rugged multi-colored bluffs border the lake; elevation 1900'.

Season, Fees & Phone: Open all year, with limited services September to May; please see Appendix for standard North Dakota state park fees and reservation information; 14-day limit; park office (701) 859-3071.

Camp Notes: This campground's designers remembered that "tent campers are people too". The lakeside, tents-only section is probably the best spot in the place. Great views.

North Dakota 2

SMISHEK LAKE
Game and Fish Department Recreation Area

Location: Northwest North Dakota northeast of Williston.

Access: From North Dakota State Highway 50 at milepost 66 +.3 (1.5 miles west of the community of Powers Lake, 5 miles west of the junction of State Highways 50 & 40 at Battleview), turn north onto Burke County Road 7 (paved) and proceed 2.6 miles; turn east (right) for 0.1 mile to the recreation area and the campground.

Facilities: Approximately 12 campsites, including a few with electrical hookups; sites are basically small, level and closely spaced; parking surfaces are grass, medium-length straight-ins/pull-offs; adequate space for medium to large tents; no fire facilities; water at a well house; vault facilities; gravel driveways; very limited supplies and services are available in Powers Lake.

Activities & Attractions: Fishing; limited boating; small boat launch; small playground.

Natural Features: Located on a short, grassy bluff above the west shore of Smishek Lake; sites receive limited shelter from a row of small hardwoods along the west edge of the line of campsites; surrounded by prairie and cropland; typically windy; elevation 2000'.

Season, Fees & Phone: Available all year, with limited services September to May; no fee (subject to change); donations are appreciated; 14-day limit; phone c/o North Dakota Game and Fish Department, Bismarck, (701) 222-6300.

Camp Notes: Considering the cost of admission, this roughcut spot might be worthy of an overnighter or a weekend. The fishing is good much of the time. On most days you can get a line from the west shore out to the middle of the lake without a boat, (or across to the east shore on a *very* windy day). Other public camps in this general area are at the city parks in Tioga and Stanley. Each has roughly a dozen sites, disposal facilities and showers. Tioga's camp costs a few bucks and seems to cater to semi-permanent campers; Stanley's requests donations and has a 4-day limit.

North Dakota 3

OLD SETTLERS
Ward County Park

Location: North-central North Dakota west of Minot.

Access: From U.S. Highways 2 & 52 at milepost 137 +.7 (1 mile west of Burlington, 9 miles west of Minot, 12 miles east of Berthold), turn north onto a frontage road which almost immediately curves east, and proceed 0.3 mile; turn north (left) onto Park Road for 0.3 mile (continuing north to a point just past the cemetery); turn left (remaining on the paved surface) for 0.2 mile, then turn left again, into the campground.

Facilities: 28 campsites, including 12 electrical hookup units; sites are basically level, vary from small to large, with good to very good separation; parking pads are gravel/grass straight-ins or pull-offs; adequate space for small to medium-sized tents; (some sites lack tables;) fireplaces or barbecue grills in some units; a very limited amount of firewood may be available for gathering, b-y-o is recommended; water at central faucets; restrooms; gravel driveways; gas and groceries in Burlington; complete supplies and services are available in Minot.

Activities & Attractions: Designated beach area (wading?); softball field; amphitheater; small playground; suspension foot bridge across the river.

Natural Features: Located in a valley woodland along a small impoundment on the Mouse River; moderately dense hardwoods provide ample shelter/shade for all sites; the area is flanked by grassy hills; elevation 1800'.

Season, Fees & Phone: May to November; no fee for a standard site (subject to change), $4.00 for an electrical hookup site; 14-day limit; (no phone).

Camp Notes: This is one of those venerable, unpretentious, local parks which you'll occasionally encounter on the prairie. As the name implies, it serves as a natural tribute to the region's pioneers (who certainly would have appreciated having this much greenery when they first settled the Great Plains).

NORTH DAKOTA

Badlands

Please refer to the North Dakota map in the Appendix

North Dakota 4

BUFFALO GAP
Little Missouri National Grassland

Location: Western North Dakota west of Dickinson.

Access: From Interstate 94 at Exit 4 (near milepost 18, 16 miles east of Beach, 23 miles west of Belfield), turn north, proceed 0.1 mile, then turn west onto a paved campground access road; proceed 0.5 mile to the campground.

Facilities: 37 campsites; sites are small to medium-sized, with nominal to fairly good separation; parking pads are paved, short to medium-length straight-ins, some are extra-wide; a little additional leveling may be required; generally small tent areas; barbecue grills; b-y-o firewood; water at several faucets; restrooms; paved driveways; holding tank disposal station; gas and groceries in Medora, 6 miles east and 2 miles south; limited supplies and services are available in Beach and Belfield.

Activities & Attractions: Self-guiding nature trail; Theodore Roosevelt National Park (South Unit) is a half-dozen miles east.

Natural Features: Located in a small basin amid tallgrass slopes and hills; campground vegetation consists of stands of large hardwoods on a grassy surface; some sites are lightly sheltered/shaded, most are quite open; elevation 2700'.

Season, Fees & Phone: May to September; $6.00; 14 day limit; Little Missouri National Grassland Headquarters (701) 225-5151.

Camp Notes: Buffalo Gap is in a classic, northern rangeland setting, and glimpses of badlands are available within a short walk or drive. You won't find a campground in North Dakota that's handier to the Interstate than this one. But with that advantage comes the turn of the coin. In this case the freeway traffic, at a distance of only a couple-hundred yards, rummmmmbles and swooooooshes by above some campsites. (Remember, though, that the campground was here first.) Arriving by four o'clock or so in midsummer will give you a better choice of sites a tad farther from I-94. Other than that, it's a good stop.

North Dakota 5

LITTLE MISSOURI
Little Missouri State Park

Location: Western North Dakota north of Dickinson.

Access: From North Dakota State Highway 22 at a point 17 miles north of Kildeer and 3 miles south of the Little Missouri River Bridge, travel east on a county road for 6 miles to the park.

Facilities: Approximately 25 primitive campsites; (several sites with electrical hookups are also available); drinking water; vault facilities; small to medium-sized parking areas.

Activities & Attractions: Hiking and equestrian trails; horse-handling facilities; horse rentals (concession); day use area with shelters.

Natural Features: Located on rolling plains along the south bank of the Little Missouri River; grassy bluffs and colorful badlands border the river; elevation 2000'.

Season & Fees: Available all year, subject to weather and road conditions, with limited services October to May; please see Appendix for standard North Dakota state park fees; 14-day limit; phone c/o Lake Sakakawea State Park (701) 487-3315.

Park Notes: With more than 75 miles of trails crisscrossing the park's 5800 acres, you could walk for many hours without passing another traveler. Plenty of elbow room here.

North Dakota 6

SQUAW CREEK
Theodore Roosevelt National Park

Location: Western North Dakota southeast of Williston.

Access: From U.S. Highway 85 at milepost 127 +.2 (0.8 mile north of the Long-X Bridge over the Little Missouri River, 15 miles south of Watford City, 53 miles north of Belfield), turn west onto the park access road and proceed 0.3 mile to the entrance station; travel 4.7 miles beyond the entrance to the campground access road; turn southwest and continue for 0.25 mile to the campground entrance station; the campground is 0.4 mile farther west (continue past the day use area on the right).

Facilities: 50 campsites; sites are level, nicely sized, with fair to excellent separation; parking pads are paved, medium straight-ins or long pull-throughs; medium to large tent areas; barbecue grills; b-y-o firewood (firewood-gathering prohibited); water at central faucets; restrooms; holding tank disposal station; paved driveways; limited supplies and services are available in Watford City.

Activities & Attractions: Visitor center; self-guiding nature trails; several backcountry trails; 15-mile scenic drive, with interpretive signs; amphitheater.

Natural Features: Located on a flat in a large grove of hardwoods near the confluence of Squaw Creek and the Little Missouri River on the river's north bank; vegetation consists primarily of light to moderately dense hardwoods and lots of grass; rugged hills and bluffs of the badlands lie in the surrounding area; elevation 2500'.

Season, Fees & Phone: May to October; $7.00, plus park entrance fee; 14 day limit; Theodore Roosevelt National Park Headquarters, Medora, (701) 623-4466.

Camp Notes: Some of the sites here are really super--larger and/or more private than you'll find in just about any other national park campground. Chances are, you'll agree that it's worth traveling an hour up the CanAm Highway from the Interstate to see this section of the park.

COTTONWOOD
Theodore Roosevelt National Park

Location: Western North Dakota west of Dickinson.

Access: From Interstate 94 at Exit 6 for Medora if eastbound (at milepost 24, 22 miles east of Beach, 17 miles west of Belfield), turn southeast onto a paved local road and proceed 1.6 miles into Medora; turn east (left) into the national park entrance and proceed 5.7 miles in a curving, generally northerly direction (across to the north side of the Interstate); turn west (left) into the campground. **Alternate Access:** From I-94 at Exit 7, if westbound, travel southwest for 2.6 miles to the north edge of Medora, then turn right into the park entrance and continue as above.

Facilities: 78 campsites, including a dozen walk-ins at the south end, in 2 loops; most sites are relatively spacious, level, with fair to very good visual separation; parking pads are gravel, short straight-ins or long pull-throughs; adequate space for a medium to large tent; barbecue grills; b-y-o firewood (firewood-gathering is prohibited); water at several faucets; restrooms; paved driveways; gas and groceries in Medora; limited supplies and services are available in Beach and Belfield.

Activities & Attractions: Several very impressive overlook points along a 36-mile loop drive; self-guiding nature trails; backcountry trails; buffalo can be viewed roaming freely within the park; visitor center near the park entrance.

Natural Features: Located in a grove of large cottonwoods mixed with junipers along the east bank of the Little Missouri River in Peaceful Valley; multi-layered, multi-colored high bluffs rise from the opposite riverbank; elevation 2600'.

Season, Fees & Phone: Open all year, with limited services October to May; $6.00, plus park entrance fee; 14 day limit; Theodore Roosevelt National Park Headquarters, Medora, (701) 623-4466.

Camp Notes: If you can secure one of the units with a pull-through parking pad, you'll probably have a really dandy campsite from a size and privacy standpoint.

SULLY CREEK
Sully Creek State Primitive Park

Location: Western North Dakota west of Dickinson.

Access: From Interstate 94 Exit 6 for Medora if eastbound (at milepost 24, 22 miles east of Beach, 17 miles west of Belfield), turn southeast onto a paved local road; proceed 1.7 miles to midtown Medora; turn southwest onto East River Road (paved for 0.4 mile, then gravel) and proceed 1.4 miles; turn west/southwest (right) onto a second gravel road; after 0.1 mile, take the right fork for 0.4 mile to the campground. **Alternate Access:** From I-94 at Exit 7, if westbound, travel southwest for 2.4 miles to Medora, and continue as above.

Facilities: 20 campsites, including several walk-ins and tent camping only units; sites are generally large, level, with fair to very good separation; parking pads are mostly medium to long, extra-wide, gravel straight-ins; adequate space for a large tent in most sites; fire rings; a very limited amount of firewood may be available for gathering, b-y-o is recommended; central water; vault facilities; gravel driveways; gas and groceries in Medora; limited supplies and services are available in Beach and Belfield.

Activities & Attractions: Equestrian facilities; horse and foot trails connect to those in nearby Theodore Roosevelt National Park.

Natural Features: Located on a large flat at the confluence of Sully's Creek and the Little Missouri River in the North Dakota Badlands; campground vegetation consists of crunchgrass, sage and several large hardwoods; elevation 2600'.

Season, Fees & Phone: Open all year, subject to weather, with limited services September to May; please see Appendix for standard North Dakota state park fees; park manager (seasonally) (701) 663-9571 or c/o Lewis and Clark State Park (701) 859-3071.

Camp Notes: This simple spot, one of the few which accommodates horses, would serve as an OK alternative to the camp in the national park, which is often filled during midsummer. B-Y-O drinking water, just in case.

BUTTE VIEW
Butte View State Campground

Location: Southeast corner of North Dakota at Bowman.

Access: From U.S. Highway 12 at milepost 35 (on the far east edge of Bowman, 1.1 miles east of the junction of U.S. 12 & 85), turn north into the campground. (Note: The traffic on this stretch of highway usually flows along at a good clip, so be watchful on the approach; look for a rail 'ranch type' gateway across the campground entrance.)

Facilities: 50 campsites with electrical hookups; sites are medium-sized, with near-zero separation; parking pads are long, gravel pull-throughs or medium straight-ins; a little additional leveling may be needed in a few units; adequate space for a large tent in most sites; fire rings or fireplaces; b-y-o firewood; water at central faucets; restrooms with showers; holding tank disposal station; gravel driveways; adequate supplies and services are available in Bowman.

Activities & Attractions: Highwayside convenience; highest point in North Dakota, White Butte (elevation 3506'), 20 miles north.

Natural Features: Located on a large plain; campground vegetation consists of a few small hardwoods and evergreens, plus rows of recently planted hardwood and pine seedlings, with sparse crunchgrass for ground cover; majority of the campsites lack shelter/shade; elevation 3000'.

Season, Fees & Phone: May to September; please see Appendix for standard North Dakota state park fees; 14 day limit; campground office, seasonally, (701) 523-9392; or c/o Lewis and Clark State Park (701) 859-3071.

Camp Notes: True to the promise of its name, there are indeed views of a pair of buttes to the north, and of a high, solitary butte to the south. Otherwise, it's the proverbial "miles and miles of miles and miles". But you're probably planning on traveling through this remote corner of the state to experience the region's classic, wide-open spaces. (Or is it just because this is the shortest route home?   Ed.)

MIRROR LAKE
Hettinger City Park

Location: Southwest North Dakota in Hettinger.

Access: From North Dakota State Highway 8 at a point 0.1 mile south of the junction of State Highway 8 & U.S. Highway 12 at the west edge of Hettinger, turn east onto a paved street and proceed 0.1 mile; turn south (right) into the park; the campground is situated on the west edge of the day use area, (south of the grain elevator).

Facilities: Approximately 15 campsites, including 7 with partial hookups; sites are small, level, with nil separation; parking surfaces are gravel, short straight-ins or driveway-side pull-offs; large, grassy tent area; a few barbecue grills; b-y-o firewood; water at several sites and at central faucets; restrooms with showers; holding tank disposal station; gravel driveways; adequate supplies and services are available in Hettinger.

Activities & Attractions: Day use area with picnic facilities, playground and fitness court; fishing; limited boating (electric, sail, people-power); swimming; baseball field.

Natural Features: Located on the north shore of 72-acre Mirror Lake; most sites have very limited shade; low, grassy hills and buttes dot the surrounding countryside; elevation 2700'.

Season, Fees & Phone: Available all year, subject to weather conditions, with limited services October to May; $4.00 for a tent, $7.00 minimum for a camper; 14 day limit; (no phone).

Camp Notes: This very small camping area has been included because (a) the overall recreational possibilities are quite good; and (b) the local scenery is certainly pleasant; and (c) quite a few campers travel U.S. 12, and the only other public campground in the neighborhood is 40 miles west of here. If you enjoy baseball, you can cheer the local teams from inside your tent or from under your awning. (Be forewarned that the lighted field may lengthen your day; and a strapping young North Dakotan might pop a homer into your potato salad.)

PATTERSON LAKE
City of Dickinson Recreation Area

Location: Western North Dakota west of Dickinson.

Access: From Interstate 94 at Exit 12 for West Dickinson (near milepost 59) turn south onto Business Route 94 and proceed south 1 mile; turn sharply west (right) onto a paved local road and continue for 1.6 miles; turn south (left) (at the west edge of the drive-in theater) and proceed on a paved road for 0.6 mile; turn west (right) into the hookup area; or turn east and proceed 0.3 mile to the standard ("tent") camping area.

Facilities: 20 partial hookup campsites, plus 40 sites in the standard/tent zone; sites are small, level and closely spaced in the hookup section; parking pads for hookups are medium-length, wide gravel straight-ins; grass surface for vehicles and tents in the standard area; adequate space for a large tent; no campsite fire facilities (barbecue grills in the day use areas); water at sites and at central faucets; restrooms with showers; holding tank disposal station; paved driveway in hookup area, gravel in standard area; complete supplies and services are available in Dickinson.

Activities & Attractions: Swimming beach; basketball court; playgrounds; fishing; boating.

Natural Features: Located on the north shore of Patterson Lake; campground vegetation consists of sparse grass, and rows of hardwoods which provide some wind shelter but limited shade for most sites; gently rolling prairie and farmland border the area; elevation 2600'.

Season, Fees & Phone: April to September; $5.00 for a standard site, $8.00 for a partial hookup unit; 7-day limit for standard sites, 3-day limit for hookup sites; (no phone).

Camp Notes: Most sites currently enjoy a lake view. This recreation complex has been undergoing extensive improvements in the "natural features" area. Many seedlings, including both hardwoods and pines, have recently been planted.

GLEN ULLIN MEMORIAL
Glen Ullin City Park

Location: Western North Dakota between Dickinson and Mandan.

Access: From North Dakota State Highway 49 at milepost 67 +.7 (at a sharp turn in the highway, on the *far* southwest corner of Glen Ullin, 32 miles north of Elgin), turn west onto a paved road for 0.1 mile, then turn south (left) into the park. (Note: It's possible to make your way to the park from Interstate 94 exits 20 or 21, then via back roads to Glen Ullin; but the sure-fire route is from Exit 22, then south and west on North Dakota State Highway 49 for 6.2 miles to the SW outskirts of town.)

Facilities: Approximately 15 campsites, including several with electrical hookups; sites are small, level and closely spaced; parking pads are gravel/grass, short to medium-length straight-ins, plus room for a few pull-along vehicles; adequate space for a medium to large tent in the sites on the south side of the camping area; small, central ramada (sun shelter); a few barbecue grills; b-y-o firewood; water at central faucets; vault facilities; holding tank disposal station; gravel driveways; limited supplies and services are available in Glen Ullin.

Activities & Attractions: Western plains environment.

Natural Features: Located on a grassy flat bordered by a small grove of hardwoods; some shelter from the wind, minimal to limited shade for campsites; hills, bluffs and buttes lie in the surrounding area; elevation 2100'.

Season, Fees & Phone: Available all year, subject to weather conditions; $3.00 for a tent, $6.00 for a trailer; park manager (701) 348-3704.

Camp Notes: Undoubtedly its proximity to the Interstate contributes to the popularity of this simple park. It also frequently serves as a rendezvous point for small groups of rv's. If you arrive in the right year of the crop rotation cycle, there will be acres of sunflowers surrounding your campsite. Good western scenery in all directions.

RIMROCK
Lake Tschida/BuRec & Grant County Recreation Area

Location: Southwest North Dakota southwest of Mandan.

Access: From North Dakota State Highway 49 at milepost 50 + .4 at the south end of Heart Butte Dam (14 miles north of Elgin, 18 miles south of Glen Ullin), turn northwest onto a gravel access road and proceed 0.2 mile to the second driveway; turn north and continue for 0.2 mile down to the campground.

Facilities: 25 camp/picnic sites; sites are small, somewhat sloped, with minimal to nominal separation; parking surfaces are grass/gravel, mostly short straight-ins/pull-offs; (larger vehicles might be accommodated in a few sites); small tent areas; fire rings; b-y-o firewood; water at a hand pump; vault facilities; holding tank disposal station at the south end of the dam; gravel driveways; limited supplies and services are available in Elgin and Glen Ullin.

Activities & Attractions: Fishing (reportedly very good for perch, walleye, northern pike, plus some smallmouth bass); boating; sailing; boat launch; designated swimming beach.

Natural Features: Located on a grassy slope among rows of hardwoods on the southeast corner of Lake Tschida (Heart Butte Reservoir); sites are well-sheltered/shaded by tall hardwoods, plus scattered pines; bordered by tree-and-grass-covered hills; typically breezy; elevation 2400'.

Season, Fees & Phone: Open all year, subject to weather and road conditions; no fee (subject to change); 14-day limit; (no phone).

Camp Notes: Simple as it is, Rimrock still is probably the best all-around campground in the area. Another camp is located on the river below the dam. (See info for Downstream). The third area--North & South Crappie Creek--is located on the northeast shore, 2 miles west of Highway 49 near milepost 55. Crappie Creek has *very* basic camping at sites scattered along both sides of a cove.

DOWNSTREAM
Lake Tschida/BuRec & Grant County Recreation Area

Location: Southwest North Dakota southwest of Mandan.

Access: From North Dakota State Highway 49 at milepost 51 + .2 at the north end of Heart Butte Dam (15 miles north of Elgin, 17 miles south of Glen Ullin), turn east onto a gravel access road and proceed 0.4 mile down to the campground.

Facilities: 12 camp/picnic sites; sites are small to large, situated in clusters of several sites, with good separation between clusters; parking surfaces are grass, tolerably level, and as large as may be required; ample space for a very large tent in each cluster; sun shelters in most clusters; fire rings; b-y-o firewood; water at a hand pump; vault facilities; holding tank disposal station at the south end of the dam; gravel driveways; limited supplies and services are available in Elgin and Glen Ullin.

Activities & Attractions: Fishing and boating on the lake.

Natural Features: Located in a shallow canyon (or a wide coulee or a narrow valley, depending upon choice of terminology) on the north bank of the Heart River, below Heart Butte Dam; Lake Tschida (also called Heart Butte Reservoir) rises behind the dam; campground vegetation consists of sections of grass bordered by hardwoods, and a few pines and junipers; bordered by rangegrass hills, and rocky bluffs; elevation 2400'.

Season, Fees & Phone: Open all year, subject to weather and road conditions; no fee (subject to change); (no phone).

Camp Notes: The campground layout is a little different from most camps. The sites are situated in good-sized "pockets" on tree-lined, grassy flats on a short shelf just above the river. Interesting. The privacy factor is good, too. The facilities have become, shall we say, "well-worn".

FORT STEVENSON
Fort Stevenson State Park

Location: Central North Dakota between Bismarck and Minot.

Access: From the junction of U.S. Highway 83 & North Dakota State Highway 37 (2.6 miles north of the Lake Sakakawea/Lake Audubon causeway, 12 miles south of Max) turn west onto ND 37 and travel 6 miles to Garrison; turn south onto Lakeview Road (County Road 15) and proceed 3.5 miles to the park entrance; continue for 0.2 mile, then turn west (right), into the campground.

Facilities: 109 campsites, nearly all with electrical hookups, plus a tent camping area; sites are level, medium-sized, with nominal separation; parking pads are medium-length, gravel straight-ins; adequate space for a medium to large tent in most units; fire rings; firewood is usually for sale, or b-y-o; water at faucets throughout; restrooms with showers, holding tank disposal station; gravel driveways; limited supplies and services are available in Garrison.

Activities & Attractions: Fishing; Governor's Cup Walleye Derby, annually in July; boating; boat launches and marina; fitness, nature, and hiking trails; swimming beach; playground; amphitheater.

Natural Features: Located on a plain on the north shore of Lake Sakakawea; campground vegetation consists of expanses of mown grass, and rows of hardwoods which provide minimal to medium shelter/shade for most sites; elevation 1900'.

Season, Fees & Phone: Open all year, with limited services October to May; please see Appendix for standard North Dakota state park fees and reservation information; 14-day limit; park office (701) 337-5576.

Camp Notes: Lake Sakakawea deserves at least one visit in a lifetime of camping (preferably with a boat). This largest of all man-made lakes in the U.S. is not unlike Lakes Mead and Powell of the southwest--but there's much more elbow room here. (Well, except when the east end of the lake is paved with boats during the fall salmon run.)

LAKE SAKAKAWEA
Lake Sakakawea State Park

Location: Central North Dakota between Bismarck and Minot.

Access: From the junction of U.S. Highway 83 & North Dakota State Highway 200 (4 miles north of Underwood, 2 miles south of Coleharbor) turn west onto ND 200 and travel 13 miles (past Riverdale and across Garrison Dam) to the east edge of Pick City; turn north onto the park access road and proceed 1.2 miles to a point just beyond the entrance station; continue ahead to a small standard ('primitive') area; or turn right and proceed 0.4 miles to the hookup areas, or 0.8 mile to the large standard area. (Note: From western North Dakota via Interstate 94, a quicker route would be I-94 Exit 22, then north through Beaulah to ND 200; then east and north to Pick City.)

Facilities: 150 electrical hookup campsites, plus about 60 standard sites, in 5 areas; sites are small+, essentially level, with nominal separation; parking pads are medium-length, gravel straight-ins; large, grassy tent areas; fire rings; b-y-o firewood; water at several faucets; restrooms with showers; holding tank disposal station; paved driveways; gas and camper supplies in Pick City and Riverdale.

Activities & Attractions: Hiking, nature, and fitness trails; swimming beach; some of the best fishing in the West; boating; boat launches; marina; amphitheater; playground.

Natural Features: Located on the south shore of Lake Sakakawea; vegetation consists of acres of grass and rows of light to medium-dense hardwoods on gently rolling terrain; minimal to light shade for most sites; elevation 1900'.

Season, Fees & Phone: Open all year, with limited services October to May; please see Appendix for standard North Dakota state park fees and reservation information; 14-day limit; park office (701) 487-3315.

Camp Notes: Fishing may very well be the #1 pastime here, but there are still plenty of other things to do if you're not inclined to angle. Room to roam.

DOWNSTREAM
Lake Sakakawea/Corps of Engineers Park

Location: Central North Dakota between Bismarck and Minot.

Access: From the junction of U.S. Highway 83 & North Dakota State Highway 200 (4 miles north of Underwood, 2 miles south of Coleharbor) turn west onto ND 200 and travel 11 miles (past Riverdale) to milepost 178 on the east end of Garrison Dam; turn southwest (i.e., left) onto a paved access road which traverses the south side of the dam and proceed 1.1 miles down to the base of the dam; turn sharply east (left), proceed 0.3 mile, then turn south (right) and continue for 1.25 miles to the campground.

Facilities: 101 campsites with electrical hookups, in 3 loops; sites are medium-sized, level, with nominal separation; parking pads are medium to long, paved straight-ins; adequate space for a large tent in most sites; fire rings; some firewood may be available for gathering in the vicinity; water at several faucets; restrooms with showers; holding tank disposal station; paved driveways; gas and camper supplies in Pick City and Riverdale, each within 2 miles.

Activities & Attractions: Riverbottom Trail; summer evening programs; playgrounds; excellent river and lake fishing; boat launch for river access; tours of the powerhouse (or "A Half-Billion Watts To Brighten Your Stay". Ed.)

Natural Features: Located on a flat near the east bank of the Missouri River below Lake Sakakawea; campground vegetation consists of short grass, and large hardwoods which provide light to moderate shelter/shade; elevation 1700'.

Season, Fees & Phone: Available all year, with limited services and no fee mid-October to mid-May; $10.00; 14 day limit; Lake Sakakawea CoE Project Office (701) 654-7411.

Camp Notes: There are as many "Downstream" campgrounds on the plains as there are streams called "Rock Creek" in the mountains. This one, typical of most "Downstream" Corps camps, has very good facilities.

North Dakota 18

CROSS RANCH
Cross Ranch State Park

Location: Central North Dakota northwest of Bismarck.

Access: From North Dakota State Highway 200 Alternate in Hensler, travel southeast on a county road for 9 miles to the park.

Facilities: Approximately 75 primitive campsites; small parking areas; drinking water; restrooms.

Activities & Attractions: Visitor center; hiking trails; cross-country ski trails; naturalist-guided nature programs in summer; fishing; boat ramp; Centennial Buffalo Herd.

Natural Features: Located on rolling prairie along the west bank and bluffs above the Missouri River; vegetation consists of unsheltered grassland and stands of large hardwoods along the river and coulees; elevation 1800'.

Season, Fees & Phone: Open all year, with limited services October to May; please see Appendix for standard North Dakota state park fees and reservation information; park office (701) 794-3731.

Park Notes: The park is situated along seven miles of the last free-flowing segment of the Missouri River, and the camping area is on a small island on the great stream. Cross Ranch encompasses one of the most expansive tracts of virgin riverbottom and prairie in North Dakota.

North Dakota 19

FORT ABRAHAM LINCOLN
Fort Abraham Lincoln State Park

Location: Central North Dakota south of Mandan.

Access: From the intersection of Main Street (Business Route I-94) & 6th Avenue SE (North Dakota State Highway 1806) in midtown Mandan, turn south onto ND 1806 and travel 5.6 miles (0.35 mile past the park visitor center) to milepost 64 +.95; turn east (left), then swing north and proceed 0.2 mile to the campground. (Note: *Probably* the easiest access from Interstate 94 is Exit 33 at the *east* end of Mandan, then west for 0.7 mile onto Main Street; avoid the nooner and afternoon rush hours, and watch for the signs. Good Luck!)

Facilities: 90 campsites, including about half with electrical hookups; sites are medium-sized, level, with nominal to fair separation; parking pads are long, gravel pull-throughs; large tent areas; fire rings; firewood is usually for sale, or b-y-o; water at several faucets; restrooms with showers; holding tank disposal station; paved driveways; complete supplies and services are available in Mandan/Bismarck.

Activities & Attractions: Restored and reconstructed military post and Indian village; interpretive trails; museum; nature and historical programs; 17-mile Roughrider Trail (designated National Recreation Trail); x-c skiing; playground.

Natural Features: Located on a densely wooded flat at the confluence of the Heart and Missouri Rivers; elevation 1700'.

Season, Fees & Phone: Open all year, with limited services October to May; please see Appendix for standard North Dakota state park fees and reservation information; 14 day limit; park office (701) 663-9571.

Camp Notes: The Cavalry and the Indians have finally come to terms in this thousand-acre park. (A sign could be posted that says "George Custer Slept Here".) After viewing the great river's valley from on top of the park's bluffs, it will become apparent to you why the people of the frontier called it "The Wide Missouri".

North Dakota 20

GENERAL SIBLEY
Burleigh County Park

Location: Central North Dakota south of Bismarck.

Access: From Interstate 94 Exit 37 at the east edge of Bismarck, turn south onto Bismarck Expressway and travel south, then west, for 5.2 miles to the south side of the city; turn south (left) onto S. Washington Street and proceed 3.4 miles; turn east (left) into the campground. **Alternate Access:** From Interstate 94 Exit 34 at the east edge of *Mandan*, turn southeast onto I-194 and proceed 1.2 miles to North Dakota Highway 810 (Bismarck Expressway); continue southeast, across the Missouri River, then east on the Expressway to S. Washington St.; continue as above. (Note that the 'Expressway' is a four-laner, not a freeway.)

Facilities: 122 electrical hookup campsites, plus a separate tent loop; sites are generally quite large, level, with fair to very good separation; parking pads are paved or gravel, long straight-ins or pull-throughs; large tent areas; barbecue grills or fire rings; b-y-o firewood; water at several faucets; restrooms with showers; holding tank disposal stations; paved driveways; complete supplies and services are available along the Bismarck Expressway.

Activities & Attractions: Playgrounds; short trails; boat dock.

Natural Features: Located on a very gently rolling, grassy flat on the east bank of the Missouri River; sites receive moderate to dense shade from large hardwoods; elevation 1800'.

Season, Fees & Phone: Open all year, with reduced services and fees mid-November to mid-April; $6.00 for a standard or tent site, $9.00 for an electrical hookup unit ($10.00 for air conditioned camping vehicles); park office (701) 222-1844.

Camp Notes: If you're willing to go the extra mile (literally) in this huge park, you'll find the campsites at the very southeast tip of the campground to be somewhat more private than those closer to the entrance. Barnum and Bailey could set up the Big Top in the tent area.

North Dakota 21

BEAVER CREEK
Lake Oahe/Corps of Engineers Park

Location: South-central North Dakota south of Bismarck and west of Linton.

Access: From the junction of North Dakota State Highways 1804 & 13 (48 miles south of Bismarck, 13 miles west of Linton), proceed west, then south, on a paved road for 2.7 miles; turn west (right) onto the campground access road and proceed 0.3 mile to the main camping area.

Facilities: 60 campsites, most with electrical hookups, in 3 areas; sites are small to medium-sized, with minimal to fairly good separation; parking pads are primarily medium-length, paved straight-ins, plus a few super long pull-throughs; pads have been reasonably well leveled, considering the terrain; medium to large tent areas, may be sloped; fire rings and barbecue grills; limited firewood may be available for gathering in the vicinity, b-y-o to be sure; water at central faucets; restrooms; holding tank disposal station; paved driveways; nearest supplies and services (limited to adequate) are in Linton.

Activities & Attractions: Boating; boat launch and dock; fishing; playground.

Natural Features: Located on a moderately steep, grassy slope on the east shore of Lake Oahe on the Missouri River; most sites are fairly well sheltered/shaded by hardwoods and a few pines; bordered by high bluffs; elevation 1700'.

Season, Fees & Phone: Available all year, subject to road and weather conditions, with limited services and no fee, mid-September to May; $8.00; 14 day limit; Lake Oahe CoE Project Office, Pierre SD, (605) 224-5862.

Camp Notes: If the main campground should be overrun, half-priced primitive camping is available on the east side of the main road. Better yet, the Hazelton area, 20 miles north of here at ND 1804 milepost 48 +.5, has a dozen gravel pads with a half-dozen tables and bbq grills, vaults, but no drinking water. There's a boat ramp 0.5 mile north of the campground. $00.00 at Hazelton.

NORTH DAKOTA
Turtle Mountains & Northeast Prairie
Please refer to the North Dakota map in the Appendix

North Dakota 22

STRAWBERRY LAKE
Turtle Mountains State Forest

Location: North-central North Dakota northeast of Minot.

Access: From North Dakota State Highway 43 at milepost 2 +.3 (2 miles east of the junction of State Highways 43 & 14 northwest of Bottineau, 21 miles west of the junction State Highway 43 and U.S. 281 north of Dunseith), turn south onto a narrow gravel access road and proceed 0.3 mile to the campground.

Facilities: 28 campsites; (an equestrian group camp area is also available); sites are generally small+, level, with fair to very good visual separation; most parking pads are short to medium-length, gravel straight-ins; enough space for only a small tent in most sites; fire rings; firewood is available for gathering in the area; water at a hand pump; vault facilities; gravel driveways; camper supplies are available in the Lake Metigoshe area, 8 miles east.

Activities & Attractions: Fishing (trout); limited boating; hiking trails; swimming beach access adjacent to the campground.

Natural Features: Located near the north shore of Strawberry Lake, high on the west slope of the Turtle Mountains; vegetation consists of tall, dense hardwoods, a few small evergreens, brush and grass; elevation 2300'.

Season, Fees & Phone: General season is late May to early September, but available at other times, depending upon weather and road conditions; $5.00; 14-day limit; North Dakota Forest Service, Bottineau, (701) 228-2277.

Camp Notes: Most commercial maps don't clearly depict this isolated, northwest-southeast range which touches the Canadian-U.S border at its northwesternmost point. On an approach to this region from the south/southwest (perhaps typical of a majority of visitors) you may at first believe you're experiencing a mirage. The Turtle Mountains rise from the immense, level plains like a great sea beast rising from the calm ocean.

North Dakota 23

HAHN'S BAY
Turtle Mountains State Forest

Location: North-central North Dakota northeast of Minot.

Access: From North Dakota State Highway 43 at milepost 8 +.2 (8 miles east of the junction of State Highways 43 & 14 northwest of Bottineau, 15 miles west of the junction State Highway 43 and U.S. 281 north of Dunseith), turn north onto a paved road and proceed 1 mile; turn east (right) onto another paved road and proceed 0.65 mile, then bear north (left) onto gravel for a final 0.45 mile to the campground.

Facilities: 31 campsites; most sites are medium-sized, somewhat sloped, closely spaced but with good visual separation; parking pads are gravel/grass, short to medium-length straight-ins; adequate space for a medium-sized tent in most sites; fire rings; gathering of firewood from forest lands prior to arrival, or b-y-o, is recommended; water at a central faucet; vault facilities; gravel/dirt driveway (a bit snug for trailers); camper supplies on the east shore of the lake; limited supplies and services are available in Bottineau, 10 miles south.

Activities & Attractions: Fishing; boating; hiking trails.

Natural Features: Located on a hillside near the southwest corner of Lake Metigoshe in the Turtle Mountains; most sites are sheltered/shaded by medium-dense, large hardwoods, plus a few evergreens; elevation 2300'.

Season, Fees & Phone: General season is late May to early September, but available at other times, subject to weather and road conditions; $5.00; 14-day limit; North Dakota Forest Service, Bottineau, (701) 228-2277.

Camp Notes: One of the best-kept secrets in the West--North Dakota has a sizeable, mountain forest and a forest service! In keeping with the long-standing tradition of forest camps in the West, this campground (as well as its sister camps here in the Turtle Mountains) provides no-frills facilities at a fairly low cost.

North Dakota 24

MAID O' MOONSHINE & WASHEGUM
Lake Metigoshe State Park

Location: North-central North Dakota northeast of Minot.

Access: From North Dakota State Highway 43 at milepost 9+ .7 (10 miles east of the junction of State Highways 43 & 14 northwest of Bottineau, 13 miles west of the junction of State Highway 43 and U.S. 281 north of Dunseith), turn north onto a paved road and travel along the east shore of the lake for 2.3 miles to the park entrance; continue beyond the entrance on the main park road for 0.3 mile; turn east (right) for 0.15 mile, then turn right into Maid O' Moonshine, or left, into Washegum.

Facilities: 88 total campsites in both areas, all with electrical hookups; sites are medium-sized, with long, gravel, pull-through parking pads in M O' M; sites in Washegum are small+, with short, gravel straight-ins; a little additional leveling may be required in some units; campsites in both areas are closely spaced, but visually well separated; small to medium-sized areas for tents; fire rings; firewood is usually for sale, or b-y-o; water at central faucets; camper supplies just south of the park; limited supplies and services are available in Bottineau, 11 miles south.

Activities & Attractions: Swimming; fishing (walleye, northerns, perch); boating; nature trail; amphitheater; x-c skiing.

Natural Features: Located on a hill a short distance from the east shore of Lake Metigoshe in the Turtle Mountains; vegetation consists of dense, large hardwoods; elevation 2300'.

Season, Fees & Phone: M O' M is open all year, with limited services September to May; Washegum is open mostly on weekends, May to September; please see Appendix for standard North Dakota state park fees and reservation information; 14 day limit; park office (701) 263-4651.

Camp Notes: Given a choice, most campers would probably choose Maid O' Moonshine (if only for the name). But there's really nothing wrong with Washegum, either. Washegum's campsites are small, but nicely private.

North Dakota 25

NORTH HILL & SOUTH HILL
Lake Metigoshe State Park

Location: North-central North Dakota northeast of Minot.

Access: From North Dakota State Highway 43 at milepost 9 +.7 (10 miles east of the junction of State Highways 43 & 14 northwest of Bottineau, 13 miles west of the junction of State Highway 43 and U.S. 281 north of Dunseith), turn north onto a paved road and travel along the east shore of the lake for 2.3 miles to the park entrance; continue beyond the entrance on the main park road for 0.45 mile; turn west (left) onto a one-way, north-to-south driveway; North Hill is 0.1 mile south of the turnoff; South Hill is 0.3 mile south of North Hill. (OK?)

Facilities: 38 total campsites in both areas; sites are small+, basically level, with minimal to fair separation; parking surfaces are grass; plenty of room for a large tent in most sites; fire rings; firewood is usually for sale, some may be available for gathering in nearby state forest lands, or b-y-o; water at several faucets; vault facilities; paved driveways; camper supplies just south of the park; limited supplies and services are available in Bottineau, 11 miles south, via paved road from near Highway 43 milepost 8.

Activities & Attractions: Swimming beach, adjacent; fishing (walleye, northern pike, perch); boating; boat launch; nature trail; amphitheater; cross-country skiing.

Natural Features: Located on a hill above the east shore of Lake Metigoshe in the Turtle Mountains; campground vegetation consists of light to medium-dense hardwoods on a grassy surface; elevation 2300'.

Season, Fees & Phone: Open all year, subject to weather conditions, with limited services September to May; please see Appendix for standard North Dakota state park fees and reservation information; 14 day limit; park office (701) 263-4651.

Camp Notes: Day-tripper traffic sometimes passes through the campground, but otherwise there's good tenting here. And it's closer to the beach than the "modern" (hookup) district.

North Dakota 26

PELICAN LAKE
Turtle Mountains State Forest

Location: North-central North Dakota northeast of Minot.

Access: From North Dakota State Highway 43 at milepost 14 +.2 (14 miles east of the junction of State Highways 43 & 14 northwest of Bottineau, 9 miles west of the junction of State Highway 43 and U.S. 281 north of Dunseith), turn south onto a gravel access road; continue for 0.9 mile to the campground.

Facilities: 5 campsites; sites are generally small, level, and quite private; parking pads are short, grass/gravel straight-ins; small tent areas; fire rings or barbecue grills; some firewood is available for gathering in the area; water at central faucets; vault facilities; narrow, gravel/dirt driveway; camper supplies are available in the Lake Metigoshe area, 4 miles west; limited to adequate supplies and services are available in Bottineau or Dunseith, about 15 miles southwest and southeast, respectively.

Activities & Attractions: Fishing on Pelican Lake and adjacent Sandy Lake (reportedly perch and a few trout); limited boating; swimming beach on Sandy Lake; day use areas.

Natural Features: Located on the north shore of Pelican Lake in the Turtle Mountains; campground vegetation consists of moderately dense hardwoods, grass and underbrush; elevation 2300'.

Season, Fees & Phone: General season is late May to early September, but available at other times, depending upon weather and road conditions $5.00; 14-day limit; North Dakota Forest Service, Bottineau, (701) 228-2277.

Camp Notes: Considering the very scenic surroundings, it's surprising that there aren't more in the way of actual campsites here. (What appears to be the picnic area at Pelican Lake is quite nice. Could it be pressed into service for camping?) It might be possible to squeeeeeeze a small trailer or motorhome into one of the campsites, but only solo cars, vans and pickups actually *fit*.

North Dakota 27

MOUNT CARMEL
Cavalier County Recreation Area

Location: Northeast North Dakota north of Langdon.

Access: From North Dakota State Highway 1 at milepost 223 (9 miles north of Langdon, 8 miles south of the U.S.-Canada border), turn east onto a paved road at a sign for "Mount Carmel Dam" and proceed 2 miles; turn north onto a gravel road and continue north 2 miles, then east for 0.5 mile to the recreation area entrance and the campground, just beyond, on the right.

Facilities: 99 campsites, including 59 with electrical hookups; sites are small to medium-sized, level, with minimal to fair separation; parking surfaces are grass straight-ins/pull-offs; adequate space for a medium to large tent in most sites; fire rings; some firewood is occasionally provided, b-y-o is recommended; water at central faucets; restrooms with showers; holding tank disposal station; paved driveways; adequate supplies and services are available in Langdon.

Activities & Attractions: Swimming; windsurfing; boating; waterskiing; fishing, primarily for walleye and northern pike.

Natural Features: Located on the west shore of a long, slender reservoir on the South Pembina (Little Pembina) River; campground vegetation consists of mown lawns, a few evergreens, and rows of hardwoods which provide light to moderate shelter/shade for most sites; surrounded by level or very gently rolling plains and agricultural land; elevation 1600'.

Season, Fees & Phone: May to mid-September; $8.00 for a standard site, $9.00 for an electrical hookup site; (no phone).

Camp Notes: This area isn't depicted on most maps, and it doesn't often show up on campground listings. But word of mouth has carried the message, nonetheless. Campers from all over the region, not just the locals, make use of this fairly simple, verdant, park-like, rec area. Reportedly, more than 300 campers commonly pack the park on holiday weekends. It's usually not quite that busy at other times, though.

North Dakota 28

RIVERSIDE
Walhalla City Park

Location: Northeast corner of North Dakota in the city of Walhalla.

Access: From North Dakota State Highway 32 at milepost 230 +.5 (at the southwest edge of the city of Walhalla), turn east onto Riverside Avenue and proceed 0.3 mile to Ninth Street; turn south (right) for 0.05 mile to the park entrance; the campground is at the southwest corner of the main park area (just south of the swimming pool). (The above access would apply to most travelers; however, if coming from north of the city, i.e., Canada, easiest access is to turn south onto Ninth Street, as the highway makes a southwesterly jog through the center of town; proceed 0.4 mile to the park.)

Facilities: 14 campsites with partial hookups; sites are medium-sized, essentially level, with nominal to fairly good separation; parking pads are mostly short to medium-length, gravel straight-ins; adequate space for a medium-sized tent in most sites; fire rings; some firewood may occasionally be provided or for sale, b-y-o to be sure; water at sites and at central faucets; restrooms with showers; holding tank disposal station; gravel driveways; nearly adequate supplies and services are available in Walhalla.

Activities & Attractions: Swimming pool; baseball field; playground; log cabin exhibits; miniature golf; hiking trails through scenic Tetrault Woods, 1.5 miles south of town.

Natural Features: Located in a grove of large hardwoods and a few spruce near the bank of the Pembina River; most sites are very well sheltered/shaded; elevation 900'.

Season, Fees & Phone: May to September; $7.00; park manager (701) 549-3666 or (701) 549-3214.

Camp Notes: Once you visit this area, it's easy to see why the town is named Walhalla. The park along the river is very pleasant indeed. And some of the surrounding countryside (especially west of town, along the back road to Mount Carmel), is worth more than just a quick pass-through.

North Dakota 29

ICELANDIC
Icelandic State Park

Location: Northeast corner of North Dakota southeast of Walhalla.

Access: From North Dakota State Highway 5 at milepost 307 +.5 (6 miles west of Cavalier, 28 miles east of Langdon), turn north onto the park access road for 0.25 mile to the entrance station; continue straight ahead across the dam for 0.4 mile; as the road curves west, turn south (left) into the standard camping area; or continue west for a final 0.4 mile to the hookup loops.

Facilities: 122 campsites in 3 loops; sites are small+ to medium-sized, with minimal to fairly good separation; parking pads are long, packed gravel pull-throughs in the hookup loops; a little additional leveling may be required; ample space for a large tent in both hookup and standard sites; fire rings; b-y-o firewood; water at several faucets; restrooms with showers, plus vault facilities; holding tank disposal station; paved driveways; limited to adequate supplies and services are available in Cavalier.

Activities & Attractions: Interpretive center; arboretum; prairie homestead; Wildwood Trail (a designated National Recreation Trail); x-c ski trails; amphitheater; swimming; playgrounds; boating; boat launch; fishing (northern pike).

Natural Features: Located on a short bluff above the north shore of Lake Renwick on the Tongue River; vegetation consists of expanses of mown grass dotted with large and small hardwoods, plus a few pines; elevation 900'.

Season, Fees & Phone: Available all year, subject to weather conditions, with limited services September to May; please see Appendix for standard North Dakota state park fees and reservation information; 14 day limit; park office (701) 265-4561.

Camp Notes: Probably the best campsites here are a number of those in the loop at the far west end of the campground, so head for there first. Nice place. Very nice.

GRAHAM'S ISLAND
Devils Lake State Park

Location: North-central North Dakota west of the city of Devils Lake.

Access: From North Dakota State Highway 19 at milepost 145 +.4 (10 miles west of Devils Lake, 7 miles east of the junction of State Highway 19 & U.S. 281 near Minnewaukan), turn south onto a gravel road and proceed 5.3 miles, then sharply east (left) for 0.5 mile; turn north (left) into the park entrance and continue for 0.25 mile to the campground.

Facilities: 82 campsites, including about 20 with electrical hookups, in 2 main loops; sites are medium-sized, with fair to very good separation; parking pads are gravel or paved, short straight-ins or long pull-throughs; a tad of additional leveling may be needed in some sites; medium to large tent areas; fire rings; firewood is usually for sale, or b-y-o; water at central faucets; restrooms with showers; holding tank disposal station; gravel driveways; adequate+ supplies and services are available in Devils Lake.

Activities & Attractions: Fishing (excellent for walleye and "Jumbo Perch"); boating; boat launch; hiking trails.

Natural Features: Located in a stand of moderately dense hardwoods on 6-Mile Bay at the west edge of Devils Lake; the multi-bayed lake's principal component, Main Bay, lies 2 miles east; elevation 500'.

Season, Fees & Phone: Available all year, subject to weather conditions, with limited services October to May; please see Appendix for standard North Dakota state park fees and reservation information; 14 day limit; park office (701) 766-4015.

Camp Notes: This former county campground has lots of recreational potential. Another state park camping area on the lake is Shelvers Grove State Recreation Area. It's a small spot with simple campsites and a swimming beach on the southeast lake shore.

LAKE AGASSIZ
Turtle River State Park

Location: Eastern North Dakota west of Grand Forks.

Access: From U.S. Highway 2 at milepost 337 +.3 (18 miles west of Grand Forks, 7 miles east of the junction of U.S 2 & North Dakota State Highway 18 near Larimore), turn north onto the park access road for 0.7 mile to the park entrance station; continue west/northwest on the main park road for 0.25 mile to a "T" intersection; turn north (right) and proceed 0.15 mile to the campground entrance station; the main campground is 0.25 mile farther.

Facilities: 80 campsites with electrical hookups in 2 loops; (a group campground is also available, by reservation); sites are medium-sized, with nominal to fairly good separation; most parking pads are long, paved pull-throughs which may require a smidgen of additional leveling; adequate space for a large tent in most sites; fire rings; b-y-o firewood; water at several faucets; restrooms with showers; holding tank disposal station; paved driveways; campers supplies at the park concession; complete supplies and services are available in Grand Forks.

Activities & Attractions: Hiking, cross-country skiing, snowmobile trails; swimming pool; amphitheater; playground; nature areas; horse rentals (concession).

Natural Features: Located amid moderately dense hardwoods within walking distance of the Turtle River; countryside consists of level woodlands and farmlands; elevation 1000'.

Season, Fees & Phone: Open all year, subject to weather conditions, with limited services October to May; please see Appendix for standard North Dakota state park fees and reservation information; 14 day limit; park office (701) 594-4445.

Camp Notes: A small primitive camp area called "Trapper's Rest" is associated with the main campground. This popular little spot has room for about a half-dozen tent campers. (Can't find Lake Agassiz? The campground's name refers to a colossal, ancient lake that is no more. The lake once covered most of eastern North Dakota and western Minnesota.)

North Dakota 32

BEAVER LAKE
Beaver Lake State Park

Location: South-central North Dakota southeast of Napoleon.

Access: From North Dakota State Highway 3 at milepost 49 + .4 (9 miles south of Napoleon, 8 miles north of the junction of State Highways 3 & 13 west of Wishek), turn east onto a paved road and travel 7 miles to a "T" intersection in the hamlet of Burnstad; turn north (left) onto a paved road, proceed 1 mile, turn east (right) and continue for another mile; turn north into the park entrance and proceed 0.3 mile to the campground.

Facilities: 42 campsites, including 25 with electrical hookups, in 3 sections; sites are small, with minimal separation; parking surfaces are grass/gravel, slightly sloped, pull-offs in the hookup sites, and short, gravel/grass straight-ins in the standard ('primitive') sites; adequate space for a small to medium-sized tent; fire rings; firewood is usually for sale, or b-y-o; water at several faucets; restrooms with showers; holding tank disposal station; gravel driveways; limited+ supplies and services are available in Napoleon.

Activities & Attractions: Fishing (walleyes and northerns); boat launch; nature trail; swimming beach; playground.

Natural Features: Located on a grassy slope above the west shore of Beaver Lake; vegetation consists primarily of tall grass and rows of hardwoods; hookup sites are minimally shaded, standard sites are lightly shaded; encircled by low, prairie hills; elevation 1900'.

Season, Fees & Phone: May to mid-September; please see Appendix for standard North Dakota state park fees and reservation information; 14 day limit; park office (701) 452-2752.

Camp Notes: Beaver Lake has somewhat less in the way of facilities than the more elaborate state parks like Turtle River and Lake Sakakawea. (But, then again, there won't be a quarter-mile-long, Friday evening waiting line at the gate, either.) Grain elevator and beauty salon in Burnstad.

North Dakota 33

CLAUSEN SPRINGS
Barnes County Park

Location: Southeast North Dakota south of Valley City.

Access: From North Dakota State Highway 1 at milepost 53 + .4 (17 miles south of Interstate 94 Exit 67 just west of Valley City, 2 miles north of the junction of State Highways 1 & 46), turn east onto a gravel road and proceed 1 mile; turn north (left) onto another gravel road and continue north for 1.65 miles then east for 0.6 mile to a "Y" intersection; turn left for 0.2 mile to the hookup area, or right for 0.3 mile to the standard ('open') camping areas.

Facilities: 10 electrical hookup campsites, plus open camping; hookup sites are small to medium-sized, with nominal separation; parking surfaces are grass, reasonably level, medium-length, straight-ins/pull-offs; adequate space for a medium to large tent in most units; central shelter; fireplaces; b-y-o firewood; water at central faucets; vault facilities; holding tank disposal station; gravel driveways; nearest reliable source of supplies (adequate+) is Valley City.

Activities & Attractions: Fishing; limited boating (no gas or diesel motors); boat launch; small playground; picnic areas.

Natural Features: Located in a hollow on a small flat along a creek (hookup area), or on a hilltop above a mile-long impoundment (standard area); large hardwoods and mown lawns in the hookup area; a few hardwoods, small pines and prairie grass in the standard area; elevation 1400'.

Season, Fees & Phone: Available all year, with limited services, October to May; $4.00 for each tent or trailer per camping night; 14 day limit; Barnes County Parks Department (701) 762-4450.

Camp Notes: Odds are that most campers would choose the hookup area for its substantial vegetation and shelter from the prairie wind. For an unrestricted view (and for those all-too-often occasions in midsummer when a stiff breeze may be welcome for several reasons), the camp areas along the rim of the lake present a good option.

LITTLE YELLOWSTONE
Barnes County Park

Location: Southeast North Dakota south of Valley City.

Access: From North Dakota State Highway 46 at milepost 66 +.8 (17 miles west of Enderlin, 4 miles east of the junction of State Highways 46 & 1, turn south into the park; the primary camping area is at the west end of the park grounds.

Facilities: Approximately 25 campsites, including 6 with electrical hookups; most sites are level, small to medium-sized, with nominal separation; most parking areas are gravel/grass straight-ins; large, grassy tent areas; fireplaces; a small amount of firewood may be available for gathering, b-y-o is recommended; water at a central faucet; vault facilities; gravel driveways; nearest reliable source of supplies (limited) is Enderlin.

Activities & Attractions: Baseball field; wading pool; small playground; fishing in the Sheyenne River.

Natural Features: Located in the Sheyenne Valley, 0.2 mile west of the Sheyenne River; large hardwoods provide adequate shelter/shade for most sites; a small creek with a little falls (Little Yellowstone Falls?) tumbles past the west edge of the park; elevation 1400'.

Season, Fees & Phone: May to mid-October; $4.00; tents limited to 5 days in one location; 14 day overall limit; Barnes County Parks Department (701) 762-4450.

Camp Notes: If you prefer a more secluded spot, there are a few small campsites on the hill behind the main campground. (The valley views are very good, but it might prove to be difficult to haul a trailer up there.) The park's drinking water has achieved a certain local renown. Each year, thousands of gallons of spring water from the taps leave here in the jugs and bottles of visitors. The true origin of the name "Little Yellowstone Park" may have been lost to posterity. Although the Sheyenne River Valley certainly is beautiful, its resemblance to the Yellowstone of the Rockies is elusive.

FORT RANSOM
Fort Ransom State Park

Location: Southeast North Dakota south of Valley City.

Access: From North Dakota State Highway 46 at milepost 65 +.6 (18 miles west of Enderlin, 5 miles east of the junction of State Highways 46 & 1, turn south onto a wide, paved road and travel 8 miles; turn east (left) onto a paved road and continue for 1.5 miles, then turn north (left) and proceed 1.2 miles to the town of Fort Ransom; the road winds through town and continues north then northwest for 1.8 miles; turn west (left) into the park and proceed 0.3 mile to the East Side camp area; or continue west, then south for 0.5 mile to the West Side (main) camp area. (There are several other accesses to the park, but this one is the most-used, and has the most miles of blacktop.)

Facilities: 20 campsites, some with electrical hookups, in 2 areas; sites are medium-sized, with nominal to fairly good separation; parking pads are mostly long, gravel pull-throughs (West Side), plus several straight-ins (East Side); medium to large tent areas; fire rings; firewood is usually for sale, or b-y-o; water at several faucets; vault facilities; gravel driveways; camper supplies in the village of Fort Ransom.

Activities & Attractions: Foot and horse trails; canoeing; playground; homesteading exhibits; museum in town.

Natural Features: Located on the east and west banks of the Sheyenne River in the Sheyenne Valley; rows of recently planted hardwoods provide limited to moderate shelter in the West Side camp loop; East Side loop is well-sheltered; heavily wooded slopes border the valley; elevation 1300'.

Season, Fees & Phone: May to October; please see Appendix for standard North Dakota state park fees and reservation information; 14 day limit; park office (701) 973-4331.

Camp Notes: This place may be a bit off the well-traveled track, but it's in one of the most beautiful valley settings in the northern plains. Worth zigzagging a few miles for.

MEL RIEMAN
Lake Ashtabula/Corps of Engineers Park

Location: Southeast North Dakota north of Valley City.

Access: From the intersection of Main Street & Central Avenue in midtown Valley City, travel north on Central Avenue for 0.85 mile; turn east onto 12th Street NE for 0.2 mile, then turn north (left) onto 5th Avenue NE; continue north for 0.8 mile (passing under the trestle, then across the railroad tracks); turn northwest (left) onto River Road and proceed for 8.5 miles (past the fish hatchery); turn northeast (right) onto a paved access road and continue up the hill, past the visitor center, for a final 0.4 mile to the campground. (Note: from Interstate 94, take Exit 68 or Exit 70, then via Business I-94 into midtown Valley City.)

Facilities: 20 campsites, including a few with electrical hookups; standard sites are small, with short, paved straight-ins; hookup units are fairly large, with long pull-throughs; most sites have reasonably good separation; some additional leveling will probably be required; small to medium-sized tent areas; fireplaces; b-y-o firewood; water at a hand pump; vault facilities; (restrooms and showers at the visitor center); paved driveways; adequate+ supplies and services are available in Valley City.

Activities & Attractions: Swimming beach; visitor center; boating; boat launch and dock, north of the campground; fishing.

Natural Features: Located on a hilltop at the southeast corner of Lake Ashtabula; most campsites are lightly sheltered by small hardwoods and a few pines; elevation 1300'.

Season, Fees & Phone: May to October; $6.00 for a standard site, $7.00 for an electrical hookup unit; 14 day limit; Lake Ashtabula CoE Project Office (701) 845-2970.

Camp Notes: From this windswept vantage point, many campsites enjoy a really good view of the lake and the nearly treeless, grassy slopes which border it. Although this spot often is busy (formerly, it was called the "Main Public Use Area"), families tend to prefer it because of the swimming beach, boat launch and availability of showers.

EGGERT'S LANDING
Lake Ashtabula/Corps of Engineers Park

Location: Southeast North Dakota north of Valley City.

Access: From the intersection of Main Street & Central Avenue in midtown Valley City, proceed north on Central Avenue for 0.85 mile; turn east onto 12th Street NE for 0.2 mile, then turn north (left) onto 5th Avenue NE; travel north on this paved road for 11.3 miles; turn west (left) onto a paved access road and proceed 0.3 mile, then turn north (right) for a final 0.2 mile to the campground (Note: from Interstate 94, take Exit 68 or Exit 70, then via Business Route I-94 to Main & Central in midtown Valley City.)

Facilities: 20 campsites, majority with electrical hookups; sites are level, small to medium-sized, with fair to very good privacy; parking pads are medium-length, gravel straight-ins; small to medium-sized areas for tents in most units; a couple of designated tents-only sites; handicapped-access site; fireplaces; limited firewood may be available for gathering in the vicinity, b-y-o to be sure; water at a hand pump; vault facilities; holding tank disposal station; gravel driveway; camper supplies at a nearby resort; adequate+ supplies and services are available in Valley City.

Activities & Attractions: Fishing; handicapped-access fishing platform; boating; boat launch and dock; fish cleaning station; day use area and playground, nearby.

Natural Features: Located on a cove along the east shore of Lake Ashtabula, a reservoir on the Sheyenne River; most campsites are well sheltered/shaded by large hardwoods; several sites are shoreside; elevation 1300'.

Season, Fees & Phone: May to October; $6.00 for a standard site, $7.00 for an electrical hookup unit; 14 day limit; Lake Ashtabula CoE Project Office (701) 845-2970.

Camp Notes: Eggert's Landing is a favorite hangout of walleye fishermen. Walleyes reportedly can be found in quantity just offshore (more or less, depending upon conditions.)

ASHTABULA CROSSING
Lake Ashtabula/Corps of Engineers Park

Location: Southeast North Dakota north of Valley City.

Access: From the intersection of Main Street & Central Avenue in midtown Valley City, proceed north on Central Avenue for 0.85 mile; turn east onto 12th Street NE for 0.2 mile, then turn north (left) onto 5th Avenue NE; travel north on this paved road for 15.6 miles to the east side of the causeway across the lake; turn north (right) into East Ashtabula Crossing; or continue for 0.3 mile to the opposite side of the lake and turn north (right again) into West Ashtabula Crossing.

Facilities: 77 campsites, including 37 in the East unit and 40 in the West unit; about one-third of the sites have electrical hookups; sites vary from small to medium+, with minimal to fair separation, and most are quite sloped; parking pads are gravel/grass, short to medium-length straight-ins; medium to large, grassy tent areas; central shelter in each area; fireplaces; b-y-o firewood; water at central faucets in the East unit, and at a hand pump on the West side; vault facilities; gravel driveways; holding tank disposal station in the West unit; camper supplies at a resort on the east side; adequate+ supplies and services are available in Valley City.

Activities & Attractions: Fishing; boating; boat launch and dock at each unit.

Natural Features: Located along the east and west shores of Lake Ashtabula; sites receive light to moderate shelter/shade from large hardwoods on a grassy surface; elevation 1300'.

Season, Fees & Phone: May to October; $6.00 for a standard site, $7.00 for an electrical hookup unit; 14 day limit; Lake Ashtabula CoE Project Office (701) 845-2970.

Camp Notes: Viewed from the center of the causeway, it would appear that these camps were nearly identical twins. Close up, they reveal subtleties in character and facilities. East is a bit more shaded, while West's campsites enjoy slightly better views. Toss-up. *Ashtabula* is said to be an Indian word that means "Fish River".

OLD HIGHWAY 26
Lake Ashtabula/Corps of Engineers Park

Location: Southeast North Dakota north of Valley City.

Access: From the intersection of Main Street & Central Avenue in midtown Valley City, proceed north on Central Avenue for 0.85 mile; turn east onto 12th Street NE for 0.2 mile, then turn north (left) onto 5th Avenue NE; travel north on this paved road (which basically parallels the east shore of Ashtabula Lake), for 15.6 miles to Ashtabula Crossing; continue for 0.3 mile across the causeway to the west shore of the lake, then north for another 2.1 miles to a crossroads; turn east (right) onto a gravel road and proceed 2 miles to the recreation area; turn south (right) for a final 0.3 mile to the campground.

Facilities: 7 campsites; sites are small, with nominal separation; most parking pads are tolerably level, gravel, medium-length straight-ins; small to medium-sized tent spots; fireplaces or fire rings; b-y-o firewood; water at a hand pump; vault facilities; camper supplies in Sibley, 5 miles north, and near East Ashtabula Crossing; adequate+ supplies and services are available in Valley City.

Activities & Attractions: Fishing (though usually not quite as good as the excellent angling on the south half of the lake); boating; small boat launch.

Natural Features: Located on the west shore of Lake Ashtabula--a half-mile-wide, 27-mile-long, flood-control reservoir on the Sheyenne River; several edgewater sites; campground vegetation consists primarily of sparse grass bordered by a few twiggy hardwoods, large bushes and tall grass; very "open" environment; elevation 1300'.

Season, Fees & Phone: Open all year, subject to weather conditions; no fee (subject to change); 14 day limit; Lake Ashtabula CoE Project Office (701) 845-2970.

Camp Notes: All CoE lakes have at least one free use area, and this is Ashtabula's freebie. It *looks* remote, it *feels* remote, and it *is* remote. They could also have named this spot "Long View".

MAYVILLE
Mayville City Park

Location: Far eastern North Dakota north of Fargo.

Access: From North Dakota State Highway 200 at the west edge of the city of Mayville (12 miles west of Interstate 29 Exit 111, 2 miles east of Portland), turn south into the campground.

Facilities: 10 electrical hookup campsites, plus additional room for standard camping; sites are small+, level, with minimal separation; parking spaces are grass, short to medium-length straight-ins/pull-offs; ample space for a large tent in most sites; barbecue grills for a few sites; b-y-o firewood; water at central faucets; restrooms with showers; holding tank disposal station; gravel driveways; adequate supplies and services are available in Mayville.

Activities & Attractions: Goose River Wildlife Park, adjacent; large day use area with playground, volleyball courts, etc., on the north side of the highway; large kitchen shelter in the camp area.

Natural Features: Located on a flat along the Goose River; campground vegetation consists of mown lawns and several large hardwoods which provide light shelter/shade for most campsites; elevation 1000'.

Season, Fees & Phone: Available all year, with limited services, October to May; $6.00 for camper camping, $4.00 for tent camping.

Camp Notes: It's fairly rare to discover a small-town campground (in this case sponsored by the Jaycees) that merits more than just a mention. The camping facilities, although quite pleasantly adequate and reasonably priced, probably wouldn't be the principal reason for spending some time here. But the small wildlife park right next to the campground (operated on a donation basis by the local Eagles lodge) and the beautifully landscaped grounds across the highway at Pioneer Park really help make the stay a worthwhile one.

LINDENWOOD
Fargo City Park

Location: Eastern North Dakota in Fargo.

Access: From Interstate 94 Exit 87 for University Drive South/U.S. 81 at the southeast corner of Fargo, turn north onto University Drive and proceed 0.4 mile to 17th Avenue South; turn east (right) onto 17th Avenue, and continue for 0.5 mile to 5th Street South; continue across 5th St.; a few yards after crossing 5th, turn south onto Roger Maris Drive and proceed south/southeast for 0.6 mile to the campground. (Note, if you're traveling I-29, get onto I-94 and go *east* to the *next* exit, then as above.)

Facilities: 67 campsites, including 46 with electrical hookups, and 20 tents-only sites, in 3 sections; sites are small in the hookup sections, medium-sized in the tent area, with minimal to nominal separation; parking pads are paved, medium to long straight-ins (which may require slight additional leveling in area B); medium to large tent spots; fire rings in some sites; b-y-o firewood; water at central faucets; restrooms with showers; holding tank disposal station; paved driveways; complete supplies and services are available within a mile.

Activities & Attractions: Huge city park complex; great playground near the camp area; paved pathways throughout the park; footbridge across the river; several regulation-size baseball fields.

Natural Features: Located along the west bank of the Red River of the North; vegetation consists primarily of moderately dense, large hardwoods and mown grass; elevation 900'.

Season, Fees & Phone: Generally available all year, with limited services October to April; $7.00 for a tent site, $8.00 for a hookup unit; park office (701) 232-3987 or (701) 232-7145.

Camp Notes: Yes, coffee pots rattle and tent flaps quiver when a big rig rumbles by on the freeway, (the price for big city convenience). But there's so much to do and see in this nice park that you probably won't even notice the traffic.

South Dakota

Public Campgrounds

The South Dakota map is located in the Appendix on page 153.

South Dakota 1

BEAR BUTTE
Bear Butte State Park

Location: Western South Dakota east of Spearfish.

Access: From Interstate 90 Exit 30 for Sturgis (18 miles southeast of Spearfish), drive east on South Dakota State Highways 34 & 79 for 5 miles; turn north (left) continuing on Highway 79 as the highways divide; proceed 3.3 miles to milepost 114 + .5; turn west (left) onto a gravel access road for 0.9 mile to the main campground, on the left.

Facilities: 15 campsites; sites are fairly good sized, with very little visual separation; parking pads are gravel, long straight-ins; some pads may require a little additional leveling; large, fairly level, grassy tent spots; fireplaces; b-y-o firewood; water at a hand pump; vault facilities; gravel driveways; adequate supplies and services are available in Sturgis.

Activities & Attractions: Boating; fishing; remains of an interesting shelter built by the WPA in 1938; playground; visitor center, east across the highway; national recreation hiking trail to the summit of Bear Butte.

Natural Features: Located near the north shore of Bear Butte Lake; reeds along the shore, prairie grass and a few scattered trees for vegetation in the wide expanse stretching in every direction; lake views from many campsites; the Black Hills are plainly visible to the southwest; to the east, Bear Butte (an eroded volcano which never actually erupted, but merely fumed and fizzled a lot), towers 1200' above the prairie, lake and camp; campground elevation 3300'.

Season, Fees & Phone: Open all year, with limited services October to May; please see Appendix for standard South Dakota state park fees and reservation information; 14 day limit; park office (605) 347-5240.

Camp Notes: Bear Butte ("Mato Paha" or "Sleeping Bear Mountain", as the Sioux called it) has been a frequently chosen campsite for *many* years. Excavations near the present-day state park have unearthed camping artifacts dating back some 4000 years. Evidently considered good then, even better now.

South Dakota 2

SPEARFISH
Spearfish City Park

Location: West-central South Dakota in Spearfish.

Access: From Interstate 90 Exit 12 for Spearfish, proceed west on Jackson Boulevard for 0.6 mile to Canyon Road; turn left (south) onto Canyon Road for 0.4 mile to the park boundary, then across the bridge to the campground.

Facilities: 57 full hookup campsites and 30+ tent sites; sites are small to medium-sized, level, with minimal to fair separation; parking pads are oiled gravel, medium to long straight-ins in the hook-up area, pull-offs (park n' walks) in the tent area; adequate space for small to medium-sized tents; barbecue grills, plus some fireplaces; b-y-o firewood is recommended; water at most sites and at several faucets; restrooms with coin-op showers; holding tank disposal station; paved driveways; adequate supplies and services are available in Spearfish.

Activities & Attractions: Fishing; adjacent day use area includes playground, tennis courts, horseshoe pits, rifle range and band shell; fish hatchery; scenic drive southward through Spearfish Canyon on Highway 14A into the Black Hills.

Natural Features: Located on a forested flat along the west bank of Spearfish Creek; a rocky bluff rises across the river to the east; Trandahl Creek flows through the campground and into Spearfish Creek; tall hardwoods and pines tower over a grassy floor; elevation 3900'.

Season, Fees & Phone: April to October; $9.00 for a tent site with a single camper, $10.00 for 2 campers, $11.00 for 3-4 campers, $1.00 for each additional camper; $14.00 for a hookup site; park office (605) 642-3744.

Camp Notes: Spearfish provides a well-used, but comfortable, campground, and (predictably) 'city park' type activities, right on the northern edge of the superscenic Black Hills.

South Dakota 3

TIMON & ROD AND GUN
Black Hills National Forest

Location: West-central South Dakota south of Spear-fish.

Access: From U.S. Highway 14A it the hamlet of Savoy (13 miles south of Spearfish, 5.5 miles northwest of Cheyenne Crossing) turn west onto Forest Road 222; proceed west for 3 miles to Rod & Gun and 4.7 miles to Timon. (The first mile from Savoy to Roughlock Falls is paved, then the road turns to gravel.)

Facilities: *Timon:* 7 campsites; sites are generally medium to large with good separation; parking pads are gravel, short to medium-length straight-ins; most pads may require additional leveling; some large, sloped, grassy tent spots; *Rod & Gun*: 7 campsites; sites are small to medium-sized, with fair separation; parking pads are gravel, short to medium-length straight-ins; small to medium-sized, acceptably level tent spots; *both camps:* fire rings; firewood is usually available for gathering in the area; water at a hand pump in each campground; vault facilities; gravel driveways; camper supplies in Cheyenne Crossing; adequate supplies and services are available in Spearfish.

Activities & Attractions: Stream fishing; Rimrock Hiking Trail connects Timon with Rod & Gun; nearby historic site of a 9-mile-long flume which brought water to 1887 placer mines; Roughlock Falls day use area, 3 miles east.

Natural Features: Located in a forested canyon along Little Spearfish Creek; tall conifers surround a grassy, sloped infield at Timon; some aspens, creekside brush and sparser grass provide a more open atmosphere at Rod & Gun; elevation 5500' at Rod and Gun, 6000' at Timon.

Season, Fees & Phone: General season is May to September; open with reduced services and no fee until snowbound; $6.00 for Rod & Gun, $7.00 for Timon; 10 day limit; Spearfish Ranger District (605) 642-4622.

Camp Notes: It would be worth traveling the extra mile+ to Timon if a more forested setting is preferred. Little Spear-fish Creek flows invitingly alongside both sets of sites.

South Dakota 4

HANNA
Black Hills National Forest

Location: West-central South Dakota south of Spear-fish.

Access: From the junction of U.S. Highways 85 & 14A (at the west edge of Cheyenne Crossing, 20 miles south of Spearfish), proceed west on U.S. 85 for 0.15 mile; turn south onto Forest Road 196 and continue for 1.9 miles; sites are along the east (left) side of the roadway.

Facilities: 13 campsites in 2 sections; sites are mostly medium-sized, with nominal to good separation; parking pads in the northern section are gravel, short to medium straight-ins; pads in the southern section are gravel park n' walks; small to medium-sized, grassy tent spots; some spots may be a bit sloped; fire rings; some firewood is usually available for gathering in the area; water at a hand pump; vault facilities; gravel/earth driveway; gas and groceries in Cheyenne Crossing, adequate supplies and services are available in the Lead-Deadwood area, 10 miles northeast.

Activities & Attractions: Catch and release fishing; hiking trail; good views from the campsites; nearby scenic drive along Highway 85 over Terry Peak Summit; tours at western hemisphere's largest gold mine, Homestake, south of Lead.

Natural Features: Located in a wide forested canyon along East Spearfish Creek in the Black Hills; vegetation along the creek is grassy and timbered; tall conifers shade some creekside sites; other sites are situated on relatively sunny, grassy slopes; elevation 5600'.

Season, Fees & Phone: May to September, with no fee and limited services later in the season; $7.00; 10 day limit; Spearfish Ranger District (605) 642-4622.

Camp Notes: Sites that are a bit farther from the roadway are walk-in sites, accessible by trip-trapping across a wooden foot bridge. (No resident trolls at last report). Don't be surprised if a thirsty deer wanders through your neat little creekside campsite--they're frequent visitors here.

South Dakota 5

ROUBAIX LAKE
Black Hills National Forest

Location: West-central South Dakota northwest of Rapid City.

Access: From U.S. Highway 385 at milepost 108 +.8 (13.5 miles south of the junction of U.S. 385 & U.S. 14A, 38 miles north of Hill City), turn west onto Forest Road 255 and proceed 1.2 miles to the campground.

Facilities: 56 campsites in 5 loops; sites are medium to large, with fair to good separation; parking pads are gravel, short to long straight-ins, and most will require additional leveling; large, somewhat sloped, tent spots; fire rings; firewood is available for gathering in the area; water at central faucets; restrooms ('mini-flush') plus auxiliary vault facilities; paved driveways; camper supplies in Brownsville, 5 miles north; adequate supplies and services are available in the Lead-Deadwood area.

Activities & Attractions: Boating; fishing; small, sandy swimming beach; picnicking along the lakeshore; hiking trails in the surrounding Black Hills area; nearby Deadwood Gulch is rich in historical attractions, including restored buildings, and Calamity Jane and Wild Bill Hickok memorabilia.

Natural Features: Located on a timbered slope above small Roubaix Lake; Middle Boxelder Creek flows nearby; medium-tall conifers shelter most campsites; low timbered hills and open meadow surround the cattail-ringed pond; elevation 4700'.

Season, Fees & Phone: Open all year, subject to weather conditions, with limited services October to May; $11.00; 10 day limit; Nemo Ranger District, Deadwood, (605) 578-2744 .

Camp Notes: This campground remains quite populated well into October. The current fee is a notch or two above many comparable forest camps in other western regions. But all those happy campers filing-in with ten bucks in hand apparently believe it's worth it. (The lake's name is pronounced like 'Row-Bay'.)

South Dakota 6

PACTOLA RESERVOIR
Black Hills National Forest

Location: West-central South Dakota west of Rapid City.

Access: From U.S. Highway 385 at milepost 95 +.1 (0.1 mile south of the Pactola Dam Visitor Center, 18 miles west of Rapid City (via South Dakota Highway 44 and U.S. Highway 385), turn west onto a paved road; proceed 1.4 miles; turn north (right) across from the small store; pass through the entrance gate and continue 0.6 mile to a fork in the road; Loops A & B are 0.5 mile to the left and Loop C is 0.1 mile to the right.

Facilities: 80 campsites in 3 loops; sites are medium to large, with fair to very good separation; parking pads are mostly gravel straight-ins, plus a few hard-surfaced pull-throughs; most pads will require additional leveling; tent spots are fairly large but sloped; (sites in Loop B are arranged in clusters especially to accommodate groups); fire rings plus a few barbecue grills; some gatherable firewood is available in the surrounding area; water at central faucets; vault facilities; paved driveways; showers and camper supplies at the store; complete supplies and services in Rapid City.

Activities & Attractions: Boating; boat launch; fishing for kokanee salmon, largemouth bass, perch, rainbow and brown trout; swimming area; hiking; visitor center nearby.

Natural Features: Located on the forested southwest shore of Pactola Reservoir; the dam on Rapid Creek has created a lake with 14 miles of forested shoreline; tall pines and grassy slopes are the predominant forms of vegetation in the campground area; elevation 4700'.

Season, Fees & Phone: May to October; $10.00, ($12.00 for a "premium" site); 10 day limit; may be operated by concessionaire; Pactola Ranger District, Rapid City, (605) 343-1567.

Camp Notes: The early settlement of Pactola was named for the "gold-bearing sand" that brought droves of prospectors here in the late 1800's. (Perhaps the "premium" sites are also situated on "gold-bearing sand". Ed.)

SHERIDAN LAKE: SOUTHSIDE
Black Hills National Forest

Location: Southwest South Dakota southwest of Rapid City.

Access: From U.S. Highway 385 at milepost 87 +.15 (1.5 miles south of the junction of U.S. Highway 385 with South Dakota Highway 228, 9 miles northeast of Hill City), turn east onto a paved road; continue (past Sheridan South Picnic Ground) for 1 mile to the campground entrance.

Facilities: 128 campsites in 5 loops; (a group camping area is available at Sheridan Lake North Cove, by reservation only); sites are medium to large, with fair to good separation; parking pads are gravel, medium to long, mostly straight-ins, plus some pull-throughs; most pads will require additional leveling; medium to large, mostly sloped, tent spots; fire rings; firewood is usually available for gathering in the area; water at central faucets; vault facilities; paved driveways; gas & camper supplies, 2 miles south; limited supplies and services are available in Keystone, 10 miles southeast.

Activities & Attractions: Boating; boat launch; fishing; swimming at adjacent day use area; short, paved nature trail; Sheridan Lake's north shore has an additional boat ramp, picnic ground and group camp; campfire programs on Saturday evenings during the summer months.

Natural Features: Located on a forested slope and ridge along the south shore of Sheridan Lake; a dam on Spring Creek has created this lake in a basin completely ringed by timbered hills; campground vegetation consists primarily of tall pines and sparse, tall grass; elevation 4600'.

Season, Fees & Phone: May to October; $10.00 ($12.00 for a "premium" site); 10 day limit; may be operated by concessionaire; Pactola Ranger District, Rapid City, (605) 343-1567.

Camp Notes: Picturesque Sheridan Lake is in a super setting--perfect for a lazy day of boating/fishing/hiking. Of the several forest camps in this part of the Black Hills, this one is probably ahead by a nose. Because it's within a few miles of the Black Hills' major attractions, it gets pretty busy in midsummer. An end-of-season visit may be a wise choice. (The prices here, like most camps in the Hills, are nearly as steep as the timbered slopes that surround them. Ed.) This area is also known as just Southside Campground.)

WHITETAIL
Black Hills National Forest

Location: Southwest South Dakota west of Rapid City.

Access: From U.S. Highway 16 & 385 at milepost 40 +.9 on Highway 16 (midtown Hill City, 14 miles north of Custer), turn west onto Harney Peak Avenue West; travel 13.6 miles to the Deerfield Lake Recreation Area boundary; proceed (past the turnoff to Dutchman) for 1.5 miles, then turn north (right) onto a gravel access road; continue for 0.9 mile to the campground. (Outside of town, Harney Peak Avenue becomes County Road C307, then C308, but the route is adequately signed).

Facilities: 17 campsites in 2 loops; sites are small to medium-sized, with nominal to fair separation; parking pads are gravel, short to medium-length straight-ins; most pads will require some additional leveling; small to medium-sized, mostly sloped tent spots; fire rings; firewood is usually available for gathering in the area; water at several faucets; vault facilities; gravel driveways; limited supplies and services are available in Hill City.

Activities & Attractions: Fishing; wakeless boating; boat launch; scenic drive through high meadow area of the Black Hills.

Natural Features: Located on the lightly-forested southern shoreline of Deerfield Reservoir; campground vegetation consists of medium to tall conifers, some low-level brush, and sparse grass; some sites have lake views through the trees; elevation 6100'.

Season, Fees & Phone: May to October; $8.00; 10 day limit; Harney Ranger District, Hill City, (605) 574-2534.

Camp Notes: Whitetail and its sister camp, Dutchman (see info) are the two most easily accessible forest camps on the reservoir. For considerably more seclusion, Custer Trail Campground, on Deerfield's north shore, is available. It's a nine-mile trip on gravel and dirt roads. A fourth forest camp in the area, Ditch Creek Campground, is 6 gravel miles southwest of Whitetail on Ditch Creek.

DUTCHMAN
Black Hills National Forest

Location: Southwest South Dakota west of Rapid City.

Access: From U.S. Highways 16 & 385 at milepost 40 +.9 on Highway 16 (midtown Hill City, 14 miles north of Custer), turn west onto Harney Peak Avenue West; travel 13.6 miles to the Deerfield Lake Recreation Area boundary; turn north (right) and continue for 1.4 miles (gravel) to the campground entrance. (Harney Peak Avenue twists and turns and becomes County Road C307, then C308, but the route to the rec area is well signed.)

Facilities: 45 campsites in 2 loops; sites are medium to fairly spacious, with fair to good separation; parking pads are gravel, medium+ straight-ins; many pads may require additional leveling; most sites, though a bit sloped, would accommodate medium or large tents comfortably; fire rings; firewood is available for gathering in the area; water at several faucets; vault facilities; gravel driveways; limited supplies and services are available in Hill City.

Activities & Attractions: Fishing; wakeless boating; boat launch, 0.5 mile west; foot trail to the lake.

Natural Features: Located on a rolling slope and forested ridge east of Deerfield Reservoir; Dutchman Creek flows nearby; campground vegetation consists of tall conifers and a few hardwoods over a fairly brush-free forest floor of pine needles and pine cones; elevation 6100'.

Season, Fees & Phone: May to September; $7.00; 10 day limit; Harney Ranger District, Hill City, (605) 574-2534.

Camp Notes: The atmosphere at Dutchman is more 'laid back' than at campgrounds in the 'thick of things' a few miles east. The road up from Hill City climbs 1000' and winds through scenic high mountain meadows and stands of conifers and hardwoods--a favorite haunt of whitetail deer and gracefully sailing hawks on the wing. Great views of the lake and surrounding terrain from the shoreline in and around the boat launch area.

HORSETHIEF LAKE
Black Hills National Forest

Location: Southwest South Dakota southwest of Rapid City.

Access: From South Dakota Highway 244 at milepost 030 (5 miles west of the Mount Rushmore Visitor Center, 6 miles east of the junction of U.S. Highways 16 & 385 with Highway 244), turn south onto a paved roadway; proceed 0.1 mile to the pay station; lower section is to the left; upper section is straight ahead.

Facilities: 35 campsites in 2 sections; sites are mostly small to medium-sized, with fair separation; most parking pads are gravel, short to medium straight-ins; many pads will require additional leveling; several nice park n' walk tent sites (some are framed and leveled); fire rings; some firewood is usually available for gathering in the area; water at several faucets; vault facilities; paved main drive; limited to adequate supplies and services are available in Keystone, 8 miles east, and Hill City, 9 miles northwest.

Activities & Attractions: Fishing; motorless boating; several hiking and nature trails in the area; Mt. Rushmore National Memorial and related attractions, 5 miles east.

Natural Features: Located on the hilly west shore of Horsethief Lake, a small lake surrounded by forested ridges and rocky outcroppings; some sites are in a forested glen near the lakeshore; other sites are perched atop a 'bench' above the lake; campground vegetation consists of pine, aspen, oak, brush, and some tall grass; elevation 5000'.

Season, Fees & Phone: May to September; $8.00 for a tent site, $10.00 for a standard site; 3 day limit; may be operated by a concessionaire; Harney Ranger District, Hill City, (605) 574-2534.

Camp Notes: Horsethief Lake, the public campground nearest to Mount Rushmore, is in a really beautiful, forested setting. This neat spot was probably even in the 'secluded' category a half century ago when Gutzon Borglum was chiseling the four famous faces on Mount Rushmore.

OREVILLE
Black Hills National Forest

Location: Southwest South Dakota north of Custer.

Access: From U.S. Highways 16 & 385 at milepost 36 on Highway 16 (5 miles south of Hill City, 9 miles north of Custer), turn east into the campground at either of the 2 entrances, 100 yards apart.

Facilities: 26 campsites in a double oval loop; sites are small to medium+, with fair to excellent separation; parking pads are mostly medium-length straight-ins; about half may need additional leveling; most sites have open spots ample enough for medium-sized tents, though many are a bit sloped; fire rings; firewood is usually available for gathering in the area; water at several faucets; vault facilities; narrow oiled-gravel driveway; limited supplies in Hill City; fairly adequate supplies and services in Custer.

Activities & Attractions: Stream fishing in the vicinity; hiking; Mount Rushmore National Memorial, 15 miles northeast; Crazy Horse Memorial and museum on Thunderhead Mountain, 5 miles south; scenic drive along U.S. 16/385.

Natural Features: Located on a slightly sloping dish-shaped flat bordered by timbered mountains/hills to the east and west; campground vegetation consists of medium-dense, tall pines and aspens on a forest floor of pine needles and grass; a number of sites are situated at the base of a forested hill; elev. 5000'.

Season, Fees & Phone: May to September; $9.00; 10 day limit; may be operated by a concessionaire; Harney Ranger District, Hill City, (605) 574-2534.

Camp Notes: This camp is conveniently situated right along the main drag connecting Mount Rushmore and Wind Cave National Park. Sites are situated away from the road, behind a small knoll. Some super sites on the upper (eastern) slope are tucked in among the aspens in very pleasant, secluded nooks.

SYLVAN LAKE
Custer State Park

Location: Southwest South Dakota northeast of Custer.

Access: From U.S. Highway 87 at milepost 73 +.1 (7 miles northeast of Custer via Highway 89, 9.4 miles southeast of Hill City), turn south onto a paved park drive into the campground. (Note: access via U.S. 87 from north and east is through very tight tunnels--or large moleholes--as narrow as 8' 7'' and as short as 10' 8"; if you drive a large rig, check with Custer Park Hq. for more information.)

Facilities: 40 campsites, including several walk-in sites; sites are small to medium-sized, with fairly good separation; parking pads are paved, medium to long, mostly straight-ins; most pads will require additional leveling; some nice, private tent spots, though mostly smallish and sloped; fireplaces; b-y-o firewood is recommended; water at several faucets; restrooms with showers; paved driveways; camper supplies at a nearby store; fairly adequate supplies and services are available in Custer.

Activities & Attractions: Several hiking trails, including Harney Peak Trail and Sunday Gulch Interpretive Trail; motorless boating; fishing; swimming; scenic Needles Highway Drive.

Natural Features: Located in a forested pocket in the Black Hills; small but picturesque Sylvan Lake is within a few hundred yards to the north; granite boulders protrude from the surrounding green hillsides; Cathedral Spires and several other curious rock formations are visible from the nearby Needles Highway; elevation 6300'.

Season, Fees & Phone: May to September; please see Appendix for standard Custer State Park fees and reservation information; 14 day limit; park office (605) 255-4515.

Camp Notes: 'Sylvan' describes this spot appropriately. Sylvan Lake seems to hold a mystic quality that coaxes you to linger--to wander once more around the lake, or to flip a dry fly out to one more trout rising on the evening water.

CENTER LAKE
Custer State Park

Location: Southwest South Dakota northeast of Custer.

Access: From U.S. Highway 87 at milepost 62 +.3, turn northeast at a junction signed for the Black Hills Playhouse; proceed 0.7 mile (past the turnoff to the playhouse); turn east (right) and continue 0.2 mile to the upper loop or 0.4 mile to the lower loop.

Facilities: 39 campsites in the lower loop, 29 sites in the upper loop, plus 7 sites designated for tents; sites are average-sized, with minimal separation; parking pads are gravel, short to medium-length straight-ins or pull-offs; many pads may require additional leveling; adequate pine-needle-covered spots for medium to large tents, may be a bit sloped; fireplaces; b-y-o firewood is recommended; water at several faucets; vault facilities; showers; paved driveways; fairly adequate supplies and services are available in Custer, 12 miles southwest.

Activities & Attractions: Swimming beach; hiking; amphitheater for evening programs; playground; limited boating (small, slow boats only); fishing; nearby Black Hills Playhouse offers theater performances June-August.

Natural Features: Located on 2 'shelves' above the west shore of Center Lake (no clear lake views from the sites); Center Lake was formed by a dam on Grace Coolidge Creek; campground vegetation consists of tall pines and hardwoods with very little underbrush; elevation 4700'.

Season, Fees & Phone: May to September; please see Appendix for standard Custer State Park fees and reservation information; 14 day limit; park office (605) 255-4515.

Camp Notes: The only road to Center Lake is the scenic (and twisty) Needles Highway. You may want to allow a tad of extra time for the trip--to stop and study some of the super sights (or in case a curious critter creates a temporary traffic tie-up).

South Dakota 14

STOCKADE LAKE
Custer State Park

Location: Southwest South Dakota east of Custer.

Access: North Unit: From U.S. Highway 16A at milepost 26 +.5 (4 miles east of Custer, 9.5 miles west of the Custer Park Visitor Center) turn south onto a paved road for 0.1 mile to the campground. **South Unit:** From U.S. 16A at milepost 26 (3.5 miles east of Custer, 10 miles west of the Custer State Park Visitor Center, a few yards west of Gordon Stockade) turn south onto County Road 341; proceed 0.7 mile south and east; turn south (right) into the campground.

Facilities: 44 campsites in the North Unit, 25 sites in the South Unit; sites are small to medium+, with nominal to fair separation; parking pads are gravel, medium to long straight-ins or pull-offs; many pads will require additional leveling; tent spots are fair-sized but most are somewhat sloped; fire rings in the northern unit; large, upright stone fireplaces in the southern unit; b-y-o firewood is recommended; water at central faucets; vault facilities; showers; paved driveways; fairly adequate supplies and services are available in Custer.

Activities & Attractions: Nearby historically significant Gordon Stockade; boating; fishing.

Natural Features: Located on the grassy, forested hills surrounding Stockade Lake; tall pines, grass and some underbrush in the camp area; elevation 5300'.

Season, Fees & Phone: May to September; please see Appendix for standard Custer State Park fees and reservation information; 14 day limit; park office (605) 255-4515.

Camp Notes: Travelers interested in the pioneers' lifestyle should enjoy the summertime exhibits presented by costumed demonstrators at the Gordon Stockade. (There's nothing like seeing how it used to be to generate a renewed appreciation for flashlights, matches, and showers.)

South Dakota 15

LEGION LAKE
Custer State Park

Location: Southwest South Dakota east of Custer.

Access: From U.S. Highway 16A at milepost 29 +.1 (7 miles east of Custer, 36 miles southwest of Rapid City), turn north into the campground. (Highways 16A and 87 merge for about 1.5 miles in this stretch; Legion Lake is midway between the 2 points of converge and diverge).

Facilities: 25 campsites; sites are small to medium-sized, with very little visual separation; parking pads are gravel, mostly level, short to medium straight-ins; good-sized tent spots on a grassy surface, but they may be a bit lumpy; fireplaces; b-y-o firewood is recommended; water at central faucets; restrooms with showers; gravel driveways; camper supplies at a small store nearby; fairly adequate supplies and services are available in Custer.

Activities & Attractions: Fishing; motorless boating; designated swimming beach; Badger Clark Historic Trail nearby; super mountain scenery along the nearby Needles Highway; Mt. Coolidge Fire Lookout accessible from Highway 87, about 3 miles south.

Natural Features: Located in a grassy draw across the highway from Legion Lake; sites are situated on a slight slope between forested hills to the west and east; the lake is visible from some of the lower sites; campground vegetation consists of grass and a few scattered trees; hardwoods and conifers grow on the adjacent slopes; elevation 5000'.

Season, Fees & Phone: May to September; please see Appendix for standard Custer State Park fees and reservation information; 14 day limit; park office (605) 255-4515.

Camp Notes: Legion Lake Campground is one of several campgrounds right along the main highway through Custer Park. It's a bit more secluded, however, than its 'cousins' to the east. And just a few hundred yards from the sites is an inviting mountain lake ringed by forested slopes.

South Dakota 16

BLUEBELL
Custer State Park

Location: Southwest South Dakota east of Custer.

Access: From U.S. Highway 87S at milepost 53 +.85 (4.2 miles south of the western junction of U.S. Highways 16A and 87S, 11 miles southeast of Custer, at a point right between the lodge and the horse stables) turn east onto a *paved* drive (if you find yourself on a gravel road, you're on the wrong trail); proceed 0.1 mile to the campground.

Facilities: 35 campsites, including some designated park n' walk sites for tents; sites are mostly medium-sized, with minimal to fair separation; parking pads are paved, short to medium-length straight-ins; many pads will require additional leveling; tent spots are fairly good-sized but a bit sloped; fireplaces; b-y-o firewood is recommended; water at central faucets; restrooms; showers; paved driveways; camper supplies at a nearby store; fairly adequate supplies and services are available in Custer.

Activities & Attractions: Hiking; playground; ranger-naturalist programs; riding stable nearby; access to Mt. Coolidge Fire Lookout Tower, 2.6 miles north; nearby 18-mile-long Wildlife Loop Road through country abundant with bison, elk, and antelope.

Natural Features: Located on a forested slope; sites are all on or near hills and ravines; campground vegetation consists of tall ponderosa pines and second growth timber; (though some of the surrounding forest shows signs of a fire, the campground itself appears unaffected); elevation 5000'

Season, Fees & Phone: May to September; please see Appendix for standard Custer State Park fees and reservation information; 14 day limit; park office (605) 255-4515.

Camp Notes: Of the many campgrounds in Custer Park, Bluebell has a definite edge in the shelter/seclusion category. It actually has all kinds of edges. It's a *nice* campground.

South Dakota 17

GRACE COOLIDGE
Custer State Park

Location: Southwest South Dakota east of Custer.

Access: From U.S. Highway 16A at milepost 33 +.4 (12 miles east of Custer, 1.5 miles west of the park visitor center), turn south into the main campground; or at milepost 34 +.6, turn north into the tent area.

Facilities: 23 campsites in the main camping area, and 9 designated tent spots in a secondary loop; sites are mostly small, level, with nominal separation; parking pads are gravel, short to long straight-ins or pull-offs; small to medium-sized tent spots; fireplaces; b-y-o firewood is recommended; water at central faucets; restrooms; showers; holding tank disposal station a few miles east at Game Lodge; gravel driveways; camper supplies at a small store to the east; fairly adequate supplies and services are available in Custer.

Activities & Attractions: Hiking; fishing; Grace Coolidge walk-in fishing area stretches along the creek for 3 miles, north toward Center Lake (lots of pools designed to harbor browns, rainbows, and brookies); evening programs at nearby Game Lodge.

Natural Features: Located on a flat along Grace Coolidge Creek, between rocky, forested hills to the north and south; some sites are in an open meadow, others are nestled along the tree-lined creek; views of stratified rocky outcroppings from most sites; elevation 4400'.

Season, Fees & Phone: Available all year, with limited services October to May; please see Appendix for standard Custer State Park fees and reservation information; 14 day limit; park office (605) 255-4515.

Camp Notes: This is one of the most easily accessible campgrounds in Custer State Park. Sites are only a few yards from a major U.S. Highway. Bison ("Tatanka") commonly roam through the adjoining meadow.

South Dakota 18

GAME LODGE
Custer State Park

Location: Southwest South Dakota east of Custer.

Access: From U.S. Highway 16A at milepost 36 +.7 (15 miles east of Custer, 28 miles southwest of Rapid City), turn south, then immediately west on a paved road and proceed 0.1 mile to the campground.

Facilities: 55 campsites; sites are small to medium-sized, level, with zero to fair separation; parking pads are paved, medium to long straight-ins or pull-offs; small to medium-sized tent spots along the creek, large tent areas in the meadow; fireplaces; b-y-o firewood; water at central faucets; restrooms with showers; holding tank disposal station; paved driveways; camper supplies at a small store, 2 miles west; fairly adequate supplies and services are available in Custer.

Activities & Attractions: Visitor center; adjacent Tatanka Theater has naturalist-directed programs, evening entertainment and a weekly barn dance; playground; stream fishing; designated swimming area; 18-mile-long Wildlife Loop Road turnoff, just east of the campground.

Natural Features: Located on a huge, grassy flat between forested ridges to the north and south; Grace Coolidge Creek flows alongside the campground; creekside vegetation consists of hardwoods, grass and small conifers; some sites are in the open meadow area, others are down along the creek; elevation 4300'.

Season, Fees & Phone: May to September; please see Appendix for standard Custer State Park fees and reservation information; 14 day limit; park office (605) 255-4515.

Camp Notes: Game Lodge is the easternmost campground in Custer Park and is at the hub of the park's activity. Nearby Peter Norbeck Visitor Center is housed in a quaint structure built by the CCC in 1938. It's now listed in the Register of National Historic Places.

South Dakota 19

BISMARCK LAKE
Black Hills National Forest

Location: Southwest South Dakota east of Custer.

Access: From U.S. Highway 16A at milepost 27 +.2 (4.8 miles east of Custer, 1.8 miles west of the western junction of U.S. Highways 16A and 87S, near the Custer State Park boundary), turn north onto a paved drive; proceed 0.3 mile to a fork in the road; the upper loop is to the left and the lower loop is down and to the right.

Facilities: 23 campsites in 2 loops; sites are small to medium-sized, with nominal separation in the lower units and fairly good separation in the upper units; parking pads are gravel, medium to long, mostly straight-ins; about half of the pads may require some additional leveling; smallish tent spots, may be a bit sloped; fire rings; firewood is usually available for gathering in the vicinity; water at several faucets; vault facilities; paved driveways; fairly adequate supplies and services are available in Custer.

Activities & Attractions: Boating; fishing; swimming; foot trail and boardwalk around the lake; Custer Park and its exhibits, geological features, and wildlife nearby.

Natural Features: Located on a bluff above, and near, the southern shore of Bismarck Lake; the lake is surrounded by grassy/forested hills; lake views from some of the sites; campground vegetation consists of light to moderately dense pines and hardwoods; elevation 5300'.

Season, Fees & Phone: Available all year, subject to weather conditions, with limited services October to May; $9.00; 10 day limit; Custer Ranger District (605) 673-4853 or (605) 673-4852.

Camp Notes: Bismarck Lake Campground is a favorite Black Hills spot in its own right. Blufftop campers can enjoy views of this beautiful lake surrounded by verdant forested shores. The Custer State Park attractions right next door are a bonus.

COMANCHE PARK
Black Hills National Forest

Location: Southwest South Dakota west of Custer.

Access: From U.S. Highway 16A at milepost 20 + .35 (6 miles west of Custer, 21 miles east of the South Dakota/Wyoming border), turn south then west onto a gravel access road and proceed 0.3 mile to the campground.

Facilities: 49 campsites in 2 loops; sites are mostly medium or better in size, with fairly good visual separation; parking pads are gravel, medium to long, fairly level straight-ins; tent spots are quite ample for medium to large tents and mostly on a forest floor of pine needles; fireplaces; firewood is available for gathering in the area; water at several faucets; vault facilities; gravel driveways; fairly adequate supplies and services are available in Custer.

Activities & Attractions: Campfire circle; forest walking; Jewel Cave National Monument, 6 miles west, offers summertime guided tours of its underground passageways and calcite crystals.

Natural Features: Located on a forested hilltop; campground vegetation consists of moderately dense, tall pines and a bit of second growth timber; a small park (meadow) and dense forest adjoin the campground; elevation 5100'.

Season, Fees & Phone: May to October; $7.00; 10 day limit; Custer Ranger District (605) 673-4853 or (605) 673-4852.

Camp Notes: Comanche Park Campground is in one of the most pleasant spots in the Hills. Open forest stretches for miles around, interspersed with areas of mountain park. Comanche Park is named for the sole survivor of the 1876 Battle of the Little Bighorn. "Comanche", the buckskin Indian pony ridden by one of Custer's officers, was the only member of the 7th Cavalry to walk away from that ill-fated encounter. Custer's entire unit, including Comanche, camped near this spot during the winter of 1874.

RIFLE PIT
Black Hills National Forest

Location: Southwest South Dakota north of Hot Springs.

Access: From U.S. Highway 385 at milepost 51 +.1 (5 miles southeast of Pringle, 15 miles north of Hot Springs), turn south (the highway follows an east/west route through this canyon) onto a steep gravel road; proceed 0.1 mile up to the sites.

Facilities: 26 campsites in 2 loops; sites are medium to large, with separation ranging from zip to fairly good; parking pads are gravel, medium to long straight-ins; many pads may require additional leveling; several large, grassy tent areas but they're quite sloped; fire rings; firewood is typically available for gathering; no drinking water; vault facilities; gravel driveways; adequate supplies and services are available in Hot Springs.

Activities & Attractions: Wind Cave National Park, 3 miles south-east; Prairie Dog Town, 2 miles southeast; Fire Lookout and hiking trail on Rankin Ridge, 9 miles northeast.

Natural Features: Located in a narrow canyon flanked by timbered ridges; dense forest borders the campground, but the sites themselves are on a somewhat open hillside; grassy, rocky terrain; some sites have limited views, while sites farthest up the hill have commanding views across the gap; elev. 4800'.

Season, Fees & Phone: Available all year, subject to weather conditions; no fee (subject to change); 10 day limit; Custer Ranger District (605) 673-4853 or (605) 673-4852.

Camp Notes: Rifle Pit is within a half hour's drive of several local attractions without being right in the thick of things--and the price is right! (It's remarkable that this steep slope was chosen as the site of a campground. Perhaps the engineers were challenged by an "it can't be done" statement.)

ELK MOUNTAIN
Wind Cave National Park

Location: Southwest South Dakota north of Hot Springs.

Access: North Entrance: From U.S. Highway 385 at milepost 48 (7.4 miles southeast of Pringle, 11 miles north of Hot Springs) turn south (right) onto the park loop road; proceed south for 0.4 mile; turn west (right) and continue 0.5 mile to the campground. **South Entrance:** From U.S. Highway 385 at milepost 47 + .2 (8.2 miles southeast of Pringle, 10.2 miles north of Hot Springs) turn north onto the park loop road; proceed 1.2 miles (past the visitor center); turn west (left) to the campground.

Facilities: 99 campsites in 3 loops and a string; sites are mostly on the small side, with nominal separation in the main section and better separation in the 'tents only' loop; parking pads are gravel, short straight-ins, or long, narrow pull-offs; most pads are level; some really nice, spacious, grassy tent spots, though some are a bit sloped; fireplaces; firewood is usually provided, or b-y-o; water at several faucets; restrooms; paved driveways; adequate supplies and services are available in Hot Springs.

Activities & Attractions: Guided tours of underground Wind Cave, 1 mile east; spelunking; amphitheater for evening naturalist programs; Elk Mountain Nature Trail.

Natural Features: Located mostly on a grassy flat between a forested hill to the south and a grassy, tree-dotted hill to the north; buffalo roam freely in the park; elevation 4400'.

Season, Fees & Phone: Open all year, with reduced services and no fee October to May; $8.00; 14 day limit; park headquarters (605) 745-4600.

Camp Notes: It almost looks as if the crew at Elk Mountain uses tweezers to pick out any unwanted dead grass. A 'neat' place, in several respects. The forested hills/rolling prairie combination makes this one of the most beautiful areas in South Dakota.

South Dakota 23

COTTONWOOD SPRINGS
Cottonwood Reservoir/Corps of Engineers Park

Location: Southwest South Dakota west of Hot Springs.

Access: From U.S. Highway 18 at milepost 31 + .5 (4.6 miles west of Hot Springs, 8.4 miles east of the junction of U.S. Highways 18 and 89), turn north onto County Road 17; proceed 1 mile to a fork in the road; take the left fork and continue north and west on County Road 17 for 0.3 mile; turn right into the recreation area (road is now paved); proceed 0.5 mile north, then turn right again, into the campground.

Facilities: 18 campsites; sites are medium+, with nominal to good separation; parking pads are paved, quite long, fairly level, mostly straight-ins (plus 1 long pull-through); grassy, good-sized tent spots, may be a bit sloped; barbecue grills and fire rings; a small amount of firewood may be available for gathering in the area, b-y-o to be sure; restrooms, plus auxiliary vaults; paved driveway; adequate supplies and services are available in Hot Springs.

Activities & Attractions: Fishing; playground; campfire circle; day use area in the valley below the campground has picnicking, shelter and playground (a caution is posted indicating that the valley area is subject to flash flooding;) south of Hot Springs is a site where mammoth skeletons are being unearthed (tours available seasonally).

Natural Features: Located on a lightly forested ridge overlooking a broad canyon, creek, dam and small Cottonwood Reservoir; some sites are situated on a large grassy slope while others are partially sheltered by conifers; red rock walls across the canyon; elevation 3800'.

Season, Fees & Phone: Open all year, with limited services in winter; no fee (subject to change); 14 day limit; (no phone).

Camp Notes: Nice place for a nice, quiet campground--golden, grassy slopes dotted with conifers. Good views, too! Nearby Coldbrook Reservoir, just north of Hot Springs, also has a few campsites, motorless boating and picnicking.

South Dakota 24

ANGOSTURA: NORTH
Angostura State Recreation Area

Location: Southwest South Dakota southeast of Hot Springs.

Access: From U.S. Highways 18 & 385 at milepost 46 + .8 on Highway 18 (7.8 miles south of Hot Springs, 15 miles north of Olerichs), turn west onto County Road 2; proceed 1.1 mile to the entrance station (road is twisty but paved); take the left fork and continue 1.6 miles; turn west (right) into the first loop or continue south to the main camping area; (sites are situated along a 2-mile stretch).

Facilities: 92 campsites in 3 loops (referred to as Campgrounds 1, 1½ and 2), including 7 tent sites at Campground 1½ and a number of electrical hookups at Campground 2; sites vary considerably in size, separation and levelness; parking pads are gravel, medium to long, mostly level straight-ins; some really fine, large grassy tent spots; many sun shelters; fireplaces; b-y-o firewood; water at central faucets; restrooms with showers; holding tank disposal station; paved driveways; adequate supplies and services are available in Hot Springs.

Activities & Attractions: Boating; nearby marina; fishing; swimming; playground; interpretive programs; hiking.

Natural Features: Located on the east shore of 5000-acre Angostura Reservoir on the Cheyenne River; sites are situated on a forested bluff, open grassland, and in a hardwood grove; sandy beach within walking distance; elevation 3200'.

Season, Fees & Phone: Open all year, with limited services in winter; please see Appendix for standard South Dakota state park fees; 14 day limit; park office (605) 745-6996.

Camp Notes: Water sports paradise. . . and good camping, too! The choice of sites in this recreation area is so diverse (especially if you include Angostura South--see separate info), that there's a spot to please almost every camper.

South Dakota 25

ANGOSTURA: SOUTH
Angostura State Recreation Area

Location: Southwest South Dakota southeast of Hot Springs.

Access: From U.S. Highways 18 & 385 at milepost 48 +.3 on Highway 18 (9.3 miles south of Hot Springs, 14 miles north of Olerichs), turn west onto County Road 1 (paved) and proceed west then south for 3.5 miles to the entrance station; Loop A and B are near the entrance and Loop C is 0.7 mile beyond.

Facilities: 74 campsites about half of them with electrical hookups, in 3 loops; sites are medium to large, with nominal to fair separation; parking pads are gravel, generally level, medium to long straight-ins; excellent tent-pitching possibilities; fire rings or fireplaces; b-y-o firewood; water at central faucets; restrooms with showers; holding tank disposal station; paved driveways; adequate supplies and services are available in Hot Springs.

Activities & Attractions: Boating (lake level subject to seasonal variations); sailing; nearby marina; fishing; playground; 1-mile Horsehead Interpretive Trail connects the northern and southern sections of Angostura Recreation Area.

Natural Features: Located on the southeast shore of Angostura Reservoir, created by a dam on the Cheyenne River; sites are situated on a grassy flat with campground vegetation of tall hardwoods in Loop C and shorter pines and hardwoods in Loops A & B; views through the trees of the lake and distant Black Hills; elevation 3200'.

Season, Fees & Phone: Open all year, with limited services in winter; please see Appendix for standard South Dakota state park fees; 14 day limit; park office (605) 745-6996.

Camp Notes: Angostura's location--where the Plains meet the Hills--provides it with somewhat of a dual personality. Although this recreation area is not technically *in* the Black Hills, those Hills are "right over yonder".

SOUTH DAKOTA
Missouri River Plains
Please refer to the South Dakota map in the Appendix

South Dakota 26

CEDAR PASS
Badlands National Park

Location: Southwest South Dakota east of Rapid City.

Access: From South Dakota Highway 240 at a point 8.6 miles south of Interstate 90 Exit 131, and 2.1 miles east of the community of Interior (via the short section of South Dakota Highway 377), turn south into the campground.

Facilities: 108 campsites in 2 loops; (a group camping area is also available); sites are small, with virtually no separation; parking pads are gravel, mostly level, short straight-ins or short to medium-length pull-offs; some spacious, mostly level tent spots on a sparse grass surface; most sites have ramadas (sun/wind shelters); no campfires permitted, (b-y-o bbq grill and charcoal is suggested); water at central faucets; restrooms (H), plus auxiliary vaults; holding tank disposal station; paved or gravel driveways; gas and camper supplies in Interior; limited+ supplies and services are available in Wall, 32 miles north.

Activities & Attractions: Visitor center with 'touch-room'; hiking trails; amphitheater for summer evening interpretive programs; guided nature walks including periodic 'Night Prowl' excursions into the surrounding habitat; scenic drive along Highway 240 (Badlands Loop) toward Wall with lots of viewing and picture-taking opportunities.

Natural Features: Located on gently rolling prairie terrain at the base of massive 'Badland' rock formations; campground vegetation consists of a bit of well-worn grass and a few planted hardwoods; impressive, far-reaching views from every site; typically sunny and breezy; elevation 2600'.

Season, Fees & Phone: Open all year, with limited services and no fee October to May; $8.00; 10 day limit June through August, 14 day limit remainder of the year; Badlands National Park Visitor Center (605) 433-5361.

Camp Notes: Imagine climbing out of your tent or camper to gaze upon this landscape! And, according to park officials, Cedar Pass is *never* full! A great park with lots of room to wander and explore.

South Dakota 27

SHADEHILL
Shadehill State Recreation Area

Location: Northwest South Dakota south of Lemmon.

Access: From South Dakota State Highway 73 at milepost 230 +.5 (in the hamlet of Shadehill, 11 miles south of Lemmon, 73 miles north of the junction of SD 73 & U.S. Highway 212 near Faith), turn southwest/west onto a paved road and travel 2.1 miles (to the end of the pavement); turn south (left) onto a paved road and proceed 1 mile; turn west (right) into the recreation area and continue for 1 mile to a "T" intersection; turn north (right) for a final 0.4 mile to the campground.

Facilities: 32 campsites, including 16 with electrical hookups; sites are medium to large, level, with some separation; parking pads are gravel, primarily medium to long straight-ins, plus several pull-throughs; large tent areas; fireplaces; a very limited amount of firewood may be available for gathering, b-y-o to be sure; water at central faucets; vault facilities; gravel driveways; camper supplies in Shadehill; adequate supplies and services are available in Lemmon.

Activities & Attractions: Swimming beaches; prairie dog town; hiking trails; fishing; boating; boat launch; small playground.

Natural Features: Located on Ketterling point near the northeast shore of 5000-acre Shadehill Reservoir, an impoundment on the North and South Forks of the Grand River; sites are moderately shaded/sheltered by large hardwoods and pines; surrounded by the rolling prairie, low hills and buttes of Grand River National Grassland; elevation 2700'.

Season, Fees & Phone: Open all year, with limited services November to May; please see Appendix for standard South Dakota state park fees and reservation information; 14 day limit; park office (605) 374-5114.

Camp Notes: The campground covers quite a large area, considering the relatively small number of sites. This is a classic, high plains setting.

South Dakota 28

LLEWELLYN JOHNS
Llewellyn Johns State Recreation Area

Location: Northwest South Dakota south of Lemmon.

Access: From South Dakota State Highway 73 at milepost 230 +.6 (at the north end of the bridge across Flat Creek Lake in the hamlet of Shadehill, 11 miles south of Lemmon, scores of miles north of Nowhere), turn west onto a gravel access road into the recreation area, then bear south (left) and up the hill to the campground.

Facilities: 10 campsites; sites are basically small and closely spaced; parking pads are gravel, medium-length straight-ins; adequate room for small to medium-sized tents in most sites; fireplaces; b-y-o firewood; water at a central faucet; vault facilities; gravel driveway; camper supplies in Shadehill; adequate supplies and services are available in Lemmon.

Activities & Attractions: Boating; boat launch; fishing for northern pike, largemouth bass, etc.

Natural Features: Located around a small, grassy flat above the south shore of Flat Creek Lake; medium to large hardwoods and pines provide light to moderate shelter/shade for most sites; elevation 2600'.

Season, Fees & Phone: Available all year, with limited services November to May; please see Appendix for standard South Dakota state park fees; 14 day limit; phone c/o Shadehill SRA (605) 374-5114.

Camp Notes: This small campground, with its reasonably pleasant surroundings, would probably serve quite well as a quick and convenient roadside stop (if you should just happen to be traveling Highway 73). There is an off-highway alternative that's just a few minutes' drive from here--Shadehill SRA (see the opposite page for info). Campgrounds are very scarce in South Dakota's sparsely populated northwest corner. There's a lot of handsome, wide-open country around here.

South Dakota 29

INDIAN MEMORIAL
Lake Oahe/Corps of Engineers Park

Location: North-central South Dakota west of Mobridge.

Access: From U.S. Highway 12 at milepost 185 +.3 (0.4 mile west of the Missouri River bridge, 4 miles west of Mobridge, 25 miles southeast of McLaughlin), turn south onto a paved access road and proceed south, east, then south again for a total of 0.3 miles to the campground.

Facilities: 81 campsites, most with electrical hookups, in 2 loops; sites are small to medium-sized, with limited to fair separation; most parking pads are paved or gravel, long, acceptably level straight-ins; medium to large tent areas; fire rings, plus a few barbecue grills; b-y-o firewood; water at central faucets; restrooms with showers; holding tank disposal station; mostly paved driveways; nearly complete supplies and services are available in Mobridge.

Activities & Attractions: Boating; boat launches; fishing; playgrounds; amphitheater.

Natural Features: Located on a grassy bluff above the west shore of Lake Oahe on the Missouri River; most sites receive light to moderately dense shade/shelter from rows of large hardwoods, bushes and some evergreens; the lake is bordered by high, grassy, nearly treeless, windswept bluffs; elevation 1700'.

Season, Fees & Phone: Open all year, with limited services and no fee, November to April; $8.00 for a standard site, $10.00 for an electrical hookup site; 14 day limit; Lake Oahe CoE Project Office, Pierre, 224-5862.

Camp Notes: This segment of the Missouri resembles, to some degree, the middle Columbia River in central Washington State or even certain portions of the Colorado River along the Arizona-California border. Near this spot is the grave of Sitting Bull, the Sioux chief who led the winning team at the Little Bighorn.

South Dakota 30

INDIAN CREEK
Lake Oahe/Corps of Engineers Park

Location: North-central South Dakota east of Mobridge.

Access: From U.S. Highway 12 at a point 1 mile east of Mobridge, 19 miles west of Selby), turn south onto a paved access road and proceed 1.3 miles; turn west (right for 0.4 mile to Loop B; or continue ahead for 0.2 mile to the main camp area in Loop A.

Facilities: 113 campsites, majority with electrical hookups; sites are medium-sized, with nominal to fair separation; parking pads are gravel, medium to long straight-ins; some pads may require a tad of additional leveling; large tent areas, though some may be slightly sloped; fire rings; b-y-o firewood; water at central faucets; restrooms with showers; holding tank disposal station; paved or gravel driveways; nearly complete supplies and services are available in Mobridge.

Activities & Attractions: Boating; boat launches; marina; fishing; large playground; amphitheater.

Natural Features: Located on a grassy bluff on the east shore of 230-mile-long Lake Oahe on the Missouri River; sites receive very light to moderately dense shade/shelter from small to large hardwoods and some pines; the lake is bordered by high, grassy, rugged bluffs; elevation 1700'.

Season, Fees & Phone: Open all year, with limited services and no fee, November to April; $8.00 for a standard site, $10.00 for an electrical hookup site; 14 day limit; Lake Oahe CoE Project Office, Pierre, 224-5862.

Camp Notes: Many campsites have *quite* a view up and down the great lake, and a number of them are along or very near the somewhat open shore. For the most part, Loop A is for shade-lovers, while Loop B is for sun-worshippers. You might note that Lake Oahe spans the borders of two great states and partly bisects them east and west. One additional observation: the capitols of The Dakotas are linked by Oahe's southernmost and northernmost shores.

South Dakota 31

LAKE HIDDENWOOD
Lake Hiddenwood State Park

Location: North-central South Dakota east of Mobridge.

Access: From the junction of U.S. Highways 12/83 & South Dakota State Highway 130 at Selby (20 miles east of Mobridge), turn east onto SD 130 and proceed 2 miles through Selby to milepost 195; turn north onto a gravel road; travel north (after 2 miles the road becomes paved) then east for a total of 3.5 miles; turn south (right) into the park entrance; continue south and east for 0.8 mile to the campground.

Facilities: 14 campsites, including 7 with electrical hookups, in 2 sections; sites are medium-sized, with nominal to fair separation; parking pads are gravel, medium-length, level or nearly level, straight-ins or pull-offs; medium to large spaces for tents, though some may be slightly sloped; fireplaces; b-y-o firewood; water at central faucets; vault facilities; gravel driveways; limited supplies and services are available in Selby.

Activities & Attractions: Swimming beach; Hidden Beauty and Blue Blanket Interpretive Trails; playground; small ball field; fishing; limited boating; boat launch; amphitheater.

Natural Features: Located on a flat and on a slight slope near the east end of Lake Hiddenwood; shade from large hardwoods varies from light to moderate; encircled by low, grassy hills/bluffs with patches of trees and bushes; elevation 2000'.

Season, Fees & Phone: Open all year, with limited services October to May; please see Appendix for standard South Dakota state park fees and reservation information; 14 day limit; phone c/o West Whitlock SRA (605) 765-9410.

Camp Notes: Tiny Lake Hiddenwood was one of the first man-made lakes in South Dakota. (A skeptic might wonder why this small, pork barrel beauty is classified as a state park when other, larger, much nicer areas, richer in history and scenic value, subsist as state recreation areas. Ed.)

South Dakota 32

WEST WHITLOCK
West Whitlock State Recreation Area

Location: Central South Dakota between Mobridge and Pierre.

Access: From U.S. Highway 212 at milepost 213 +.3 (3 miles east of the Missouri River Bridge, 6 miles west of the junction of U.S. 212 & South Dakota State Highway 83 west of Gettysburg), turn north onto South Dakota State Highway 1804 and travel 3.4 miles to milepost 311 +.9; turn west (left) onto a paved access road and proceed 4 miles to the recreation area entrance; continue for another 0.3 mile to the main loop, on the right; or for 0.1 mile beyond the main loop to an auxiliary loop.

Facilities: 100 campsites, including 50 with electrical hookups; sites are medium to large, level, with fairly good separation; parking pads are gravel, medium to long straight-ins; adequate space for large tents; fire rings; firewood is usually for sale, or b-y-o; water at central faucets; restrooms with showers; holding tank disposal station; paved driveways; camper supplies at an adjacent resort; limited+ supplies and services in Gettysburg.

Activities & Attractions: Fishing (reportedly excellent for walleye, northern pike, chinook salmon, among others); boating; boat launch and docks; fitness trail; swimming beach; playground; amphitheater.

Natural Features: Located on the east shore of Lake Oahe on the Missouri River; large hardwoods provide ample shelter/shade for most sites; high, grassy, treeless bluffs border the lake; typically breezy; elevation 1700'.

Season, Fees & Phone: Open all year, with limited services November to May; please see Appendix for standard South Dakota state park fees and reservation information; 14 day limit; park office (605) 765-9410.

Camp Notes: This area might remind a well-traveled camper of certain camps on Lake Powell and Lake Mead in the Southwest. Fishing is indubitably the #1 pastime here.

South Dakota 33

DOWNSTREAM: NORTH
Lake Oahe/Corps of Engineers Park

Location: Central South Dakota on the west edge of Pierre.

Access: From U.S. Highway 14 & South Dakota State Highway 34 at a point 1.2 miles west of the Missouri River Bridge and 3 miles west of Pierre, turn north onto State Highway 1806; proceed north for 3.9 miles; turn northeast (right) onto a paved project road; proceed 0.6 mile east to a "T" intersection; turn south (right) and continue for 0.45 mile; turn west (right) to the campground entrance station; "Campground #1" is to the right and "Campground #2" is to the left.

Facilities: 161 campsites, including 120 with electrical hookups; sites are medium to large, with nominal to fairly good separation; parking pads are paved, medium to very long straight-ins; minor additional leveling may be required; large, grassy tent spots; fireplaces; b-y-o firewood; water at central faucets; restrooms (H) with showers; paved driveways; campground attendant; nearly complete supplies and services are available in Pierre.

Activities & Attractions: Boating; marina; fishing; playground; amphitheater; Cottonwood Path Nature Trail; day use area with shelter; nearby archery and rifle ranges; Oahe Dam Visitor Center across the dam on the east bank.

Natural Features: Located on a gently rolling grassy flat near the west bank of the Missouri River; campground vegetation consists of mown grass, huge cottonwoods, and some smaller hardwoods; surrounding terrain includes riverside marsh and barren bluffs which border the river; elevation 1400'.

Season, Fees & Phone: May to October; $8.00 for a standard site, $10.00 for an electrical hookup site; 14 day limit; Lake Oahe CoE Project Office 224-5862.

Camp Notes: There's plenty of room for big rv's and tents among the tall cottonwoods. You're camping in good company here: the Lewis & Clark Party lingered along this same riverbank in 1804.

South Dakota 34

DOWNSTREAM: SOUTH
Lake Oahe/Corps of Engineers Park

Location: Central South Dakota on the west edge of Pierre.

Access: From U.S. Highway 14 & South Dakota State Highway 34 at a point 1.2 miles west of the Missouri River Bridge and 3 miles west of Pierre, turn north onto State Highway 1806; proceed north for 3.9 miles; turn northeast (right) onto a paved project road; continue for 0.15 mile, then turn south/southeast (right) for 0.6 mile; turn left into the campground.

Facilities: 45 campsites in a loop and a string; sites are small to large, with average to good separation; parking pads are mostly paved (some are gravel), level, medium to huge, straight-ins or pull-throughs; large, level, grassy tent spots; fire rings; b-y-o firewood is recommended; water at central faucets; restrooms with showers; holding tank disposal station near the highway; paved driveways; camper supplies at a nearby marina; nearly complete supplies and services are available in Pierre.

Activities & Attractions: Dam tours; boating; fishing (boat ramp and marina at Downstream North); playground; day use area with shelter; ORV area nearby off Highway 1806.

Natural Features: Located on the west bank of the Missouri River, just south of (below) Oahe Dam; most sites are situated on a grassy, tree-covered flat; some are along the riverfront; cottonwoods, grass and smaller planted trees comprise the vegetation; river views through the trees from most campsites; elevation 1400'.

Season, Fees & Phone: Open all year; $8.00; 14 day limit; Lake Oahe CoE Project Office 224-5862.

Camp Notes: Of the two main camps in this area, Downstream South and Downstream North, the atmosphere is usually more 'relaxed' at South. (Many boaters prefer staying at Downstream North because it's 2 miles closer to the boat ramp/marina and there are electrical hookups available.) Downstream South is also known as "Campground 3".

COW CREEK
Lake Oahe/Corps of Engineers Park

Location: Central South Dakota north of Pierre.

Access: From South Dakota State Highway 1804 at milepost 264 +.4 (14 miles north of Pierre, 7.8 miles north of the Oahe Dam Visitor Center), turn west onto a paved road and proceed 0.7 mile; turn north (right) and continue for 0.9 mile north, then west toward the camp area.

Facilities: 20 or more campsites in 2 sections; parking pads are gravel/grass, short to long straight-ins; many pads will require a little additional leveling; some large grassy tent areas; bbq grills at some sites; b-y-o firewood; many sites lack tables; central water (at the fish cleaning station); vault facilities; gravel driveways; camper supplies at a small marina, 2 miles southwest near Spring Creek; nearly complete supplies and services are available in Pierre.

Activities & Attractions: Boating; boat launch; marina nearby at Spring Creek; fishing; nearby Oahe Dam Visitor Center and tours of the Oahe Dam Power Plant.

Natural Features: Located on a peninsula near the southeast corner of Lake Oahe on the Missouri River; sites along the shore are wind-swept, very lightly sheltered, and have sweeping views to the north across the inlet; those away from the waterfront are on a grassy bluff tucked in among bushes and small trees planted as a wind break; elevation 1600'.

Season, Fees & Phone: Available all year, subject to weather conditions; no fee (subject to change); 14 day limit; Lake Oahe CoE Project Office 224-5862.

Camp Notes: The camping here is very basic, but for a camper with simple requirements who's looking for a good compromise between easy accessibility and remoteness, it's worth checking out. Another basic, open camping area, Spring Creek, is situated on another inlet just about 2 miles south of Cow Creek.

FARM ISLAND
Farm Island State Recreation Area

Location: Central South Dakota southeast of Pierre.

Access: From South Dakota State Highway 34 at milepost 213 +.5 (3 miles southeast of Pierre), turn south onto a paved access road and continue for 0.4 mile to the campground entrance.

Facilities: 70 campsites, including 30 with electrical hookups; sites are medium to large, with fair to good separation; parking pads are gravel, level, medium to long, straight-ins; generally excellent tent pitching possibilities; several sites have ramadas (sun/wind shelters); mostly fireplaces, plus some fire rings; firewood is usually for sale, or b-y-o; water at central faucets; restrooms with showers; holding tank disposal station; paved driveways; nearly complete supplies and services are available in Pierre.

Activities & Attractions: Boating; boat ramps; fishing (especially for walleye and northern pike); 500-foot-long sandy swimming beach; playground; amphitheater; visitor center with historical/natural displays; nature trails; junior ranger program.

Natural Features: Located on a flat along the north bank of the Missouri River (Lake Sharpe); sites are situated on a grassy floor sheltered by tall cottonwoods; a causeway connects the campground (on the mainland) with Farm Island; excellent, sheltered, sandy beach on Hipple Lake, a small, backwater impoundment created by the land bridge from the mainland to Farm Island; elevation 1400'.

Season, Fees & Phone: Open all year, with limited services November to May; please see Appendix for standard South Dakota state park fees and reservation information; 14 day limit; park office (605) 224-5605.

Camp Notes: Farm Island is a fantastic, 1200-acre park with seemingly something for everyone. The roomy, sheltered camping facility is, in itself, worth the trip.

WEST BEND
West Bend State Recreation Area

Location: Central South Dakota southeast of Pierre.

Access: From South Dakota State Highway 34 at milepost 239 +.3 (29 miles southeast of Pierre, 18 miles west of the junction of South Dakota Highways 34 and 47) turn south onto a gravel road; continue south/southeast for 9 miles; turn east (left) onto a paved park access road; camp #3 is to the left; camps #1 & #2 are a few hundred yards farther east.

Facilities: 127 campsites, including many with electrical hookups; sites are medium to large, with nominal to very good separation; parking pads are gravel, medium to long straight-ins; some pads may require additional leveling; some excellent tent-pitching opportunities; many sites have ramadas (sun shelters); fire rings or fireplaces; firewood is usually for sale, or b-y-o; water at central faucets; restrooms with showers; paved main driveways; camper supplies in Big Bend, 7 miles north; nearly complete supplies and services are available in Pierre.

Activities & Attractions: Boating; boat launch; fishing; Ox Bow Trail; playground; day use area with shelter.

Natural Features: Located on the grassy west bank of Lake Sharpe, an 80-mile-long, 2-mile-wide reservoir on the Missouri River; vegetation along the shore is very sparse, but the sites a few yards from the shore are shaded/sheltered by mature hardwoods; sites in Loop 3 are situated in a dense oak grove along a (dry) creekbed; elevation 1400'.

Season, Fees & Phone: Open all year, with limited services November to May; please see Appendix for standard South Dakota state park fees and reservation information; 14-day limit park office (605) 875-3220.

Camp Notes: West Bend offers quite a variety of good campsites: open beachside sites, or tree-sheltered sites fairly near the shore, or very secluded sites. Walleye fishing is reportedly excellent in the waters off West Bend.

South Dakota 38

TAILRACE
Lake Sharpe/Corps of Engineers Park

Location: Central South Dakota southeast of Pierre.

Access: From the junction of South Dakota State Highways 47 & 34 at milepost 249 on Highway 34 (north edge of Fort Thompson, 25 miles north of Chamberlain), proceed south and west on Highway 47 for 2.8 miles; turn southeast and continue 0.7 mile down to the campground.

Facilities: 63 electrical hookup campsites, including 22 double sites; sites are small to medium-sized, with very little visual separation; parking pads are paved, medium to very long, level, parallel pull-throughs; very large, level, grassy tent spots; ramadas (sun shelters) and cement table pads; barbecue grills and fireplaces; b-y-o firewood; water at central faucets; restrooms with showers; holding tank disposal station; paved driveways; limited supplies and services are available in Fort Thompson.

Activities & Attractions: Boating; boat launches and docks for river access; (boat access to Lake Sharpe is available at Good Soldier boat ramp, west 0.5 mile, on the south/west shore of the lake;) fishing; playgrounds; designated swimming beach; visitor center has wildlife and interpretive displays.

Natural Features: Located on a grassy point of land extending into the Missouri River; Big Bend Dam is immediately behind the campground to the northwest; a few planted trees are scattered over the mown grass flat; Eagle Island is just offshore to the south; typically breezy; elevation 1400'.

Season, Fees & Phone: Open all year, with limited services November to May; $9.00; 14 day limit; Lake Sharpe CoE Project Office (605) 734-6772.

Camp Notes: This is probably the most highly developed of the campgrounds on this section of the Missouri River. It has many of the comforts of home. A substantial number of campers enjoy watching the bald eagles known to make a migratory rest stop on the nearby island.

South Dakota 39

AMERICAN CREEK
Lake Francis Case/Corps of Engineers Park

Location: South-central South Dakota in Chamberlain.

Access: From South Dakota State Highway 50 on the north edge of Chamberlain at the corner of Jasper and G Avenue, turn west into the campground. (Note: from Interstate 90 *westbound*, access is from Exit 263 for Chamberlain (1 mile east of the Missouri River Bridge), then north on Business Route I-90 for 3.5 miles through town; *eastbound* access is from Exit 260 (on the west side of the river), then northeast on Biz I-90 for 4.5 miles.)

Facilities: 62 campsites, including 10 with full hookups and about 40 with electrical hookups; sites are small to medium-sized, with nominal separation; parking pads are gravel, medium to long, fairly level, mostly straight-ins, plus several parallel pull-throughs; good, level spots for medium-sized tents; barbecue grills and fireplaces; b-y-o firewood; water at central faucets; restrooms with showers; holding tank disposal station; paved or gravel driveways; adequate supplies and services are available in Chamberlain.

Activities & Attractions: Swimming beach; boating; fishing; waterskiing; playground.

Natural Features: Located on the east bank of Lake Francis Case on the Missouri River; campground vegetation consists of worn grass, tall cottonwoods, and a few other smaller planted hardwoods; tree-dotted, grassy bluffs are visible across the river; elevation 1400'.

Season, Fees & Phone: May to November; $8.00 for a standard site; $10.00 for an electrical hookup site; 14 day limit; Lake Francis Case CoE Project Office (605) 487-7844.

Camp Notes: The well-worn facilities at American Creek are reportedly filled by Thursday evening on most summer weekends. Considering that it's just a few minutes' drive off the Interstate (unless you elect to take the grand tour through town), it's not surprising that it's a popular place.

South Dakota 40

WEST CHAMBERLAIN
Lake Francis Case/Corps of Engineers Park

Location: South-central South Dakota west of Chamberlain.

Access: From Interstate 90 Exit 260 (34 miles east of Presho, 2 miles west of the Missouri River Bridge), turn north and immediately east onto Business Route I-90; proceed east for 2.3 miles (through the small community of Oacoma); turn north (left) onto a paved/gravel road; and continue for 0.7 mile; turn east (right) and immediately south (right again) into the campground.

Facilities: 40 campsites; sites are large, with nominal to fair separation; parking pads are paved, mostly long straight-ins; many pads may require some additional leveling; large, grassy tent spots, may be a bit sloped; several ramadas (sun shelters); fire rings, plus some barbecue grills; b-y-o firewood is recommended; water at central faucets; restrooms (H) with showers; holding tank disposal station; paved driveways; adequate supplies and services are available in Chamberlain.

Activities & Attractions: Boating; gravel boat launch and dock; playground; day use area adjacent; fishing for channel cat, walleye, pike, sauger, white bass, crappie, sheepshead, and sturgeon; waterskiing.

Natural Features: Located on a grassy slope on the west shore of 100-mile-long Lake Francis Case on the Missouri River; campground vegetation consists of prairie grass and some small/medium planted hardwoods; short, grassy, evergreen-dotted bluffs are visible across the river; elevation 1400'.

Season, Fees & Phone: May to September; $8.00; 14 day limit; Lake Francis Case CoE Project Office (605) 487-7844.

Camp Notes: If you don't need a hookup, check out West Chamberlain before settling into the more popular American Creek Campground (see separate information) across the river. The atmosphere at West Chamberlain seems quite different--more open and low-keyed--even though it's just the opposite shore of the same lake.

South Dakota 41

SNAKE CREEK
Snake Creek State Recreation Area

Location: South-central South Dakota southeast of Chamberlain.

Access: From South Dakota Highway 44 at milepost 291 + .8 (15 miles west of Platte, 0.2 mile east of the Missouri River Bridge), turn south into the campground.

Facilities: 96 campsites in a terraced arrangement; sites are medium to large, with average to good separation; parking pads are gravel, medium to long straight-ins, plus a few long pull-throughs; many pads may require some additional leveling; medium to large tent spots, may be a bit sloped; fire rings; b-y-o firewood; restrooms (H) with showers; water at central faucets; holding tank disposal station; paved driveways; limited supplies and services are available in Platte.

Activities & Attractions: Boating; fishing for walleye, crappie, etc.; scenic overlook, day use area and boat ramp are north across the highway; playground; hiking trail.

Natural Features: Located on a tree-covered, grassy hillside above the east bank of 100,000-acre Lake Francis Case on the Missouri River; Snake Creek is about midway between the northern tip and the southern (dam side) end of the lake; campground vegetation consists of rows of tall hardwoods and patches of worn grass; terrific lake views from a number of lakeside sites and from many others farther up the hillside; elevation 1400'.

Season, Fees & Phone: Open all year, with limited services October to April; please see Appendix for standard South Dakota state park fees and reservation information; 14 day limit; park office (605) 337-2587.

Camp Notes: There's no doubt about it--this place is a long way from the cradle of civilization. (Some campers are apprehensive about tangling with the reptiles here. Not to worry. A few years ago, most of the critters shed their skins, put on three-piece pinstripe suits, and migrated to D.C. Ed.)

South Dakota 42

PLATTE CREEK
Platte Creek State Recreation Area

Location: South-central South Dakota southeast of Chamberlain.

Access: From South Dakota State Highway 44 at milepost 297 +.8 turn south onto State Highway 1804; travel south for 8.2 miles; at a "T" intersection, turn west (right, continuing on the paved route 1804) and proceed west for 1.8 miles to the entrance station.

Facilities: 72 campsites, including a number with electrical hookups; sites vary from small and closely spaced to large and well separated; parking pads are gravel, short to medium-length, pull-offs or straight-ins; most pads will require additional leveling; most tent areas are small and sloped; several sites have ramadas (sun/wind shelters); fire rings or fireplaces; b-y-o firewood; water at central faucets; restrooms with showers; disposal station; mostly gravel driveways; gas and camper supplies at the marina; limited supplies and services are available in Platte.

Activities & Attractions: Boating; boat launch and dock; good fishing; small amphitheater; playground; hiking trail.

Natural Features: Located on the hilly, grassy, east shoreline of Lake Francis Case on the Missouri River; sites stretch for over a mile in 2 strings north and south of the Platte Creek inlet; prairie grass and a few small trees and bushes for vegetation; wide vistas up and down the lake and across to the 1000' bluffs on the opposite bank; elevation 1400'.

Season, Fees & Phone: Open all year, with limited services October to April; please see Appendix for standard South Dakota state park fees and reservation information; 14 day limit; phone c/o Snake Creek SRA (605) 337-2587.

Camp Notes: A number of sites are built on a very steep slope with an elaborate system of steps and timbers bordering the table areas. Before settling into a spot, you may want to scout the entire area--there are some really nice, spacious sites toward the south end.

South Dakota 43

BURKE LAKE
Burke Lake State Recreation Area

Location: South-central South Dakota near the South Dakota-Nebraska border near the town of Burke.

Access: From U.S. Highway 18 at milepost 286 +.2 (at the southern edge of Burke, 23 miles east of the junction of U.S. Highways 18 & 183, 45 miles west of the Missouri River near Pickstown), turn north onto Main Street; proceed north for 0.3 mile (5 blocks); turn east (right) onto 7th Street; continue for 0.8 mile, then turn south (right) onto a gravel access road; continue south for 1.55 miles (paved again after 1 mile of gravel); turn west (right) into the camping area.

Facilities: 15 campsites; sites are quite roomy, level and well separated; parking pads are paved, medium to long straight-ins; some excellent tent-pitching opportunities; fireplaces; b-y-o firewood; water at central faucets; vault facilities; paved driveway; limited supplies and services are available in Burke.

Activities & Attractions: Limited boating/sailing; fishing for northern pike, largemouth bass, perch, bluegill; swimming beach and bathhouse; playground; day use area; hiking trail around the lake.

Natural Features: Located in a wooded glen in a grassy basin surrounded by miles of prairie and agricultural land; small, but picturesque, 25-acre Burke Lake is visible through the trees from many of the sites; pines and hardwoods provide a considerable amount of shelter and separation for the sites; elevation 2300'.

Season, Fees & Phone: Available all year, subject to weather conditions, with limited services October to May; please see Appendix for standard South Dakota state park fees; 14 day limit; phone c/o Snake Creek SRA (605) 337-2587.

Camp Notes: This is one of the nicest little hidden treasures in the state of South Dakota! It must surely be a welcome, forested retreat in the heat of the summer, and also a colorful scene in the autumn months. This a definite 'find'.

South Dakota 44

NORTH POINT
Lake Francis Case/Corps of Engineers Park

Location: Southeast South Dakota near the South Dakota-Nebraska border.

Access: From U.S. Highway 18 at milepost 333 +.8 (1 mile north of the junction of South Dakota Highway 46 & U.S. Highways 18/281, 5 miles south of Lake Andes), turn west onto a paved access road; proceed 1.8 miles to the campground entrance station.

Facilities: 75 campsites with electrical hookups; sites are average to spacious, level, with fair to very good separation; parking pads are paved, long to very long straight-ins or pull-throughs; medium to large, grassy tent spots; fire rings, plus a few barbecue grills; b-y-o firewood is recommended; water at central faucets; restrooms (H) with showers; holding tank disposal station; paved driveways; campground attendant; gas and camper supplies in Pickstown; limited supplies and services are available in Lake Andes.

Activities & Attractions: Boating; boat launch and dock; fishing; day use area with shelters; playground; swimming beach; hiking; biking; interpretive displays; rifle range; tours of Fort Randall dam, 1 mile south.

Natural Features: Located on the southeast shore of Lake Francis Case on the Missouri River, on a grassy flat just above the rocky shore; the lake stretches for more than 100 miles to the north; extensive lawns bordered by mature conifers and hardwoods which provide ample shelter/shade for most sites; elevation 1400'.

Season, Fees & Phone: Open all year, with limited services November to May; $10.00; 14 day limit; Lake Francis Case CoE Project Office (605) 487-7844.

Camp Notes: This is the heartland/prairie version of camping on the ocean. From one of the many lakeside sites, it's very easy to envision yourself listening to the breakers crash upon the rocky Pacific Coast.

South Dakota 45

RANDALL CREEK
Lake Francis Case/Corps of Engineers Park

Location: Southeast South Dakota near the South Dakota-Nebraska border.

Access: From U.S. Highway 18 at milepost 329 +.75 (at the west edge of the dam and the Missouri River Bridge, 45 miles east of Burke, 1.4 miles west of Pickstown), turn south onto a paved project road; continue south and east for 0.85 mile; turn south (right) and continue for 0.3 mile; turn right again to the campground entrance station.

Facilities: 134 campsites with electrical hookups, in several loops stretching for over a mile; sites are average to spacious, level, with fair to excellent separation; parking pads are paved, medium to very long straight-ins; most sites have large, grassy tent spots; fire rings and barbecue grills; b-y-o firewood is recommended; water at central faucets; restrooms with showers; holding tank disposal station; paved driveways; gas and camper supplies in Pickstown.

Activities & Attractions: Boating; boat launch for river access nearby; Lake Francis Case boat ramp across the highway to the north; fishing; playgrounds; large day use area with chimneyed shelters and team sports equipment; Fort Randall ruins; dam tours.

Natural Features: Located on a wooded flat along the west bank of the Missouri River, just downstream of Fort Randall Dam and Lake Francis Case; lush grass and medium to tall hardwoods in the camp area; roughcut banks are visible across the river; there are a number of enormous riverside sites; elevation 1300'.

Season, Fees & Phone: May to September; $10.00; 14 day limit; Lake Francis Case CoE Project Office (605) 487-7844.

Camp Notes: Randall Creek Campground is a superb facility... a real CoE showplace. Obviously, a lot of planning and work went into creating this recreation complex. (The place is so big that you actually could get *lost* on a long walk away from your campsite.) Terrific.

LAKE LOUISE
Lake Louise State Recreation Area

Location: Central South Dakota northwest of Huron.

Access: From South Dakota State Highway 45 at milepost 119 +.5 (6 miles north of Miller, 20 miles south of the junction of SD 45 & U.S. 212 west of Redfield), turn west onto a paved road and proceed 7.7 miles; turn north (right) into the recreation area, then east (right) for 0.6 mile to the campground.
Alternate Access: From U.S. 14 at milepost 289 +.7 (11 miles west of Miller, 12 miles east of Highmore), turn north onto a paved road and zigzag north, zig east, zag north, zig east again, and zag into the park for a total meander of 9.9 miles from the highway.

Facilities: 28 campsites, including 15 with electrical hookups; sites are medium+, with fair to excellent separation; parking pads are paved, level, short+ to medium+, mostly straight-ins, plus a few pull-offs; medium to large tent spots; some sites have small ramadas (arched, sun/wind shelters); fireplaces; b-y-o firewood is recommended; water at central faucets; restrooms with showers; paved driveways; limited+ to adequate supplies and services are available in Miller.

Activities & Attractions: Swimming beach; hiking trails; playground; amphitheater; fishing; boating; boat launch.

Natural Features: Located near the east shore of serpentine Lake Louise; campground vegetation consists of light to fairly dense hardwoods, cedars, pines, and mown grass; surrounding countryside is classic prairie; elevation 1400'.

Season, Fees & Phone: Open all year, with limited services October to May; please see Appendix for standard South Dakota state park fees and reservation information; 14 day limit; park office (605) 853-2533.

Camp Notes: There are some *nice* camp spots tucked into their own little nooks among the trees here. But if you prefer something a little more open, that's available too. Lake Louise is shaped like a boa that just ate an island for lunch.

SOUTH DAKOTA
Northeast Prairie
Please refer to the South Dakota map in the Appendix

MINA LAKE
Mina Lake State Recreation Area

Location: Northeast South Dakota west of Aberdeen.

Access: From U.S. Highway 12 at milepost 277 +.8 (1 mile east of Mina, 12 miles west of Aberdeen), turn north onto Nesbitt Drive (Edmunds County Road 35) for 1.7 miles to a "T" intersection; turn west (left) onto a paved road for 0.8 mile; turn south (left) onto Edmunds County Road 33 (paved); continue on pavement south, east, and south again for 1.3 miles to the entrance station; the campground is just beyond, to the west (right). **Alternate Access:** From U.S. 12 at milepost 275 +.9 (1 mile west of Mina), turn north onto a paved road and proceed north for 1.2 miles, then east for 0.9 mile to County Road 33; turn south (right) and continue as above.

Facilities: 36 campsites, including 19 with electrical hookups; sites are medium-sized, with fair separation; parking pads are paved/gravel, mostly long, level straight-ins; large tent areas, some slightly sloped; a few sites have ramadas (small, sun/wind shelters; fire rings; b-y-o firewood; water at central faucets; restrooms with showers; paved driveway; complete supplies and services in Aberdeen.

Activities & Attractions: Interpretive trail; swimming beach; playground; fishing; boating; boat launch.

Natural Features: Located on a grassy shelf at the tip of a long peninsula a few feet above the north shore of Mina Lake; sites receive light to moderate shelter/shade from large hardwoods, plus a few evergreens; lake views; elevation 1300'.

Season, Fees & Phone: Open all year, with limited services October to May; please see Appendix for standard South Dakota state park fees and reservation information; 14 day limit; phone c/o Richmond Lake SRA (605) 225-5325.

Camp Notes: The peninsula on which the recreation area is situated nearly bisects this horseshoe-shaped lake, so the campground is *almost* on the *south* shore. The camp and its associated lake views are really quite nice.

South Dakota 48

RICHMOND LAKE
Richmond Lake State Recreation Area

Location: Northeast South Dakota west of Aberdeen.

Access: From U.S. Highway 12 at milepost 284 +.4 (6 miles west of Aberdeen, 7 miles east of Mina), turn north onto Brown County Road 6 and travel 5 miles to Brown County Road 13; turn west (left) onto Road 13 and proceed west 1 mile, then north 1 mile; as the road turns west at this point, continue straight ahead, into the recreation area and a final zigzag 0.3 mile around the one-way drive to the campground. **Alternate Access:** From U.S. 281 at milepost 200 +.2 (5 miles north of Aberdeen), turn west onto Brown County Road 13 and proceed west 5 miles, then north 1 mile to the recreation area.

Facilities: 25 campsites, some with electrical hookups; sites are medium to large, slightly sloped, with fairly good separation; parking pads are paved/gravel, medium to long, mostly straight-ins, plus a few pull-offs; adequate space for medium to large tents; fireplaces; b-y-o firewood; water at central faucets; restrooms; paved driveways; nearest supplies and services (complete) are in Aberdeen.

Activities & Attractions: Richmond Lake Hiking Trail; swimming beach; playground; amphitheater; fishing; boating.

Natural Features: Located on a wooded slope near the south shore of long, slender, branched, 800-acre Richmond Lake; sites are moderately sheltered/shaded by large hardwoods on mown grass; elevation 1300'.

Season, Fees & Phone: Open all year, with limited services October to May; please see Appendix for standard South Dakota state park fees and reservation information; 14 day limit; park office (605) 225-5325.

Camp Notes: Richmond Lake hasn't any really special attributes; but its quick-and-easy access makes it a good place to stay in the Aberdeen area. Most of the countryside west of Aberdeen looks as if a gargantuan slab of slate was laid down and planted with prairie grass. It's that flat.

South Dakota 49

MELGAARD
Aberdeen City Park

Location: Northeast South Dakota in Aberdeen.

Access: From U.S. Highway 12 on the east end of Aberdeen (by the airport) turn south onto Melgaard Road/Brown County Road 19 and proceed 1 mile, then the road curves west; continue west for 2.2 miles; turn north (right) onto South Lloyd Street, then a quick left into the campground. **Alternate Access:** From U.S. 281 at milepost 193 +.2, on the far southwest corner of Aberdeen, turn east onto 18th Avenue SW/Road 19 and proceed 1.8 miles to South Lloyd Street and the park.

Facilities: 14 campsites with electrical hookups, plus a tent camping area; sites are generally small, level, closely spaced; trees provide visual separation between some sites; parking pads are paved, medium-length straight-ins or long pull-throughs; adequate space for large tents in the grassy tent zone; no fire facilities in campground, barbecue grills and fireplaces in adjacent day use area; b-y-o charcoal; water at central faucets; restrooms with showers; holding tank disposal station; paved driveway; complete supplies and services are available within 3 miles.

Activities & Attractions: Spacious park grounds; shelters in the day use area; playground.

Natural Features: Located on the east side of a large city park complex; campsites are sheltered/shaded by light to medium-dense, large hardwoods and pines; elevation 1300'.

Season, Fees & Phone: April to November; $6.50 for a tent site, $8.00 for an electrical hookup unit; 5 day limit; park office (605) 622-7015.

Camp Notes: The area immediately adjacent to the park is heavily residentialized. Nonetheless, there are open fields to the south, beyond a row of houses, so the park area is semi-rural. (Aberdeen is the corporate headquarters of a very large, well-known, economy motel chain. But the campground here is even more economical--if you can make-do without cable TV and free popcorn. Ed.)

South Dakota 50

FISHER GROVE
Fisher Grove State Park

Location: Northeast South Dakota north of Huron.

Access: From U.S. Highway 212 at milepost 314 +.6 (8 miles east of Redfield, 3 miles west of Frankfort), turn north onto a paved park access road and proceed 0.4 mile to the park entrance station; turn west and continue for 0.1 mile across the bridge over the river to the campground.

Facilities: 28 campsites, including 12 with electrical hookups; (a group camping area is also available); sites are medium to medium+, essentially level, with minimal to nominal separation; parking pads are gravel, long straight-ins; very good to excellent tent-pitching possibilities; fireplaces, plus a few barbecue grills; firewood is usually for sale, or b-y-o; water at several faucets; restrooms with showers; holding tank disposal station; paved driveways; adequate supplies and services are available in Redfield.

Activities & Attractions: Dakota Interpretive/Hiking Trail; visitor center; historical sites; canoeing, floating; boat landing; playground.

Natural Features: Located on a large, grassy flat on the north bank of the James River; sites receive minimal to light shelter/shade from large and small hardwoods; elevation 1300'.

Season, Fees & Phone: Open all year, with limited services November to May; please see Appendix for standard South Dakota state park fees and reservation information; 14 day limit; park office (605) 472-1212.

Camp Notes: The river in this segment is generally canoeable through midsummer, and floatable in an inflatable for a little longer. (Pundits have referred to the historic James as the world's longest unnavigable river.) The park's small visitor center is distinctively different from the typical arched doorway/cathedral ceiling/glass wall approach of visitor centers in many state and national parks in the West. Fisher Grove's VC is in an old country schoolhouse. Appropriate. And neat!

South Dakota 51

FORT SISSETON
Fort Sisseton State Park

Location: Northeast South Dakota west of Sisseton.

Access: From South Dakota State Highway 10 at a point 7 miles northwest of Lake City, 11 miles southeast of Britton), turn south onto Marshall County Road 5 and proceed 7 miles; turn west into the park; the campground is on the west side of the fort. (Note: this is the most straightforward access from a major highway; access is possible from 3 other points--from U.S. 12 in Webster, north on SD 25 11 miles, then continue north on county roads for 10 miles; or from SD 25 in Eden, west for 5.5 miles on Marshall County Road 16 to County Road 5, then north 3 miles; or from SD 27, east on Marshall County 16 for 11 miles to County Road 5, then north. Got that??)

Facilities: 12 campsites; sites are medium-sized, basically level, with minimal separation; parking surfaces are grass and generally as large as needed; good-sized, grassy tent areas; fireplaces; b-y-o firewood; water at a central faucet; vault facilities; gravel driveway; nearest source of supplies (a small market, 3 bars and a bank) is Eden, 9 miles SE.

Activities & Attractions: Restored/well maintained buildings and grounds of a large, frontier military outpost; visitor center; interpretive programs in summer; annual festival in June.

Natural Features: Located in a small grove of hardwoods; sites are lightly sheltered/shaded; park grounds include acres of mown lawns; surrounded by prairie interspersed with stands of trees; elevation 1200'.

Season, Fees & Phone: Open all year, with limited services October to May; please see Appendix for standard South Dakota state park fees; 14 day limit; phone c/o Roy Lake SP (605) 448-5701.

Camp Notes: Sure, this isn't the * * * * camping that's found in other state parks. But where's that spirit of adventure? Just imagine that you're part of a cavalry patrol out on bivouac. (Now...where did I leave my carbine and canteen? Ed.)

ROY LAKE: WEST
Roy Lake State Park

Location: Northeast South Dakota west of Sisseton.

Access: From South Dakota State Highway 10 at milepost 337 +.5 (1.7 miles west of the junction of State Highways 10 & 25 near Lake City, 17 miles southeast of Britton), turn south onto a paved park access road and proceed 1.5 miles to the park entrance; turn west (right) for 0.3 mile to the campground. (Note: access is also possible from milepost 211 on SD 25, then west 3 miles around the north shore of the lake to the campground.)

Facilities: 39 campsites, most with electrical hookups, plus a small tent camping area; sites are medium to fairly large, with fair to good separation; parking pads are gravel, long, respectably level straight-ins; enough room for large tents in most units; fireplaces; b-y-o firewood; water at central faucets; restrooms with showers; (holding tank disposal station in the East unit); paved driveways; gas and camper supplies at the park concession, limited groceries in Lake City.

Activities & Attractions: Swimming beach; Roy Island Trail; fishing; boating; boat launches; playground; amphitheater.

Natural Features: Located on gently sloping terrain on a point on the north shore of Roy Lake; sites are quite well sheltered/shaded by large hardwoods; a few sites have lake views through the trees; a bay and marsh border the campground on the northwest; elevation 1300'.

Season, Fees & Phone: Open all year, with limited services November to May; please see Appendix for standard South Dakota state park fees and reservation information; 14 day limit; park office (605) 448-5701.

Camp Notes: This campground is adjacent to the concession area and is much handier to the swimming beach than Roy Lake-East (see info). The marshy bay and its assorted critters might be a consideration for some campers. A foot bridge spans the bay to the trail on the circular island.

ROY LAKE: EAST
Roy Lake State Park

Location: Northeast South Dakota west of Sisseton.

Access: From South Dakota State Highway 25 at milepost 211 +.4 (1 mile south of the junction of State Highways 25 & 10 near Lake City, 6 miles north of Eden), turn west onto the park access road and proceed 0.6 mile; turn south (left) into the campground. (Note: access is also available from SD 10 at milepost 337 +.5, then south 1.5 miles to the park's north entrance, then east along the lake's north shore for 2 miles to the campground.)

Facilities: 36 campsites with electrical hookups, plus a dozen park n' walk tent sites; sites are medium to large, basically level, with fair to good separation; parking pads are packed gravel, mostly medium to long straight-ins; adequate space for large tents; fireplaces; b-y-o firewood; water at central faucets; restrooms with showers; holding tank disposal station; paved driveways; gas and camper supplies at the park concession, limited groceries in Lake City.

Activities & Attractions: Prairie Pond Interpretive Trail; swimming beach; playground; fishing; boating; boat launches; cross-country skiing.

Natural Features: Located on a grassy slope and flat on the east shore of Roy Lake in the Glacial Lakes Region; sites receive moderate shelter/shade from large hardwoods, plus pines along the edge of the campground; elevation 1300'.

Season, Fees & Phone: Open all year, with limited services November to May; please see Appendix for standard South Dakota state park fees and reservation information; 14 day limit; park office (605) 448-5701.

Camp Notes: The terrain and campground vegetation are generally similar to the West Unit at Roy Lake (see separate information). But this camp is (subjectively) superior because of it's greater area, considerably better lake views, and terrific tent camping area on the lakeshore.

PICKEREL LAKE: WEST
Pickerel Lake State Recreation Area

Location: Northeast South Dakota south of Sisseton.

Access: From U.S. Highway 12 at milepost 355 (1.5 miles east of Waubay, 11 miles west of Interstate 29 Exit 207), turn north onto a paved county road and travel 12.5 miles; turn east (right) onto a paved park access road and proceed 0.4 mile to the campground. (Note: access is also possible from I-29 Exit 234, southeast of Sisseton; travel west on a paved county road for about 14 miles to a point 0.2 mile west of YMCA Camp Wisagoma; turn south onto a paved county road for 2 miles to the rec area access road; the county roads around here aren't well-signed.)

Facilities: 42 campsites, including 39 with electrical hookups, in 2 loops; sites are medium to large, with fair to good separation; most parking pads are gravel, medium+ to long straight-ins, plus a few pull-offs; half of the pads are tolerably level, others may require additional leveling; adequate space for large tents, though may be slightly sloped; fireplaces; a limited amount of gatherable firewood may be available in the vicinity, b-y-o to be sure; water at a central faucet; restrooms with showers; holding tank disposal station; paved driveways; camper supplies at nearby lodges; limited supplies and services in Waubay.

Activities & Attractions: Nature/hiking trail; swimming area; playgrounds; amphitheater; fishing; boating; boat launch.

Natural Features: Located on rolling terrain above the west shore of Pickerel Lake in the Glacial Lakes Region; vegetation consists of a mixture of large hardwoods, cedars and pines on a surface of mown grass; elevation 1500'.

Season, Fees & Phone: Available all year, with limited services November to May; please see Appendix for standard South Dakota state park fees and reservation information; 14 day limit; park office (605) 486-4753.

Camp Notes: Of the pair of camps on Pickerel Lake, this is probably the one of choice. Very "piney" environment.

PICKEREL LAKE: EAST
Pickerel Lake State Recreation Area

Location: Northeast South Dakota south of Sisseton.

Access: From U.S. Highway 12 at milepost 355 (1.5 miles east of Waubay, 11 miles west of I-29 Exit 207), turn north onto a paved county road and travel 10.5 miles to an intersection; turn east (right) onto Day County Road 6 (paved) and proceed east, then north, for 2.6 miles; turn west (left) onto the park access road for 0.9 mile to the campground. (Note: access is also possible from I-29 Exit 234, south of Sisseton; travel west on a paved county road for about 14 miles to a point 0.2 miles west of YMCA Camp Wisagoma; turn south onto a paved road for 3.9 miles to Day County Road 6 and continue as above.)

Facilities: 18 campsites, including 17 with electrical hookups; sites are medium-sized, with nominal to fair separation; parking pads are paved/oiled gravel straight-ins; some pads may require additional leveling; adequate space for medium to large tents, though may be slightly sloped; fireplaces; some firewood may be available for gathering, b-y-o to be sure; water at a hand pump; vault facilities; paved driveways; camper supplies nearby; limited supplies and services are available in Waubay.

Activities & Attractions: Glacial Mounds Interpretive Trail; playground; swimming area; fishing; boating; boat launch.

Natural Features: Located on the sloping east shore of Pickerel Lake; campground vegetation consists of light to moderately dense, large hardwoods and mown grass; elevation 1500'.

Season, Fees & Phone: Available all year, with limited services November to May; please see Appendix for standard South Dakota state park fees and reservation information; 14 day limit; park office (605) 486-4753.

Camp Notes: Probably the majority of visitors come here for the very good fishing (especially for walleyes, white bass, smallmouth bass). But this is really a nice, tucked-out-of-the-way camp for anyone. Lake views through the trees.

HARTFORD BEACH
Hartford Beach State Park

Location: Northeast corner of South Dakota northeast of Watertown.

Access: From South Dakota State Highway 15 at milepost 189 + .9 (18 miles east of Interstate 29 Exit 213 for Wilmot, 13 miles west of the South Dakota-Iowa border), turn north onto the paved park access road and proceed 0.3 mile to the entrance station and a "T" intersection; turn east (right) and proceed 0.2 mile to a fork: bear left for 0.1 mile down to the campground. (Note: the turnoff is about 15 miles north of the city of Milbank.)

Facilities: 37 campsites, majority with electrical hookups; sites are generally small, sloped, with little separation; parking pads are gravel, short to medium-length straight-ins; adequate space for small to medium-sized tents; fireplaces or fire rings; b-y-o firewood; water at several faucets; restrooms, plus auxiliary vaults; holding tank disposal station; paved driveway; limited supplies and services are available in Wilmot.

Activities & Attractions: Swimming beach; interpretive and hiking trails; historical sites; interpretive programs; boating; boat launch; fishing.

Natural Features: Located on a rather steep hillside above the south/west shore of 40-mile-long, 22,000-acre Big Stone Lake (the headwater of the Minnesota River); sites are well sheltered/shaded by large hardwoods and a few evergreens; views of the lake from most sites; elevation 1000'.

Season, Fees & Phone: Available all year, with limited services November to May; please see Appendix for standard South Dakota state park fees and reservation information; 14 day limit; park office (605) 432-6374.

Camp Notes: Even though there's a substantial tilt to most of the campsites, the woods-and-water setting is beautiful enough to overcome that consideration. There also is a small, tent camping section on a grassy flat near the day use area and the long, sandy beach.

SANDY SHORE
Sandy Shore State Recreation Area

Location: Northeast South Dakota west of Watertown.

Access: From U.S. Highway 212 at milepost 370 + .3 (5 miles west of Watertown), turn north onto South Dakota State Highway 139 and proceed 0.15 mile; turn east (right) onto a paved county road and continue for 0.3 mile to the recreation area entrance; most campsites are on the west side of the park (left of the entrance); a few sites are situated to the east (right) of the entrance.

Facilities: 21 campsites, including 12 with electrical hookups; sites are`small, level, with minimal separation; parking surfaces are paved/gravel/grass, short to medium-length straight-ins; small tent spots; fire rings; b-y-o firewood; water at central faucets; restrooms (H) with showers; paved driveway; complete supplies and services are available in Watertown.

Activities & Attractions: Swimming; playsets; fishing; boat launch.

Natural Features: Located at the southwest tip of Lake Kampeska; sites are sheltered/shaded by a row of large hardwoods and a few pines; all sites have a lake view; elevation 1700'.

Season, Fees & Phone: Available all year, with limited services November to May; please see Appendix for standard South Dakota state park fees and reservation information; 14 day limit; phone c/o State Parks District Manager, Watertown, (605) 886-4769.

Camp Notes: At only 8 acres, this is the smallest unit in South Dakota's state park and recreation area system. Since it's within a few minutes' drive of one of the state's larger cities, it *does* get busy. If more solitude is your preference, you might try nearby Pelican Lake SRA, a much larger area but with much less in the way of camping facilities. Pelican Lake has a small designated camping area, central shelter and a sandy beach. To get there, take the paved road signed for Pelican Lake from U.S. 212 at milepost 372 + .5, (2 miles east of Sandy Shore), south and east 5 miles to the recreation area, on the lake's south shore.

ULVEN
Clear Lake City Park

Location: East-central South Dakota southeast of Watertown.

Access: From South Dakota State Highway 15 at a point 0.4 mile north of midtown Clear Lake, 7 miles south of Altamont, turn east onto an access road (starts as paved, shortly becomes gravel), and proceed 1.9 miles east and south; turn west (right) into the campground.

Facilities: Approximately 10 campsites, including 8 with electrical hookups; sites are small+, with minimal separation; parking surfaces are grass, reasonably level straight-ins/pull-offs; adequate space for large tents; fireplaces or barbecue grills; b-y-o firewood; water at a hand pump; vault facilities; gravel driveway; limited+ supplies and services are available in Clear Lake.

Activities & Attractions: Playground; day use area.

Natural Features: Located on a grassy flat on a small point on the east shore of Clear Lake; sites receive light to moderate shelter/shade from large hardwoods, plus a few pines scattered around the area; most sites have a lake view through the trees; elevation 1800'.

Season, Fees & Phone: Available all year, with limited services October to May; $4.00; (no phone).

Camp Notes: For a few bucks, you get fairly good views during the day and the glint of small town lights on the lake at night. This is, by most standards, the better of the two municipal camping areas in the Clear Lake vicinity. The other spot primarily consists of a gravel parking lot with water, vaults and a dump station. It's situated on the west side of the highway at the north edge of town, a few hundred yards south of the turnoff to Ulven Park.

LAKE COCHRANE
Lake Cochrane State Recreation Area

Location: Eastern border of South Dakota southeast of Watertown.

Access: From South Dakota State Highway 22 at milepost 380 +.5 (10 miles east of the city of Clear Lake, 3 miles west of the South Dakota-Minnesota border), turn south onto a gravel road and proceed 2.2 miles; turn east (left) onto a paved road for 0.25 miles, then turn south (right) to the recreation area entrance; turn east (left) to the campground.

Facilities: 15 campsites, including 8 with electrical hookups; sites are medium-sized, essentially level, with nominal separation; parking pads are gravel, medium to long straight-ins; large, grassy, tent areas; all sites have ramadas (arched, sun/wind shelters); fireplaces; b-y-o firewood; water at central faucets; vault facilities; paved/oiled gravel driveway; limited+ supplies and services are available in Clear Lake.

Activities & Attractions: Swimming beach; fishing for walleyes, bass, northerns, perch; limited boating; day use area.

Natural Features: Located on the north shore of Lake Cochrane, on a grassy knoll dotted with medium-height hardwoods and a few pines; Lake Oliver lies just to the north of the campground; elevation 1800'.

Season, Fees & Phone: Available all year, subject to weather conditions, with limited services November to May; please see Appendix for standard South Dakota state park fees and reservation information; 14-day limit; phone c/o State Parks District Manager, Watertown, (605) 886-4769.

Camp Notes: Although the fishing is supposedly pretty decent here, this doesn't appear to be one of those places you'd go out of your way just to camp in. (That's not a negativism, merely an observation.) Good facilities, good lake views.

LAKE POINSETT
Lake Poinsett State Recreation Area

Location: East-central South Dakota northwest of Brookings.

Access: From U.S. Highway 81 at milepost 131 +.7 (12 miles north of Arlington, 27 miles south of Watertown), turn east onto Brookings County Road 2 (paved) and travel 2.3 miles to the entrance station; proceed 0.3 mile to Camp #1, or continue for another 0.4 mile to Camp #2.

Facilities: 93 campsites, the majority with electrical hookups, in 2 loops; sites vary from small to large, with generally good separation; most parking pads are gravel, medium to long straight-ins or pull-offs; some pads may require a tad of additional leveling; enough space for medium to large tents on a grassy surface; ramadas (small sun/wind shelters) for some sites; fireplaces; b-y-o firewood; water at central faucets; restrooms with showers; holding tank disposal station; paved driveways; gas and camper supplies at nearby resorts; gas and groceries in Arlington.

Activities & Attractions: Very long, sand/gravel beach; boating; boat launch; fishing; playground; amphitheater.

Natural Features: Located along or near the south shore of Lake Poinsett, an 8000-acre glacial lake; shelter/shade from tall hardwoods and evergreens varies from limited along the shore in camp #1, to moderately dense away from the shore in camp #2; mown lawns; elevation 1700'.

Season, Fees & Phone: May to November; please see Appendix for standard South Dakota state park fees and reservation information; 14 day limit; phone c/o Oakwood Lakes SP (605) 627-5441.

Camp Notes: Many of the campsites in Camp #1 are close enough to the lake that you may need to squeegee your window or sponge your tent floor when a norther blows. Nearly all sites in that loop have fine lake views. But also check out Camp #2--its sites are somewhat more sheltered and private than those in Camp #1.

South Dakota 61

OAKWOOD LAKES
Oakwood Lakes State Park

Location: East-central South Dakota northwest of Brookings.

Access: From Interstate 29 Exit 140 (7 miles north of Brookings), turn west onto South Dakota State Highway 30 for 1 mile; continue west on Brookings County Road 6 (paved) and travel 11.5 miles; turn north onto the park access road and proceed 2.3 miles; turn east (right) into the campground. **Alternate Access:** From U.S. 81 at milepost 123 +.7 (3 miles north of Arlington, 36 miles south of Watertown), turn east onto Brookings County Road 6 and travel 7.4 miles to the park access road; continue as above.

Facilities: 71 campsites, including about a third with electrical hookups; sites are medium-sized, with fair to good separation; parking pads are gravel, medium to long straight-ins which may need a bit of additional leveling; medium to large tent areas; fireplaces; firewood is usually for sale, or b-y-o; water at central faucets; restrooms with showers; holding tank disposal station; paved driveways; gas and groceries in Volga, 10 miles south/southeast.

Activities & Attractions: Historical and natural exhibits; swimming beach; hiking trails; cross-country skiing; playground, volleyball courts; limited boating; fishing.

Natural Features: Located in a woodland on grassy, gently rolling terrain; most sites are well sheltered by large hardwoods and several types of large evergreens; 8 lakes, including large Lake Tetonkaha (just across the main road from the campground) provide the water interest; elevation 1800'.

Season, Fees & Phone: Open all year, with limited services November to May; please see Appendix for standard South Dakota state park fees and reservation information; 14 day limit; park office (605) 627-5441.

Camp Notes: This very pretty park seems to be a favorite place of pro and amateur entomologists. (Buzzzzz. Whack! Ed.)

SOUTH DAKOTA
Southeast Prairie

Please refer to the South Dakota map in the Appendix

South Dakota 62

LAKE MITCHELL
Mitchell City Park

Location: Southeast South Dakota north of Mitchell.

Access: From South Dakota State Highway 37 at milepost 76 +.6 (2 miles north of midtown Mitchell, 4 miles north of Interstate 90), turn west into the campground. (Note: If westbound on I-90, take Exit 332, then north on Highway 37; if eastbound on I-90, take Exit 330, then north on Omaha Street and east on Havens Avenue to connect with Highway 37 in midtown Mitchell.)

Facilities: 74 campsites, most with full or partial hookups, and including about a dozen designated tent sites; many units have cable TV hookups; sites are very small to small+, basically level, and closely spaced; parking pads are grass/gravel, short straight-ins; mostly small to medium-sized tent areas; fire rings, fireplaces or barbecue grills; firewood is usually for sale, or b-y-o; water at faucets throughout; restrooms with showers; gravel driveways; complete supplies and services are available in Mitchell.

Activities & Attractions: Swimming beach; boating; fishing.

Natural Features: Located on the southeast shore of Lake Mitchell, an impoundment on the Firesteel River; most sites receive light to moderate shelter/shade from large hardwoods; bordered by level prairie and cropland; elevation 1300'.

Season, Fees & Phone: May to September; $7.50 for a tent site, $9.50 for a standard site, $11.00 for an electrical hookup site, $12.00 for an electrical & sewer hookup site; $1.50 for cable TV; site fees include charges for 2 persons--add $1.00 for each additional person; campground office (605) 996-9643 or park office (605) 996-7180.

Camp Notes: Some of the best campsites here are several of the tent sites just above the lakeshore. The fees (as of this writing) are just about the highest in South Dakota for the facilities provided. (But where else can you switch to cable TV and watch reruns of *Dallas* and *Dynasty* when you grow weary of watching the sunset over the lake? Ed.)

South Dakota 63

LAKE HERMAN
Lake Herman State Park

Location: East-central South Dakota northwest of Sioux Falls.

Access: From U.S. 81/South Dakota State Highway 34 at milepost 92 +.6 (2 miles west of Madison, 5 miles east of Junius) turn south/southwest off the highway for a few yards, then turn south/southeast (left) and follow the east shore of the lake for 1.6 miles to the park entrance; proceed 0.6 mile to the main camp loop, or continue east for another 0.5 mile to the east loop.

Facilities: 69 campsites, some with electrical hookups, in 2 loops; sites are medium to large, essentially level, with fairly good to excellent separation; parking pads are gravel, medium to long straight-ins; good to excellent tent-pitching opportunities; fire rings; b-y-o firewood; water at central faucets; restrooms with showers; holding tank disposal station; paved or gravel driveways; adequate+ supplies and services are available in Madison.

Activities & Attractions: Sandy swimming beach; hiking, fitness, and cross-country ski trails; playground; amphitheater; boating; boat launch and dock; fishing.

Natural Features: Located in stands of large hardwoods, plus some evergreens, near the east shore of Lake Herman; Herman Slough is an adjacent pond which may be the seasonal residence of all kinds of wildlife; elevation 1700'.

Season, Fees & Phone: Available all year, with limited services November to May; please see Appendix for standard South Dakota state park fees and reservation information; 14 day limit; park office (605) 256-3613.

Camp Notes: All of the sites here are quite nice. But for privacy, many of the campsites in the densely forested east loop would be hard to beat. The park area's recorded history dates back to 1870, when one Herman N. Luce took up squatter's rights on the lakeshore near this spot.

South Dakota 64

WALKERS POINT
Walkers Point State Recreation Area

Location: East-central South Dakota northwest of Sioux Falls.

Access: From South Dakota State Highway 19 at milepost 94 +.4 (2.5 miles south of the junction of State Highways 19 & 34 southeast of Madison, 5 miles north of Franklin), turn east onto Lake County Road 44 (paved); proceed 2 miles, then turn north (left) onto a gravel road; continue for 0.5 mile, then turn east (right) into the recreation area; proceed east 0.2 mile, then turn south (right) into the campground.

Facilities: 29 campsites; sites are small+ to medium-sized, with nominal separation; parking pads are gravel, tolerably level, medium-length straight-ins or pull-offs; adequate space for large tents in most sites, though may be slightly sloped; fire rings; b-y-o firewood is recommended; water at central faucets; restrooms with showers; gravel driveways; adequate+ supplies and services are available in Madison.

Activities & Attractions: Fishing; boating; boat launch.

Natural Features: Located on the west shore of Madison Lake; sites receive minimal to light shelter/shade from hardwoods and tall brush; residences and farms are situated around the lakeshore; elevation 1600'.

Season, Fees & Phone: Available all year, with limited services November to May; please see Appendix for standard South Dakota state park fees; 14 day limit; phone c/o Lake Herman SP (605) 256-3613.

Camp Notes: This recreation area (which was formerly just a fishing and boating access site) is currently undergoing expansion and improvement (more sites, new boat ramp, road surfacing, etc.). All sites are shoreside or within a few yards of the lake.

LAKE VERMILLION
Lake Vermillion State Recreation Area

Location: Southeast South Dakota west of Sioux Falls.

Access: From Interstate 90 Exit 374 (Montrose Exit, 25 miles west of Sioux Falls, 42 miles east of Mitchell), turn south onto a local highway and travel 5 miles; turn east onto a paved park access road for 0.2 mile to the entrance station; continue for another 0.4 mile, then turn south (right) into the campground.

Facilities: 24 campsites; sites are medium-sized, with minimal separation; parking pads are paved, long straight-ins or pull-offs; a little additional leveling may be required; adequate space for large tents, though some spots may be slightly sloped; ramadas (small sun/wind shelters) for most sites; fire rings; firewood is usually for sale, or b-y-o; water at central faucets; restrooms with showers; paved driveways; camper supplies at a nearby private campground; gas and limited groceries in Montrose and Canistota, (both within 7 miles).

Activities & Attractions: Swimming beach; playground; boating; boat launch and dock; fishing (reportedly good to very good) for walleyes, northerns, largemouth bass, panfish.

Natural Features: Located on the north shore of Vermillion Lake, an impoundment on the East Fork of the Vermillion River; campground vegetation consists of mown grass and a few small hardwoods and evergreens; encircled by gently rolling prairie; elevation 1400'.

Season, Fees & Phone: Available all year, with limited services November to April; please see Appendix for standard South Dakota state park fees; 14-day limit; park office (605) 296-3643.

Camp Notes: Camping facilities here recently underwent a major facelift. Although the sites are very well suited to both tent or rv camping, no hookups are provided (possibly be-cause these services are available at the nearby private campground). Excellent lake views from all sites.

PALISADES
Palisades State Park

Location: Southeast South Dakota northeast of Sioux Falls.

Access: From South Dakota State Highway 11 at milepost 90 +.3 (at the corner of a right angle turn in the highway, 0.5 mile south of Garrison, 9.5 miles northeast of Interstate 90 Exit 406 for Corson-Brandon), turn southeast onto a paved road which becomes gravel and proceed southeast, then south for 1.25 miles; turn west (right) onto a paved park road for 0.3 mile to the park entrance station, then a final 0.1 mile to the campground.

Facilities: 38 campsites, including several park n' walks; sites are small to medium-sized, with nominal to fairly good separation; parking pads are paved, medium to long straight-ins or pull-offs which will probably require additional leveling; small to medium-sized, sloped tent spots; fire rings or fireplaces; b-y-o firewood; water at central faucets; restrooms; paved/loose gravel driveways; gas and groceries are available in Garretson.

Activities & Attractions: Trails; playground; interpretive programs; amphitheater; limited stream fishing.

Natural Features: Located on a grassy, tree-dotted slope in a valley along Split Rock Creek; sites receive light to moderate shelter/shade from hardwoods and a few cedars; the stream has exposed and eroded the rock in the area into lines of cliffs which fancifully resemble fortifications; elevation 1400'.

Season, Fees & Phone: May to October; please see Appendix for standard South Dakota state park fees and reservation information; 14 day limit; park office (605) 594-3824.

Camp Notes: The small (110-acre) park's 'theme' (if that's the correct term) seems to be one of simplicity, and appreciation of the natural environment. This is the closest public campground to the state's largest city.

NEWTON HILLS
Newton Hills State Park

Location: Southeast South Dakota southeast of Sioux Falls.

Access: From Interstate 29 Exit 56 (9 miles north of Beresford, 22 miles south of Sioux Falls), turn east onto Lincoln County Road 140 and travel 12 miles to County Road 135; turn north (left) onto Road 135 and proceed 0.3 mile; turn west (left) into the park; continue ahead 0.2 mile, then left to the campground.
Alternate Access: From U.S. 18 in midtown Canton, turn south onto South Cedar Street (County Road 135) and drive 6.8 miles to the park.

Facilities: 111 campsites, about half with electrical hookups, in 5 loops; (group camping areas and an equestrian camp are also available); sites are medium to large, essentially level, with good to excellent separation; parking pads are gravel, medium to long straight-ins; ample space for tents; some sites have ramadas (sun/wind shelters); fireplaces or fire rings; b-y-o firewood; water at central faucets; restrooms with showers; disposal station; paved driveways; adequate supplies and services in Canton.

Activities & Attractions: Hiking and nature trails; Indian lookout tower; interpretive shelter; amphitheater; playground; swimming, limited boating (electric motors, oars and paddles) at adjacent, 90-acre Lake Lakota.

Natural Features: Located atop the Newton Hills area of the *Coteau des Prairies* ("Hills of the Prairie") region; pines, cedars, large hardwoods, and acres of lawns provide campsite environments of privacy or spaciousness; elevation 1500'.

Season, Fees & Phone: Principal season is May to November; please see Appendix for standard South Dakota state park fees and reservation information; 14 day limit; park office (605) 987-2263.

Camp Notes: Newton Hills is one of those radiant parks with a nicely trimmed look. The camp loops have been dubbed with avian names: Bluejay, Flicker, Robin, Cardinal and Bluebird. (Grouchy campers stay in the Buzzard Loop. Ed.)

UNION COUNTY
Union County State Park

Location: Southeast corner of South Dakota south of Sioux Falls.

Access: From Interstate 29 Exit 38 (12 miles north of Junction City, 9 miles south of Beresford), turn east onto a local paved road and proceed 0.6 mile to an intersection; turn south (right) onto Union County Road 1C and continue for 2.2 miles; turn east (left) into the park entrance and proceed 0.45 mile to the main campground.

Facilities: 25 campsites; sites are small to medium-sized, with some separation; parking pads are gravel, short to medium-length, of all varieties; a little additional leveling will probably be required in some sites; small, generally sloped, tent areas; fireplaces; b-y-o firewood; water at central faucets; restrooms; paved driveways; nearest reliable source of supplies (limited+) is Beresford.

Activities & Attractions: Nature trails, hiking and horse trails; arboretum; simple equestrian facilities.

Natural Features: Located on a timbered hilltop (a densely forested island on the plains, so to speak); campsites are well sheltered by rows of pines; hardwoods predominate on the lower slopes; typically breezy; elevation 1500'.

Season, Fees & Phone: May to November; please see Appendix for standard South Dakota state park fees and reservation information; 14 day limit; park office (605) 253-2370.

Camp Notes: The county-wide panorama from this piney perch is exceptional for this part of the state. The lower-level, dense hardwoods form 'tunnels' over the roads and trails. This may not be a tent camper's delight in relation to space available--it might be a snug squeeze for even a backpack tent in all except a handful of sites (unless one of the larger parking pads was pressed into service). In the horse area there's a corral, shelter, plus a few tables and bbq grills (in case your mount wants to char a steak for dinner.)

South Dakota 69

CLAY COUNTY
Clay County State Recreation Area

Location: Southeast corner of South Dakota southeast of Yankton.

Access: From South Dakota State Highway 50 Business Route at milepost 407 + .9 (2 miles west of Vermillion, 24 miles east of Yankton), turn west/southwest onto Timber Road and proceed 1.8 miles; turn south (left) onto a paved road and proceed 1.15 miles; turn west (left) onto a gravel access road and continue for 0.1 mile, then bear right, into the campground.

Facilities: 9 campsites; sites are medium+ to very large, level and well-separated; parking pads are gravel, medium-length straight-ins; excellent tent-pitching possibilities; fireplaces; some firewood is available for gathering in the area; water at a central faucet; vault facilities; gravel driveway; nearly complete supplies and services are available in Vermillion.

Activities & Attractions: Boating; boat launch; fishing; hiking trails.

Natural Features: Located on a forested flat near the north bank of the Missouri River; campground vegetation consists of tall cottonwoods and a few cedars on a grassy surface; dense timber, brush and tall grass encircle the campground; surrounding countryside is level prairie and farmland; elevation 1100'.

Season, Fees & Phone: Open all year, subject to weather conditions; please see Appendix for standard South Dakota state park fees; 14 day limit; phone c/o Newton Hills State Park (605) 987-2263.

Camp Notes: The heavily timbered, hushed atmosphere here is very appealing. If you're looking for a place far from the madding crowd (except possibly on summer weekends) it would be a good spot to check out. This small (120-acres) recreation area is quite undeveloped--primitive even. (Many arguments could be advanced in favor of it remaining in that condition. Note that some official literature lists this as a simple "Lakeside Use Area" or "LUA", which could explain the rustic facilities.)

South Dakota 70

SPRINGFIELD
Lewis and Clark State Recreation Area

Location: Southeast South Dakota west of Yankton.

Access: From South Dakota State Highway 37 (Walnut Street) just north of midtown Springfield, turn east onto 10th Street and proceed 0.5 mile to the recreation area; swing north and continue for 0.3 mile through the day use area; turn left into the hookup loop, or turn right for 0.1 mile to a small area with standard sites.

Facilities: 15 campsites, including 11 with electrical hookups; sites are medium-sized, with nominal to fair separation; parking pads are gravel, basically level, medium-length straight-ins; ample space on a grassy surface for large tents in all units, though standard area tent spots are slightly sloped; fireplaces; b-y-o firewood; water at central faucets and at a hand pump; vault facilities; holding tank disposal station; gravel driveways; limited+ supplies and services are available in Springfield.

Activities & Attractions: Swimming beach and bathhouse; large playground; small golf course, 'just over the hill' from the campground; boating; boat launch, marina; fishing.

Natural Features: Located on a flat (hookups) and on a hillside on a small bay at the west end of Lewis and Clark Lake on the Missouri River; sites are moderately sheltered/shaded by rows of large hardwoods, plus some pines and cedars, on a grassy surface; a small stream flows through the campground; a half-dozen islands (the large lake's only isles) are a short distance offshore; elevation 1200'.

Season, Fees & Phone: Open all year, with limited services October to May; please see Appendix for standard South Dakota state park fees; 14 day limit; park office (605) 668-3435.

Camp Notes: The islands, plus high, colorful, eroded bluffs, add substantial interest to the local shoreline. The several standard campsites on the hillside actually have a slightly better view than the hookup sites. (Oh, one more thing: don't pick up any hitchhikers in the Springfield area.)

GAVINS POINT
Lewis and Clark State Recreation Area

Location: Southeast South Dakota west of Yankton.

Access: From South Dakota State Highway 52 at a point 2.9 miles west of Gavins Point Dam, 8 miles west of Yankton, 3.5 miles south of the junction of State Highways 52 & 50 southeast of Tabor, turn southwest onto the recreation area access road and proceed 0.4 mile to the entrance station; turn south then east to the campground; the campsites are located over the next mile of parkland. (Note that Highway 52 is "L"-shaped in this section and that the turnoff is at the bend in the "L").

Facilities: 76 campsites, many with electrical hookups; sites are medium to large, with fair to excellent separation; parking pads are paved, medium to long straight-ins which may require a little additional leveling; large, possibly slightly sloped, tent areas; fireplaces; b-y-o firewood; water at central faucets; restrooms with showers; paved driveways; gas and groceries, 3 miles east on 52; complete supplies and services are available in Yankton, 12 miles.

Activities & Attractions: Swimming beach; archery range; paved hike/bike path; playground; boating; boat launch; fishing.

Natural Features: Located on the north shore of Lewis and Clark Lake; sites are generally well-sheltered/shaded by rows of large hardwoods, plus smaller hardwood bushes and evergreens; expansive tree-dotted or open lawns; many sites have good lake views; elevation 1200'.

Season, Fees & Phone: May to November; please see Appendix for standard South Dakota state park fees and reservation information; 14 day limit; park office (605) 668-3435.

Camp Notes: Of the trio of full service campgrounds in Lewis and Clark Recreation Area, this is the most 'primitive'. (Yeah, right.) If you plan to come to the lake seeking solitude and an exclusively 'natural' environment, this may not be the place for you. But it might be difficult to resist staying in these remarkably beautiful surroundings.

MIDWAY
Lewis and Clark State Recreation Area

Location: Southeast South Dakota west of Yankton.

Access: From South Dakota State Highway 52 at a point 1.7 miles west of Gavins Point Dam, 7 miles west of Yankton, 4.7 miles southeast of the junction of State Highways 52 & 50 southeast of Tabor, turn south, then west for 0.2 mile to the entrance station; continue 0.2 mile, west or south, into the camp loops.

Facilities: 135 campsites, half with electrical hookups, plus primitive camping; sites are medium to large, with fairly good to excellent separation; most parking pads are paved, long straight-ins; large, possibly slightly sloped, tent areas; fireplaces; firewood is usually for sale, or b-y-o; water at central faucets; restrooms with showers; paved driveways; gas and groceries, 3 miles east on 52; complete supplies and services are available in Yankton, 10 miles.

Activities & Attractions: Swimming beach; paved hike/bike path; playground; boating; sailing; boat launch; fishing.

Natural Features: Located on the north shore of Lewis and Clark Lake, formed by Gavins Point Dam on the Missouri River; sites are well-sheltered/shaded by rows of large hardwoods and evergreens; expansive tree-dotted or open lawns; several superb campsites are on a lightly sheltered section of shoreline; elevation 1200'.

Season, Fees & Phone: Open all year; principal season is May to November; please see Appendix for standard South Dakota state park fees and reservation information; 14 day limit; park office (605) 668-3435.

Camp Notes: If you camp here in October, you'll be treated to what may be the most gratifying, sparkling, spectacular, dazzling, captivating, or_____(enter your own adjective) collage of green and blue and gold and yellow and crimson in the West. This is *worth* the trip.

YANKTON
Lewis and Clark State Recreation Area

Location: Southeast South Dakota west of Yankton.

Access: From South Dakota State Highway 52 at a point 0.4 mile west of Gavins Point Dam, 5 miles west of Yankton, 6 miles southeast of the junction of Highways 52 & 50 southeast of Tabor), turn south into the recreation area entrance, then west for 0.4 mile to the campground.

Facilities: 78 campsites, about half with electrical hookups; sites are large, level, with fair to excellent separation; parking pads are paved, mostly long straight-ins; ample space for large tents; fireplaces; b-y-o firewood; water at central faucets; restrooms with showers; holding tank disposal station, 0.6 mile west on Highway 52; paved driveways; gas and groceries, 0.5 mile east; complete supplies and services are available in Yankton.

Activities & Attractions: Visitor center; sandy swimming beach; paved hike/bike path; playground; boating; sailing; boat launch, marina; fishing.

Natural Features: Located on the north shore of Lewis and Clark Lake; vegetation consists of large hardwoods, evergreens and expansive, mown lawns; elevation 1200'.

Season, Fees & Phone: Open all year; principal season is May to November; please see Appendix for standard South Dakota state park fees and reservation information; 14 day limit; park office (605) 668-3435.

Camp Notes: This is the Taj Mahal of western public campgrounds. Certainly there are many fine campgrounds in the West, particularly in Washington, Oregon and, of course, California. Lewis and Clark's are *at least* the equal of (and most likely superior to) any of the others. The recreation area *is* undergoing commercial and quasi-commercial development; but if you enjoy camping amidst acres and acres of exquisitely landscaped parklands, this is the place to visit. Highly and decidedly recommended.

PIERSON RANCH
Lewis and Clark Lake/Corps of Engineers Park

Location: Southeast South Dakota west of Yankton.

Access: From South Dakota State Highway 52 at a point 0.35 mile east of Gavins Point Dam, 5 miles west of Yankton, turn south onto a paved access road and proceed 0.4 mile south, then west (around the large day use area); turn north (right) into the campground.

Facilities: 68 campsites with electrical hookups in 2 loops; sites are small to medium-sized and somewhat closely spaced; parking pads are paved, medium-length straight-ins which may require a bit of additional leveling; large tent areas; fireplaces; b-y-o firewood; water at central faucets; restrooms with showers; disposal station near the day use area; paved driveways; gas and groceries, east on Highway 52; complete supplies and services in Yankton.

Activities & Attractions: Gavins Point National Fish Hatchery and Aquarium, adjacent; paved hike/bike path; tennis and basketball courts, softball field in adjoining day use area; fishing; limited boating (electric motors, hand-propulsion) on Lake Yankton); unlimited boating/sailing on Lewis and Clark Lake.

Natural Features: Located on a slight slope above the northwest corner of Lake Yankton, a small, secondary impoundment below Gavins Point Dam and Lewis and Clark Lake on the Missouri River; sites are lightly sheltered/shaded by large hardwoods and a few pines on a grassy surface; a split rail fence adds the "ranch" touch; elevation 1200'.

Season, Fees & Phone: May to September; $10.00; 14 day limit; Lewis and Clark Lake/Gavins Point Dam CoE Project Office (402) 667-7873.

Camp Notes: Perhaps the deciding factor in electing to stay here is the camp's location within somewhat of a high-traffic zone. A considerable amount of traffic passes by across the dam and through the day use area. But you won't find a spot that's handier to the aquarium, tennis courts, ball diamond and basketball hoops.

COTTONWOOD
Lewis and Clark Lake/Corps of Engineers Park

Location: Southeast South Dakota west of Yankton.

Access: From South Dakota State Highway 52 at a point 0.35 mile east of Gavins Point Dam, 5 miles west of Yankton, turn south onto a paved access road and proceed 1.7 miles south, west, then south along the base of Gavins Point Dam; turn east (left) into the campground. (The campground is also conveniently accessible from Nebraska State Highway 121; proceed north on the road across the dam for 0.4 mile; then angle northeast off the top of the dam on a paved access road for 0.2 mile down to the 'base' road, then 0.7 mile north to the campground.)

Facilities: 78 campsites, most with electrical hookups; sites are small to medium-sized, essentially level, with nominal to fair separation; most parking pads are paved, medium-length straight-ins; adequate space for large tents; fireplaces; b-y-o firewood; water at central faucets; restrooms with showers; mostly paved driveways; gas and groceries on SD 52 and NE 121; complete supplies and services are available in Yankton.

Activities & Attractions: Playground; boating (electric, manual on Lake Yankton); boat launch; fishing; large day use area.

Natural Features: Located on a flat in a stand of very tall cottonwoods on the west shore of Lake Yankton, a small, secondary impoundment just below Gavins Point Dam and Lewis and Clark Lake, the major flatwater in the area; elevation 1200'.

Season, Fees & Phone: Open all year, with limited services October to April; $7.00 for a standard site, $10.00 for an electrical hookup site; 14 day limit; Lewis and Clark Lake/Gavins Point Dam CoE Project Office (402) 667-7873.

Camp Notes: Although the campground is only a few yards from the base of the dam, the grassed embankment is relatively unobtrusive. There are a half-dozen nice sites right along the grassy shore of Lake Yankton, and virtually all campsites have some sort of lake view.

CHIEF WHITE CRANE
Lewis and Clark Lake/Corps of Engineers Park

Location: Southeast South Dakota west of Yankton.

Access: From South Dakota State Highway 52 at a point 0.35 mile east of Gavins Point Dam, 5 miles west of Yankton, turn south onto a paved access road and proceed 2.2 miles south, west, then south along the base of Gavins Point Dam; turn east (left) onto a paved road which traverses a dike along the north bank of the outlet channel and continue for 1.1 miles to the campground. (Note: The campground is also easily accessible from Nebraska State Highway 121; just start north on the road across the dam for 0.4 mile; then angle northeast off the top of the dam on a paved access road for 0.2 mile down to the 'base' road; turn east and continue across the dike to the campground.)

Facilities: 116 campsites, most with electrical hookups, in 3 loops; sites are medium-sized, basically level, with nominal to fair separation; parking pads are paved, medium+ to long straight-ins; adequate space for large tents in most sites; large, central shelters; fireplaces; b-y-o firewood is recommended; water at central faucets; restrooms with showers; holding tank disposal station; paved driveways; complete supplies and services are available in Yankton.

Activities & Attractions: Fishing; handicapped-access fishing pier; limited boating on Lake Yankton; playgrounds.

Natural Features: Located in a grove of tall cottonwoods on the southeast shore of Lake Yankton, a small, backwater impoundment along the Missouri River below Gavins Point Dam and Lewis and Clark Lake; most sites are well sheltered/shaded; elevation 1200'.

Season, Fees & Phone: Open all year, with limited services November to April; $7.00 for a standard site, $10.00 for an electrical hookup unit; 14 day limit; Lewis and Clark Lake/Gavins Point Dam CoE Project Office (402) 667-7873.

Camp Notes: Chances are that a poll among campers would award First Place among the Corps camps in this area to Chief White Crane. Some excellent lakefront sites here. Chief Martoree ("White Crane") was a "second chief" of a Sioux tribe who met with Lewis and Clark along the Missouri on August 31, 1804 as the expedition was headed upriver. According to the Lewis and Clark Journals, White Crane made a short "speech" representing the 'great chief" of his band of Sioux to the expedition leaders. But White Crane apparently was a man of few words: he left most of the talking to the "third chief".

Nebraska

Public Campgrounds

The Nebraska map is located in the Appendix on page 155.

NEBRASKA
Panhandle
Please refer to the Nebraska map in the Appendix

Nebraska 1

FORT ROBINSON
Fort Robinson State Park

Location: Northwest corner of Nebraska southwest of Chadron.

Access: From U.S. Highway 20 at milepost 32 (4 miles west of Crawford, 23 miles east of Harrison), turn southwest onto a paved park access road and proceed 0.1 mile; turn west (right) into the main (hookup) loop; tent camping ('primitive') area is at the southwest corner of the campground, via a railroad underpass (9-foot clearance).

Facilities: 77 electrical hookup campsites, plus approximately 20 tent sites, in 2 sections; sites are small, essentially level, and closely spaced; parking pads are primarily medium-length, gravel straight-ins; adequate space for a medium to large tent in most sites; barbecue grills; b-y-o firewood; water at central faucets; restrooms with showers, plus auxiliary vaults; holding tank disposal station; paved or gravel driveways; limited+ supplies and services are available in Crawford.

Activities & Attractions: Maintained/restored, post-bellum military complex; museums, nature trails, fishing, scenic drives, rides, playhouse, campfire programs, you name it.

Natural Features: Located on a gently rolling, highwayside flat; sites receive limited to moderate shelter/shade from large hardwoods on a surface of sparse grass; Soldier Creek meanders past the west edge of the campground; pine-dotted hills and buttes border the park; elevation 3900'.

Season, Fees & Phone: Principal season is mid-April to mid-November, but may be available at other times with limited services, subject to weather conditions; please see Appendix for standard Nebraska state park fees; park office (308) 665-2660.

Camp Notes: Fort Robinson is Nebraska's largest state park. (Considering the stagecoach rides, tennis courts, theater, swimming pool, jeep jaunts, hot dogs, etc., visitors with just the right amount of cynicism might say it's the largest state-owned amusement park as well. Ed.) The northwest corner is one of the most beautiful regions in Nebraska.

Nebraska 2

CHADRON
Chadron State Park

Location: Northwest corner of Nebraska south of Chadron.

Access: From U.S. Highway 385 at milepost 159 + .6 (8 miles south of Chadron, 29 miles north of the junction of U.S. 385 & State Highway 87 east of Hemingford), turn west into the park.

Facilities: 70 campsites with electrical hookups; sites are small, acceptably level, with minimal separation; parking pads are straight-ins or pull-offs of assorted lengths; sufficient space for a medium to large tent; barbecue grills; firewood may be provided, b-y-o to be sure; water at several faucets; restrooms and showers; holding tank disposal station; paved driveways; nearly complete supplies and services are available in Chadron

Activities & Attractions: Hiking and nature trails; trail rides; fishing for stocked trout in the lagoon; swimming pool; evening campfire programs; scenic drive.

Natural Features: Located along Chadron Creek on Pine Ridge; vegetation consists primarily of light to medium-dense hardwoods and conifers, and grass; small pond (lagoon); elevation 4300'.

Season, Fees & Phone: Principal season is May to October, but available at other times with limited services, subject to weather conditions; please see Appendix for standard Nebraska state park fees; 14 day limit; park office (308) 432-6167.

Camp Notes: Chadron was established in 1921 as Nebraska's first state park. And no wonder: the Pine Ridge region is superscenic!

Box Butte
Box Butte State Recreation Area

Location: Northwest corner of Nebraska south of Chadron.

Access: From U.S. Highway 385 at milepost 141 +.3 (28 miles south of Chadron, 9 miles north of the junction of U.S. 385 & State Highway 87 east of Hemingford), turn west onto a paved road and proceed 5 miles to a "T" intersection; turn north (right) onto a paved road for 0.65 mile; turn west (left) onto a paved-then-gravel road and proceed 0.4 mile to the camping area, along the next 0.6 mile. **Alternate Access:** From Nebraska State Highways 2 & 87 in midtown Hemingford, turn north onto Box Butte Avenue and travel 10 paved miles to the campground turnoff.

Facilities: Approximately 35 campsites; sites vary from small to large, with fair to very good separation; parking surfaces are sandy gravel/grass, and vary in length and type; some maneuvering will probably be necessary for leveling; adequate space for a medium to large tent in most sites, though it may be sloped; a few small sun shelters; barbecue grills; b-y-o firewood is recommended; water at hand pumps; vault facilities; gravel driveways; limited supplies and services are available in Hemingford.

Activities & Attractions: Fishing; boating; boat launch.

Natural Features: Located on the north shore of Box Butte Reservoir; vegetation consists of a line of tall hardwoods along the lake shore, and a surface of short crunchgrass; most sites receive limited to moderate shelter/shade; encircled by grassy slopes and hills; elevation 4000'.

Season, Fees & Phone: Open all year, subject to weather conditions; please see Appendix for standard Nebraska state park fees; 14 day limit; phone c/o Chadron State Park (308) 432-6167.

Camp Notes: Probably the best time to visit is prior to mid-summer. Depending upon time of year and precipitation levels, a site here might be 3 or 300 yards from the water.

Walgren Lake
Walgren Lake State Recreation Area

Location: Northwest Nebraska southeast of Chadron.

Access: From U.S. Highway 20 at milepost 82 (3 miles east of Hay Springs, 9 miles west of Rushville), turn south onto a gravel road and proceed 3.3 miles; turn east (left) onto a gravel road and continue for 0.25 mile, then turn south (right) into the recreation area; camping areas are situated on the north, west and south shores of the lake, within 0.5 mile of the entrance.

Facilities: Approximately 50 campsites; sites are medium-sized, essentially level to slightly sloped, with fair visual separation but generally good spacing; parking pads are gravel, medium-length straight-ins/pull-offs; adequate space for a medium to large tent in most sites; large, central, rustic stone shelter; barbecue grills; b-y-o firewood; water at a hand pump; vault facilities; gravel driveways; gas and groceries and a few other assorted services in Hay Springs; limited+ supplies and services are available in Rushville.

Activities & Attractions: Fishing; small boat launch; playground.

Natural Features: Located on the shore of 50-acre Walgren Lake; campground vegetation consists of light to medium-dense, large hardwoods, and sparse grass; gently rolling plains and cropland encircle the recreation area; elevation 3800'.

Season, Fees & Phone: Open all year, subject to weather conditions; please see Appendix for standard Nebraska state park fees; 14 day limit; phone c/o Nebraska Game & Parks Commission District I Office, Alliance, (308) 762-5605.

Camp Notes: Virtually every campsite has a lake view. Sites on the west and south shores are lakeside, but are also closer to the main driveway. On the other hand, a group of sites in a stand of trees on the north shore are a little farther from the water's edge, but are more private and shaded. If you catch a glimpse of the local 'legendary' prehistoric monster-in-residence, you can file a report at the pub in Hay Springs. (Or have you been there already? Ed.)

RIVERSIDE
Scottsbluff City Park

Location: Northwest Nebraska in Scottsbluff.

Access: From Nebraska State Highway 71 at milepost 60 +.8 at the southwest corner of Scottsbluff, turn south into the park entrance and proceed around the east end of the zoo, then south again for 0.3 mile; turn east (left) into the campground. (Note that the highway, which is basically a north-south road, makes an east-west jog in this area, around the west side of the city.)

Facilities: 40 campsites, including 20 with electrical hookups and a few full hookup units; sites are small+, level and closely spaced; parking pads are sandy gravel, medium-length straight-ins or long pull-throughs; adequate space for large tents; barbecue grills; b-y-o firewood; water at faucets throughout; restrooms with showers; holding tank disposal station; sandy gravel driveways; complete supplies and services are available in Scottsbluff.

Activities & Attractions: Small (but quite nice) zoo; playground; Scotts Bluff National Monument, 6 miles south.

Natural Features: Located on a flat near the north bank of the North Platte River; sites are lightly sheltered/shaded by hardwoods on a sparse grass surface; elevation 3900'.

Season, Fees & Phone: May to mid-September; $7.00 for a site with 4 persons, $8.00 for an electrical hookup site, $9.00 for a full hookup unit, $1.00 extra for each additional person over 13 years, $1.00 extra for a vehicle using an air conditioner; 14 day limit; park office (308) 632-4136.

Camp Notes: Scotts Bluff (the geological feature) is plainly visible from in or near the camp area. It's much larger and more fascinating than most photographs depict. Because a large day use area is just across the driveway from the camp, the park gets a little busy at times. But the views of the Bluff overshadow (pardon the pun) that disadvantage. Very primitive, no fee camping is available not far from Riverside Park in the scenic Wildcat Hills State Recreation Area, off Highway 71, 12 miles south of Scottsbluff.

LAKE MINATARE
Lake Minatare State Recreation Area

Location: Northwest Nebraska north of Scottsbluff.

Access: From Nebraska State Highway 71 at milepost 66 +.2 (3 miles north of Scottsbluff, ?? miles south of nowhere), turn east onto Lake Minatare Road (paved) and travel 8.3 miles to a "T" intersection; turn north (left) and proceed 1 mile, then turn southeast (right) into the recreation area entrance; continue for 0.5 mile to the campground. **Alternate Access:** From U.S. Highway 26 at milepost 33 in the hamlet of Minatare (10 miles east of Scottsbluff), turn north onto Stonegate Road (paved) and proceed 7 miles to South Gate; bear left and continue for 2.25 miles to the main park entrance.

Facilities: 52 campsites with electrical hookups in 2 sections; sites are medium-sized, with fair to good separation; parking pads are gravel, medium to long straight-ins; some additional leveling will probably be required; adequate space for large tents; fire rings; b-y-o firewood is recommended; restrooms with showers; holding tank disposal station nearby; gravel driveways; complete supplies and services are available in Scottsbluff.

Activities & Attractions: Fishing for walleye, perch, crappie, smallmouth bass, channel cat; boating; boat launch; large, stone lighthouse built by the WPA (but why?).

Natural Features: Located on Lighthouse Point on the northwest shore of 2200-acre Lake Minatare amid rolling prairie and agricultural land; the lake is ringed by large, hardwoods which provide ample shelter/shade for most sites; elevation 4000'.

Season, Fees & Phone: April to October; please see Appendix for standard Nebraska state park fees; 14 day limit; park office (308) 783-2911.

Camp Notes: Camping is also available in several small areas around the lake shore. In the bright sun of early evening, the lake is a big brilliant blue button sewn to a swatch of gold cloth.

BRIDGEPORT
Bridgeport State Recreation Area

Location: Northwest Nebraska southeast of Scottsbluff.

Access: From U.S. Highway 26 at milepost 61 (on the west edge of Bridgeport, 36 miles southeast of Scottsbluff), turn north onto F Street and continue for 0.65 mile to the recreation area entrance at the end of the pavement; turn right or left to the campsites.

Facilities: Approximately 35 campsites; sites are generally medium+, level and fairly well separated; parking spaces are sandy gravel, medium-length straight-ins or pull-offs; enough space for small to medium-sized tents; some sites lack tables; barbecue grills or fire rings; b-y-o firewood is recommended; water at a hand pump; vault facilities; holding tank disposal station; gravel driveways; adequate supplies and services are available in Bridgeport.

Activities & Attractions: Sandy beach; fishing (reportedly for largemouth and smallmouth bass, walleye, northern pike, bluegill and rainbow trout, depending upon the individual lake); boating (some restrictions); small boat launch and dock; Chimney Rock National Historic Site, 15 miles west.

Natural Features: Located along the shores of 1 large lake and 4 small lakes on the high plains; campsites receive minimal to light shelter/shade from large hardwoods on a surface of sparse grass; virtually all sites have a lake view; the North Platte River flows past just north of the area; elevation 3700'.

Season, Fees & Phone: Open all year, subject to weather conditions; please see Appendix for standard Nebraska state park fees; 14 day limit; phone c/o Nebraska Game & Parks Commission District 1 Office, Alliance, (308) 762-5605.

Camp Notes: The country just west of here sports an assortment of rugged buttes, bluffs, ridges and chimneys. To a well-traveled camper, the rock formations might resemble those in a beige, pine-dotted Monument Valley.

OLIVER RESERVOIR
Oliver Reservoir State Recreation Area

Location: West-central Nebraska near the Nebraska-Wyoming border.

Access: From Interstate 80 (westbound) Exit 20 for Kimball, turn north onto Nebraska State Highway 71 and proceed 1.3 miles into midtown Kimball; turn west (left) onto U.S. Highway 30 and proceed 9 miles to milepost 13; turn south into the main camping area. **Alternate Access:** From Interstate 80 (eastbound) Exit 8 for Bushnell, turn north onto Nebraska Route 53-C Link (L-53-C) for 2.4 miles to Bushnell; turn east onto U.S. 30 and proceed 3.5 miles to milepost 13; turn south into the camping area.

Facilities: Approximately 50 campsites in a more or less open camping arrangement; sites are level, and about as large as may be required; parking surfaces are grass or gravel; ample space for large tents; a few barbecue grills; water at central faucets; vault facilities; gravel driveways; adequate supplies and services are available in Kimball.

Activities & Attractions: Day use area; designated swimming area; boating; boat launch; fishing for bass, walleye, blue-gill, crappie, some trout.

Natural Features: Located on a large, grassy flat along the northwest shore of 270-acre Oliver Reservoir on Lodgepole Creek on the high plains; large hardwoods line the lake shore; hardwood saplings have been planted on the flat; bordered by low, virtually treeless hills and bluffs; elevation 4900'.

Season, Fees & Phone: Open all year, subject to weather conditions; please see Appendix for standard Nebraska state park fees; 14 day limit; phone c/o Nebraska Game & Parks Commission District 1 Office, Alliance, (308) 762-5605.

Camp Notes: At this time, the most pleasing parcel of property is the picnic area--it's on a nicely sheltered bay with a hardwood-covered shoreline. This recreation area is in such a strategic location (the most Interstate-accessible spot in the Nebraska Panhandle), that it's surprising the camping facilities haven't received more attention.

Nebraska 9

COTTONWOOD LAKE
Cottonwood Lake State Recreation Area

Location: Northwest Nebraska between Chadron and Valentine.

Access: From U.S. Highway 20 at milepost 136 +.9 (1 mile east of Merriman, 22 miles west of Cody), turn south onto a gravel road and proceed 0.5 mile to the recreation area and the principal camping area; or turn east and proceed 0.2 mile to several park n' walk sites.

Facilities: Approximately 20 campsites; sites vary from small to large, with minimal to fair separation; parking surfaces are gravel/grass, straight-ins or pull-offs; room for a few larger vehicles, but parking spots are mostly small; adequate space for a medium-sized tent in most sites; central ramada (sun shelter); barbecue grills; a small amount of firewood may be available for gathering in the vicinity, b-y-o is recommended; water at hand pumps; vault facilities; gravel driveways; gas and snacks in Merriman; nearest source of adequate supplies and services is Gordon, 31 miles west.

Activities & Attractions: Fishing; boating; small boat launch; Arthur Bowring Sandhills Ranch State Historical Park, northeast of Merriman.

Natural Features: Located on the north shore of Cottonwood Lake at the north edge of the Sandhills region; sites are lightly sheltered/shaded by large hardwoods on a grass and sand surface; elevation 3200'.

Season, Fees & Phone: Open all year, subject to weather conditions; please see Appendix for standard Nebraska state park fees; 14 day limit; phone c/o Arthur Bowring Sandhills Ranch SHP (308) 684-3428.

Camp Notes: The small group of park n' walk sites, located on a small point, are perhaps the best of the camp spots here. This would be a handy place to camp while visiting the nearby state historical park noted above. The property was recently willed to the state by former U.S. Senator Eve Bowring to serve as an exemplary Nebraska working ranch.

Nebraska 10

STEER CREEK
Samuel R. McKelvie National Forest

Location: North-Central Nebraska southeast of Valentine.

Access: From U.S. Highway 20 at milepost 167 in the hamlet of Nenzel (30 miles west of Valentine), turn south onto Nebraska Route 16-F Spur (S-16-F, paved); travel 18.1 miles to a point 1 mile past the national forest ranger station; turn west (right) into the campground. (Note: the main road narrows markedly to what really amounts to a wide one-laner just before the campground, so watch for oncoming traffic.)

Facilities: 23 campsites; sites are large, level, with fair to very good separation; parking pads are long, wide, gravel straight-ins; ample space for a medium-sized tent in most sites; fire rings and barbecue grills; firewood is often provided, or b-y-o; water at a hand pump; vault facilities; paved driveway; nearest reliable source of supplies and services is Valentine.

Activities & Attractions: Unique forest environment; excellent fishing and boating on Merritt Reservoir, 15 miles southeast.

Natural Features: Located on a forested flat in the Sandhills region; sites are quite well sheltered/shaded by tall ponderosa pines; elevation 3100'.

Season, Fees & Phone: Available all year, subject to weather conditions, but principal season is May to October; no fee (subject to change); 14 day limit; phone c/o Bessey Ranger District, Halsey, (308) 533-2257.

Camp Notes: Ten campers, even on a holiday weekend, would constitute a crowd at this remote, yet quite accessible, spot. (Mucho mosquitoes in late June and July, though.) Steer Creek lies within one of Nebraska's more unusual features, a 2300-acre man-made forest. The original trees were planted in 1915. Now the forest is an evergreen island on a rolling, inland sea of sand and grass. Beautiful spot.

SNAKE RIVER
Merritt Reservoir State Recreation Area

Location: North-central Nebraska southwest of Valentine.

Access: From Nebraska State Highway 97 at milepost 110 +.4 (32 miles southwest of Valentine, 43 miles north of Mullen), turn west onto Recreation Road 16-C (paved) and proceed 2.9 miles; turn northwest onto a gravel access road for a final 0.1 mile to the campground.

Facilities: Approximately 20 campsites in somewhat of an "open camping" arrangement; any-which-way-you-can, any-size, parking areas on a grassy slope; large, though mainly sloped, spots for tents; ramada (sun shelter); a few barbecue grills; b-y-o firewood; water at a hand pump; vault facilities; holding tank disposal station; gravel driveways; gas and camper supplies at a small store, 5 miles north; next-nearest supplies and services (adequate+) are in Valentine.

Activities & Attractions: Fishing (one of the country's best producers of large walleyes, plus white bass, perch, etc.); boating; paved boat launch.

Natural Features: Located on an open, grassy slope above the east shore of Merritt Reservoir on the Snake River in the Sandhills region; a few small evergreens and hardwoods dot the slope; elevation 3100'.

Season, Fees & Phone: Open all year, subject to weather conditions; please see Appendix for standard Nebraska state park fees; 14 day limit; c/o Nebraska Game & Parks Commission District II Office, Bassett, (402) 684-2921.

Camp Notes: Snake River is probably the most popular camping area on the reservoir. It's as rustic and basic as its description (although anything can change). The other camp areas--Cedar Bay, near mile 113, Beed's Landing, at mile 112, and Boardman, near mile 111--provide fewer "comforts" than Snake River. The rugged Sandhills views at Snake River and Cedar Bay are excellent, however, and chances are you'll mainly come here to fish, anyway.

VALENTINE
Valentine City Park

Location: North-central Nebraska in Valentine.

Access: From U.S. Highway 20 in midtown Valentine, turn north onto Main Street and proceed 1.4 miles to just beyond the far north end of town; after crossing the bridge over the stream, the road curves to the east; turn southeast (right) into the park.

Facilities: Approximately 20 campsites; sites are medium-sized, with limited to fair separation; parking spaces are mostly medium-length, sand/grass pull-offs which may require a little additional leveling; ample space for a medium to large tent; central shelter; barbecue grills; b-y-o firewood; water at several faucets; restrooms with showers; holding tank disposal station in town, near the hospital; paved/sand driveway; adequate+ supplies and services are available in Valentine.

Activities & Attractions: Playground; horseshoe pits; Sandhills Museum in Valentine.

Natural Features: Located in a narrow valley along Minnichaduza Creek; most campsites are quite well sheltered/shaded by large hardwoods; elevation 2600'.

Season, Fees & Phone: May to September; no fee (subject to change); (donations are appreciated); Valentine City Hall (402) 376-2323.

Camp Notes: Although the park's main driveway passes by most of the campsites, the traffic is restricted to campers-only at night. For a town with an official population of only 2800+, Valentine has a surprisingly good re-supply potential for campers traveling the Nebraska Highline. (Its closest rivals along Nebraska's northern edge are Chadron, 140 miles west, and O'Neill, 110 miles east.) (If you were to judge the community solely by the simple, but unique, design on all of the city's street signs--a bright red heart next to the name of the street--you might draw the conclusion that there are 2800+ congenial people here. Ed.)

KELLER PARK
Keller Park State Recreation Area

Location: North-central Nebraska between Valentine and O'Neill.

Access: From U.S. Highway 183 at milepost 202 +.5 (8.5 miles north of the junction of U.S. Highways 183 & 20 east of Ainsworth, 12 miles south of Springview), turn west onto a gravel access road and proceed 0.5 mile to a fork in the road; take the right fork into the campground.

Facilities: 25 campsites with electrical hookups; sites are medium-sized, essentially level, with minimal separation; parking pads are medium to long, gravel straight-ins; enough space for a medium-sized tent in most units; barbecue grills; a limited amount of firewood may be available for gathering in the vicinity, b-y-o is suggested; water at central faucets; vault facilities (H); holding tank disposal station; gravel driveways; adequate supplies and services are available in Ainsworth.

Activities & Attractions: Fishing in 5 stocked ponds in 2 areas (largemouth bass, bluegill, channel catfish in 4 ponds, rainbow trout in the 5th); trails; long, arched bridge over the stream.

Natural Features: Located on bottomland along the south bank of Bone Creek; campground is bordered by dense hardwoods, cedars (junipers) and pines; most campsites lack midday shade; elevation 2500'.

Season, Fees & Phone: Open all year, with limited services, October to May; please see Appendix for standard Nebraska state park fees; 14 day limit; c/o Nebraska Game & Parks Commission District II Office, Bassett, (402) 684-2921.

Camp Notes: This isn't just a place to seek refuge from the prairie wind on the flatland above the valley. It's a really nice spot with a definite "park" atmosphere. There are only a handful of locations in the state where trout and bass can be caught within a few yards of each other, and this is one of them.

LONG PINE
Long Pine State Recreation Area

Location: North-central Nebraska between Valentine and O'Neill.

Access: From U.S. Highway 20 at milepost 249 +.8 (1 mile west of the community of Long Pine, 8 miles east of Ainsworth), turn south onto a gravel road and proceed 0.2 mile; turn east to a "T" intersection; turn north or south for 0.3 mile to either of the 2 camping areas.

Facilities: Approximately 25 campsites; sites are small to medium-sized, sloped, with minimal to fairly good separation; most parking pads are paved, short to medium-length straight-ins; small tent areas; barbecue grills, plus a few fire rings; a limited amount of firewood may be available for gathering, b-y-o is recommended; water at a hand pump; vault facilities; pack-it-in/pack-it-out system of trash removal; mostly paved driveways; adequate supplies and services are available in Ainsworth.

Activities & Attractions: Fishing.

Natural Features: Located on a valleyside above Long Pine Creek; campground vegetation consists of dense pines and cedars, a few hardwoods, and sections of grass; a few sites are situated on a small, creekside flat; elevation 2500'.

Season, Fees & Phone: Open all year, subject to weather conditions; please see Appendix for standard Nebraska state park fees; 14 day limit; c/o Nebraska Game & Parks Commission District II Office, Bassett, (402) 684-2921.

Camp Notes: Long Pine appears to be used as a fishing camp more than anything else. (Judging from the terrain and the amount of natural cover available, it might also harbor deer and game birds.) Getting out of here in snowy or even rainy weather might pose a problem for anything but a solo 4X4. (No sweat sliding *in*!) Bring a winch and a grappling hook, just in case. Remarkably pleasant, timbered setting.

ATKINSON LAKE
Atkinson Lake State Recreation Area

Location: North-central Nebraska west of O'Neill.

Access: From U.S. Highway 20 at milepost 288 +.1 at the far west edge of the city of Atkinson (18 miles west of O'Neill), turn south onto a sandy gravel road; proceed 0.1 mile, across the railroad tracks and half-way past the marble orchard, to an intersection; turn west (right) onto a paved road and continue for 0.45 mile; turn north (right) into the recreation area; the primary campground is just inside the entrance; a few additional sites are on the north side of the area.

Facilities: Approximately 30 campsites, including a half-dozen with electrical hookups; sites are basically small, level, and closely spaced; parking surfaces are grass, with enough room for large vehicles; ample room for a large tent; barbecue grills and fireplaces; b-y-o firewood; water at a hand pump; vault facilities; gravel driveways; limited+ supplies and services are available in Atkinson.

Activities & Attractions: Fishing (maybe).

Natural Features: Located principally on a large, grassy flat along a small stream; campsites are lightly sheltered/shaded by large hardwoods; elevation 2100'.

Season, Fees & Phone: Open all year, subject to weather conditions; please see Appendix for standard Nebraska state park fees; 14 day limit; c/o Nebraska Game & Parks Commission District II Office, Bassett, (402) 684-2921.

Camp Notes: Be advised (perhaps *forewarned* might be more appropriate) that this camp has been included mainly as a public service to travelers of U.S. 20 who might need a quick hookup or a tent spot before moving on to bigger and better places. (And if you're temporarily between paychecks, you'd have a fortnight to decide where to flop next.) To be fair about the place, you *are* in a good neighborhood--the local country club is right next door.

Nebraska 16

BESSEY
Nebraska National Forest Recreation Area

Location: Central Nebraska northwest of Broken Bow.

Access: From Nebraska State Highway 2 at milepost 226 (1.5 miles northwest of Halsey, 16 miles southeast of Thedford), turn south onto Nebraska Route 86-B Spur (S-86-B, paved) and proceed 0.35 mile to the campground, at the south edge of the recreation complex.

Facilities: 31 campsites in 3 loops; (a group campground is also available, by reservation); sites are generally small to medium-sized and quite private; parking pads are mostly short, gravel or paved straight-ins, plus a few medium to long pull-offs; a little additional leveling may be necessary; small tent spots; fireplaces, fire rings, or barbecue grills; some firewood is provided; water at central faucets; restrooms, plus auxiliary vaults; holding tank disposal station; gravel or paved driveways; gas and groceries+ are available in Halsey.

Activities & Attractions: Scott Lookout National Recreation Trail; Bessey Arboretum; tennis courts, swimming pool, and day use area, adjacent.

Natural Features: Located at the base of a forested hillside in the Sandhills region; sites are quite well sheltered/shaded by an assortment of hardwoods and evergreens; Middle Loup River flows by a few yards north; elevation 2800'.

Season, Fees & Phone: Open all year, subject to weather conditions, with limited services October to May; $6.00; 14-day limit; Bessey Ranger District, Halsey, (308) 533-2257.

Camp Notes: Two of the campground's loops are quite appropriately named "Hardwoods" and "Cedars". The third small, as yet unnamed, loop could readily be called "Pines". (Incidentally, the recreation area was named in recognition of the efforts of Dr. Charles Bessey, a long-time professor of botany at the University of Nebraska. Bessey convinced Theodore Roosevelt to establish the Nebraska National Forest back in '02. Furthermore, he swayed the USDA into planting what have now become 22,000-acres of man-made forest in this region.)

Nebraska 17

VICTORIA SPRINGS
Victoria Springs State Recreation Area

Location: Central Nebraska northwest of Broken Bow.

Access: From Nebraska State Highway 2 at milepost 258 +.3 in Anselmo (21 miles northwest of Broken Bow, 21 miles southeast of Dunning), turn east onto Nebraska Route 21-A Spur (S-21-A, paved) and proceed 6.2 miles (0.1 mile past the main entrance, across Victoria Creek); turn south (right) into the campground.

Facilities: 30 campsites, including 15 with electrical hookups; sites are medium+, level, with nominal separation; parking surfaces are grass, principally medium to large straight-ins/pull-offs; ample space for large tents; barbecue grills; b-y-o firewood; water at central faucets; restrooms with showers; gravel driveway; gas and groceries in Anselmo; nearly complete supplies and services are available in Broken Bow.

Activities & Attractions: Mineral springs; original log cabins; country schoolhouse; fishing for largemouth bass, bluegill, channel catfish in the lake, small trout in the creek; limited boating on the lake (electric, person-propulsion); ball field.

Natural Features: Located on a short shelf above the east bank of Victoria Creek in the Sandhills region; sites are lightly sheltered/shaded by rows of hardwoods; a small lake is adjacent to the picnic area west of the camp; elevation 2700'.

Season, Fees & Phone: Available all year, with limited services mid-September to mid-May; please see Appendix for standard Nebraska state park fees; 14 day limit; park office (308) 749-2235.

Camp Notes: The ball field is right next to the campground, so be sure to listen for a "batter up" or "heads up" or "fore" or whatever. It's worth travelling a few miles off the main drag to come to this neat little spot in Nebraska's vast, golden Sandhills country. Lots of water, lots of greenery.

Nebraska 18

HOMESTEAD KNOLLS
Calamus Reservoir State Recreation Area

Location: Central Nebraska northwest of Burwell.

Access: From the junction of Nebraska State Highways 91 & 11 in Burwell, travel north/northwest on a paved local road for 5.5 miles to a 'T" intersection just below the dam; turn northeast (right) and proceed to the end of the dam, then northwest along the lake shore for 1 mile; turn west (left) into the campground.

Facilities: 83 campsites with electrical hookups; sites are small+, basically level, with minimal separation; parking pads are paved, medium to long straight-ins; adequate space for large tents; fire rings; b-y-o firewood; water at central faucets; restrooms with showers; holding tank disposal station at Little York Point, 0.5 mile southeast; paved driveways; limited supplies and services are available in Burwell.

Activities & Attractions: Sandy swimming beach; fishing, reportedly very good to excellent for largemouth bass, walleye, northern pike; boating; paved boat launches; Fort Hartstuff State Historical Park, southeast of Burwell, is a restoration of an 1870's frontier post with exhibits and self-guided tours.

Natural Features: Located on a slightly rolling flat above the northeast shore of Calamus Reservoir, a major (5000-acre) irrigation impoundment on the Calamus River; sites are very lightly sheltered/shaded by planted hardwoods on a grassy surface; elevation 2200'.

Season, Fees & Phone: Open all year, with limited services October to April; please see Appendix for standard Nebraska state park fees; 14 day limit; park office (308) 346-5666.

Camp Notes: In addition to the main campground detailed here, camping is also available at a smaller area, Nunda Shoal, on the opposite (southwest) shore. Calamus Reservoir is one of the newest state recreation areas in Nebraska. Remote...with excellent recreational potential.

NEBRASKA
Southwest Plains
Please refer to the Nebraska map in the Appendix

Nebraska 19

CEDAR VIEW
Lake McConaughy State Recreation Area

Location: West-central Nebraska northwest of Ogallala.

Access: From Nebraska State Highway 92 at milepost 125 (12 miles southeast of Lewellen, 12 miles northwest of the junction of State Highways 92 & 61 north of Ogallala), turn south onto Road 13 and proceed 0.5 mile; turn west (right) and continue for 0.1 mile to the campground.

Facilities: 117 campsites, including 80 with electrical hookups, in 2 loops; sites are small and closely spaced; parking pads are paved, medium-length straight-ins; some pads may require a little additional leveling; adequate space for a medium to large tent in most sites; barbecue grills; water at several faucets; restrooms with showers; holding tank disposal station; paved driveways; gas, camper supplies and laundromat nearby on the highway.

Activities & Attractions: Boating; sailing; boat launch and dock; very good to excellent boat fishing; waterskiing.

Natural Features: Located on a short bluff above the north shore of Lake McConaughy on the North Platte River; sites receive minimal to light shelter/shade from large hardwoods, plus small pines and cedars; sandy beach; evergreen and hardwood-dotted hills and bluffs border the lake; lake views from many campsites; elevation 3400'.

Season, Fees & Phone: Open all year, with limited services November to April; please see Appendix for standard Nebraska state park fees; 14 day limit; park office (308) 284-3542.

Camp Notes: As long as the lake's water level isn't too high, there'll be a magnificent, wide, sandy beach to loaf on. Indeed, in late summer or fall, the stretch of snow white sand and turquoise water just below the campground rivals or even surpasses many Pacific Ocean beaches. Nebraska's largest reservoir has been nicknamed (ready?) "Big Mac".

MARTIN BAY
Lake McConoughy State Recreation Area

Location: West-central Nebraska north of Ogallala.

Access: From Nebraska State Highway 61 near the north end of Kinsley Dam (at either of 2 points, 0.25 mile or 0.75 mile south of the junction of State Highways 61 & 92, 12 miles north of Ogallala), turn west for 0.2 mile to the recreation area.

Facilities: Approximately 40 camp/picnic sites; sites are small to medium-sized, slightly sloped, with minimal to fair separation; parking surfaces are sandy gravel, straight-ins, pull-offs; small to medium-sized tent areas; several ramadas (sun shelters); no fire facilities; water at central faucets and a hand pump; restrooms and vault facilities; holding tank disposal station; gravel driveways; gas and camper supplies within 0.5 mile.

Activities & Attractions: Boating; boat launch and dock; fishing for most major warm water species, plus rainbow trout.

Natural Features: Located at the northeast corner of Lake McConoughy; large hardwoods provide fair to good shelter/shade for most sites; sandy beach; elevation 3400'.

Season, Fees & Phone: Open all year, subject to weather conditions; please see Appendix for standard Nebraska state park fees; 14 day limit; park office (308) 284-3542.

Camp Notes: This is the largest and best-equipped of nearly a dozen areas on Lake McConoughy which offer only basic camping at bargain basement prices. (The lake's most complete campground is Cedar Vue--see separate info.) On a busy weekend, it might be in the midst of the storm of popularity on the lake. Camping here also provides the most convenient access to the excellent spring walleye fishing along the face of the dam. (The present Nebraska record walleye--16+ lbs.--came from this lake.) For more deluxe camping in this vicinity, Lake Ogallala Campground is a short drive away (see info).

LAKE OGALLALA
Lake Ogallala State Recreation Area

Location: West-central Nebraska north of Ogallala.

Access: From Nebraska State Highway 61 at the north end of Kinsley Dam (1 mile south of the junction of State Highways 61 & 92, 12 miles north of Ogallala), turn east onto a paved access road and proceed 1.6 miles (the road zigzags a bit); turn south (right) at a point just beyond the private campground into the public camp.

Facilities: 82 campsites, including 18 with electrical hookups, in 3 loops, plus primitive camping; sites are small to medium-sized, level, with nominal to fairly good separation; parking pads are medium to long, paved straight-ins; very good tent-pitching possibilities; barbecue grills; b-y-o firewood; water at several faucets and at hand pumps; rest-rooms with showers; paved driveways; several stops for gas and camper supplies within 1 mile.

Activities & Attractions: Fishing for most major warm water species, plus rainbow trout; boating; boat launch.

Natural Features: Located on a flat at the west end of Lake Ogallala on the North Platte River just below Kingsley Dam; (the dam impounds the river upstream of this point and forms giant Lake McConoughy to the west); vegetation consists of lots of grass and hardwoods; elevation 3300'.

Season, Fees & Phone: Open all year, with limited services November to April; please see Appendix for standard Nebraska state park fees; 14 day limit; phone c/o Lake McConaughy SRA (308) 284-3542.

Camp Notes: Tiny Lake Ogallala is an indirect result of the creation of Lake McConoughy. The cavernous excavation left behind when material was removed for the big lake's dam has filled with water to become Lake Ogallala. In some respects, the little lake could be considered merely an afterthought; but the campground is on par with most other full-service sra camps. Many good waterfront sites.

Nebraska 22

SUTHERLAND
Sutherland State Recreation Area

Location: Central Nebraska west of North Platte.

Access: From Nebraska State Highway 25 at milepost 98 +.3 (at the southwest corner of Sutherland Reservoir, 4.5 miles south of Interstate 80 Exit 158 for Sutherland, 18 miles north of the junction of State Highways 25 & 23 near Wallace), turn east onto a gravel access road and proceed 0.2 mile to the campground.

Facilities: 15 campsites; sites are small+, with minimal to fair separation; parking surfaces are grass/gravel, mostly medium-length straight-ins; adequate space for a large tent in most sites; some sites lack tables; barbecue grills; a small amount of firewood may be available for gathering, b-y-o is recommended; water at a hand pump; vault facilities; gravel driveway; limited supplies and services are available in Sutherland, just north of the freeway.

Activities & Attractions: Fishing for walleye, perch, white bass; boating; boat launches; small golf course.

Natural Features: Located near the southwest shore of 3000-acre Sutherland Reservoir; large hardwoods and some cedars provide limited to fairly good shelter/shade; surrounded by gently rolling plains; elevation 3100'.

Season, Fees & Phone: Open all year, subject to weather conditions; please see Appendix for standard Nebraska state park fees; phone c/o Nebraska Game & Parks Commission District IV Office, North Platte, (308) 535-8025.

Camp Notes: In addition to this campground at the "Inlet" unit, and a couple of other small state areas, there's a small camp on the north shore (next to the golf course) that's run by the public power company. The cost there is about the same as the state camps. If you tire of fishing, boating or watching the lake's power plant spout steam, try a round of prairie golf. Depending upon which hole is being played, and the velocity and direction of the seemingly ceaseless crosswind over the open slope, you may find that you've suddenly acquired a severe 'slice' or a heckuva 'hook'.

Nebraska 23

CODY
North Platte City Park

Location: Central Nebraska in North Platte.

Access: From U.S. Highway 83 (North Jeffers Street) at milepost 84 +.5 at the northwest corner of the large city park complex (0.6 mile north of midtown North Platte, 2.9 miles north of Interstate 80 Exit 177), turn east into the campground. (Note: U.S. 83 takes a short jog west, then north, while passing through midtown, so watch the highway signs carefully and follow Jeffers Street north out of downtown.)

Facilities: 36 campsites; sites are small, level and closely spaced; parking pads are short to scant medium-length gravel/paved straight-ins; space for a small tent in most sites; barbecue grills or fireplaces in some sites; b-y-o firewood; water at several faucets; restrooms; paved driveway; complete supplies and services are available in North Platte.

Activities & Attractions: Swimming pool; museum and train display; playground; small wildlife park; Buffalo Bill Ranch State Historical Park, 3 miles west.

Natural Features: Located on a grassy flat along the south bank of the North Platte River; sites receive adequate shelter/shade from large hardwoods; elevation 2800'.

Season, Fees & Phone: May to mid-October; $5.00; 7 day limit; North Platte Recreation Department (308) 534-4772.

Camp Notes: Most of the campground is quite visible from, and within earshot of, the highway. (Since the camp loop lies perpendicular to the main road, selecting a spot at the far end should minimize the effect of passing traffic.) Although the campsites are quite small, there's lots of room to roam on the adjoining park grounds. If your campmates include kids (no matter what age!), the local activities make it one of the better stops in the state.

Nebraska 24

KANSAS POINT
Lake Maloney State Recreation Area

Location: Central Nebraska south of North Platte.

Access: From U.S. Highway 83 at milepost 76 + .9 (4.6 miles south of Interstate 80 Exit 177 at North Platte, 14 miles north of the junction of U.S. 83 & Nebraska State Highway 23 near Wellfleet), turn west onto a paved access road and proceed 0.7 mile to the Outlet area; continue for 2 miles northwest, west, then south across the inlet channel to the campground.

Facilities: 58 campsites with electrical hookups; sites are small to medium-sized, basically level, with nominal separation; parking pads are gravel, medium to long straight-ins; adequate space for tents on a grassy surface; fire rings; b-y-o firewood; water at hand pumps; vault facilities; holding tank disposal station at the Outlet area; gravel driveways; complete supplies and services are available in North Platte.

Activities & Attractions: Fishing for walleye, crappie, white bass and drum); boating; boat launches; playsets.

Natural Features: Located on the west shore of 3000-acre Lake Maloney, a reservoir with diversion canals that serve as the inlet and the outlet streams; hardwoods plus a few cedars and pines provide very light to moderate shade/shelter for most sites; elevation 3100'.

Season, Fees & Phone: Available all year, with limited services in winter; please see Appendix for standard Nebraska state park fees; phone c/o Nebraska Game & Parks Commission District IV Office, North Platte, (308) 535-8025.

Camp Notes: Kansas Point is the most highly developed of the three camp areas on the lake. Semi-open camping is also available at the adjacent Jaycee Park area, and at the Main (Outlet) area, located just inside the main entrance. The Main area has a few advantages: it's more easily accessible, has water at a central faucet, is a couple of bucks cheaper, and provides a little more shelter than Kansas Point.

Nebraska 25

GOTHENBURG
Gothenburg City Park

Location: Central Nebraska southeast of North Platte.

Access: From Nebraska State Highway 47 (Lake Avenue) at the north edge of Gothenburg (1.1 miles north of midtown, 2.2 miles north of Interstate 80 Exit 211), turn west onto 27th Street (gravel) and proceed 0.1 mile; turn south (left) into the campground.

Facilities: 24 campsites, including several with electrical hookups; sites are small+, level, with minimal to fair separation; parking pads are short to medium-length, gravel straight-ins; ample space for a medium to large tent in most sites; barbecue grills; b-y-o firewood; water at several faucets; restrooms; holding tank disposal station; paved or gravel driveways; adequate supplies and services are available in Gothenburg.

Activities & Attractions: Situated adjacent to Lake Helen Recreation Area--small lake, volleyball courts, playground, covered bridge, shelters, very limited boating and fishing, lots of grass; original Pony Express Station at the city park in midtown Gothenburg.

Natural Features: Located in a grove of hardwoods on a surface of sparse grass; sites are moderately shaded by rows of large trees; surrounding countryside is comprised of level plains and agricultural land; elevation 2600'.

Season, Fees & Phone: April to November; $6.00; 5 day limit; park manager (308) 537-3867.

Camp Notes: Actually, the campground's facilities are worn and simple, so don't expect the Central Plains Waldorf (unless a major face-lift was accomplished recently). But what would probably make a stay worthwhile is the really nice recreational complex just south of the camping area. This park is also known as Lafayette Park.

Nebraska 26

JOHNSON LAKE
Johnson Lake State Recreation Area

Location: South-central Nebraska west of Kearney.

Access: From U.S. Highway 283 at milepost 48 (8 miles south of Interstate 80 Exit 237 for Lexington, 6 miles north of Elwood), turn northwest onto a paved access road and proceed 0.2 mile; turn west (left) onto a gravel roadway to the campground entrance.

Facilities: 110 campsites, including 81 with electrical hookups; sites are small+, level, with nominal separation; parking pads are medium-length, gravel straight-ins; sufficient space for medium-sized tents (large, if squeezed a bit) on a grassy surface; barbecue grills; b-y-o firewood; water at central faucets; restrooms with showers; auxiliary vault facilities; holding tank disposal station; gravel driveways; camper supplies and laundromat nearby; limited supplies in Elwood; adequate supplies and services are available in Lexington.

Activities & Attractions: Swimming; fishing for white bass, walleye, drum; boating; boat launch.

Natural Features: Located on the east shore of 2100-acre Johnson Lake; sites are adequately sheltered by rows and rows and rows of large hardwoods; virtually all sites have some sort of a lake view; surrounding area consists of plains and agricultural land; elevation 2600'.

Season, Fees & Phone: Open all year, with limited services November to May; please see Appendix for standard Nebraska state park fees; 14 day limit; park office (308) 785-2685.

Camp Notes: Johnson Lake is one of Nebraska's so-called "Chain O' Lakes" and is the largest in this area. The campground is laid out much like a drive-in theater. Instead of scratchy, crackling speakers, the wind in the trees provides the audio portion of the show. And there's a different movie every evening. Try to get here early on summer weekends in order to get a front row seat.

Nebraska 27

CHAMPION LAKE
Champion Lake State Recreation Area

Location: Southwest Nebraska southwest of Imperial.

Access: From U.S. Highway 6 at the south edge of Imperial, turn southwest onto Nebraska Route 15-A Spur (S-15-A) and proceed 7 miles to the village of Champion; turn north (right) onto an unnamed street which passes through midtown, and proceed 0.3 mile (the first block is paved, remainder is gravel) to a "T"; turn west (left) for a final 0.15 mile to the recreation area.

Facilities: Approximately 12 campsites; sites are very small, level and closely spaced; parking surfaces are gravel/grass, short straight-ins/pull-offs; space for small to medium-sized tents; barbecue grills for a few sites; b-y-o firewood; water at a hand pump; vault facilities; (restrooms in the state historical park, adjacent); gravel driveways; gas and a small market in Champion; adequate supplies and services are available in Imperial.

Activities & Attractions: Champion Mill State Historical Park (adjacent); Chase County Historical Museum; possibly fishing.

Natural Features: Located on the north shore of 10-acre Champion Lake on the Frenchman River on the high plains; sites are lightly sheltered/shaded by large hardwoods on patches of grass; gently rolling plains and agricultural land surround the recreation area; elevation 3300'.

Season, Fees & Phone: Open all year, subject to weather conditions; please see Appendix for standard Nebraska state park fees; 14 day limit; phone c/o Champion Mill SHP (308) 882-5860.

Camp Notes: The tiny lake is really the mill pond for the historical park's restored, water-powered grain mill--the last of its genre in Nebraska. The old mill is just a short walk around the lake shore and across the outlet stream from the camping area.

ENDERS
Enders State Recreation Area

Location: Southwest Nebraska southeast of Imperial.

Access: From Nebraska State Highway 61 at a point 0.1 mile southwest of the junction of Highway 61 & U.S. Highway 6 (11 miles southeast of Imperial, 27 miles north of Benkelman), turn northwest into the recreation area.

Facilities: Approximately 35 camp/picnic sites, plus open camping at several other points around the shore; site size and separation varies; parking surfaces are gravel or grass, generally long enough for large vehicles; adequate space for tents; barbecue grills; some firewood is available for gathering in the vicinity; water at central faucets and at hand pumps; restrooms; disposal station; campers supplies in the town of Enders, 1 mile north; limited supplies and services are available in Imperial.

Activities & Attractions: Fair to good fishing for white bass, walleye, crappie; boating; boat launches; playground.

Natural Features: Located on the east shore of Enders Reservoir, a flood control and irrigation impoundment on the Frenchman River; vegetation mainly consists of range grass, yucca, sage and light to medium dense hardwoods; much of the lake shore is timbered; elevation 3200'.

Season, Fees & Phone: Open all year, subject to weather conditions; please see Appendix for standard Nebraska state park fees; 14 day limit; phone c/o Nebraska Game & Parks Commission District IV Office, North Platte, (308) 535-8025.

Camp Notes: Except for its highwayside convenience, there really isn't a lot to recommend this as a place at which to *plan* to camp, particularly in a dry year. By the same token, there aren't any significantly *better* places within an hour's drive, either. Enders and its sister reservoirs in Nebraska's southwest--Swanson, Butler and Strunk--are collectively known locally as the "Little TVA" or the "Great Lakes of Nebraska". The future of Enders, particularly, is uncertain: the flow of water into the reservoir has dwindled in recent years because of shifts in regional farming methods.

ROCK CREEK LAKE
Rock Creek Lake State Recreation Area

Location: Southwest corner of Nebraska south of Imperial.

Access: From U.S. Highway 34 at milepost 19 (11 miles west of Benkelman, 19 miles east of the Nebraska-Colorado border), turn north onto a gravel access road and proceed 0.4 mile to a "T" intersection in the hamlet of Parks; turn west (left) and continue for 0.35 mile through downtown Parks to the west end of town; turn north (right) onto a gravel road and proceed 2.7 miles; turn west (left) for a final 1.7 miles to the camping area, on the west side of the lake.

Facilities: Approximately 15 campsites in a semi-open camping arrangement; sites vary from small to large, with minimal to good separation; parking surfaces are grass or gravel; small tent areas; barbecue grills; a small amount of firewood may be available for gathering, b-y-o to be sure; water from a spring; vault facilities; gravel driveways; limited+ supplies and services are available in Benkelman.

Activities & Attractions: Rock Creek Fish Hatchery (open to the public during normal business hours); fishing for warm water species; limited boating (12-volt or 2-handed power).

Natural Features: Located along the shore of Rock Creek Lake on the high plains; sites are very lightly sheltered/shaded by a few large hardwoods and cedars; elevation 3200'.

Season, Fees & Phone: Open all year, subject to weather conditions; please see Appendix for standard Nebraska state park fees; 14 day limit; phone c/o Nebraska Game & Parks Commission District IV Office, North Platte, (308) 535-8025.

Camp Notes: The fish hatchery is the only one in Nebraska where you'll find newborn trout. Sorry, but you'll have to trip over to the tiny trout lake at Two Rivers SRA near Omaha, and a few other areas, to catch them. Camping at Rock Creek Lake is as rough hewn as it gets in Nebraska.

MACKLIN BAY
Swanson State Recreation Area

Location: Southwest Nebraska west of McCook.

Access: From U.S. Highway 34 at milepost 56 +.4 (5 miles west of Trenton, 9 miles east of Stratton), turn south onto a gravel access road and proceed 0.1 mile; turn west for 0.1 mile to the entrance, at the west end of the campground.

Facilities: 17 campsites with electrical hookups; sites are small, with limited separation; parking pads are gravel, short to medium-length straight-ins plus a few long pull-throughs; slight additional leveling may be needed; adequate space for small, perhaps medium-sized, tents; barbecue grills; b-y-o firewood is recommended; water at central faucets; restrooms with showers; holding tank disposal station; gravel driveways; limited supplies and services are available in Trenton and Stratton.

Activities & Attractions: Convenient highwayside stop; fishing; boating; boat launch and dock.

Natural Features: Located on a high bluff above small Macklin Bay on the north shore of Swanson Reservoir, an impoundment on the Republican River; sites are lightly sheltered/shaded by medium-height hardwoods on a surface of sand and grass; breezy; elevation 2600'.

Season, Fees & Phone: Open all year, with limited services October to April; please see Appendix for standard Nebraska state park fees; 14 day limit; phone c/o Nebraska Game & Parks Commission District IV Office, North Platte, (308) 535-8025.

Camp Notes: Don't plan on launching a cabin cruiser at the boat ramp on the bay. The passage under the railroad bridge to open water is s-n-u-g. The Republican Valley, particularly east of here, is certainly one of Nebraska's most beautiful regions. The original Indian name for the Republican River was Manure River. Honest. (You may enter your own editorial comments in the following space: _____ Ed.)

SPRING CANYON
Swanson State Recreation Area

Location: Southwest Nebraska west of McCook.

Access: From U.S. Highway 34 at milepost 58 +.1 (3 miles west of Trenton, 9 miles east of Stratton), turn south onto Recreation Road 44-B and travel 2 miles across Swanson Dam; turn west (actually continuing on 44-B) and proceed 0.7 mile; turn south (left) into the campground. **Alternate Access:** From Nebraska State Highway 25 at milepost 10 +.2 (4 miles south of Trenton, 10 miles north of the Nebraska-Kansas border), turn west onto the access road and continue as above.

Facilities: 37 campsites, most with electrical hookups; sites are tiny to small and closely spaced; parking pads are gravel, short straight-ins or pull-offs; a tad of additional leveling may be required; small tent areas; barbecue grills; a limited amount of firewood may be gathered by doing some local brush-busting; water at central faucets and at a hand pump; restrooms; holding tank disposal station; gravel driveways; camper supplies at a marina; limited supplies and services are available in Trenton.

Activities & Attractions: Boating; boat launch, docks; marina fishing (especially northerns and walleye); day use area.

Natural Features: Located in a shallow draw along a bay on the south shore of Swanson Reservoir; sites are adequately sheltered/shaded by large hardwoods; elevation 2600'.

Season, Fees & Phone: Open all year, with limited services mid-November to April; please see Appendix for standard Nebraska state park fees; 14 day limit; phone c/o Nebraska Game & Parks Commission District IV Office, North Platte, (308) 535-8025.

Camp Notes: Should you decide to stay in the Swanson Reservoir area, and the wind is blowing (usual), this camp will provide considerably more shelter than the lake's other campground at Macklin Bay (see info). Besides, if you need a cup of sugar or some refreshments, you can tap the neighbors in the trailer court next door for a loan.

WILLOW VIEW
Red Willow State Recreation Area

Location: Southwest Nebraska north of McCook.

Access: From U.S. Highway 83 at milepost 27 +.5 (12 miles north of McCook, 19 miles south of the junction of U.S. 83 & Nebraska State Highway 20 near Maywood), turn west onto a paved access road and proceed 0.5 mile; turn north (right) for 0.1 mile, then west into the campground.

Facilities: 49 campsites, most with electrical hookups; sites are small+, essentially level, with nil visual separation; parking pads are gravel/grass, medium-length straight-ins; ample space for large tents; barbecue grills; b-y-o firewood or chips; water at central faucets; restrooms with showers; holding tank disposal station; gravel driveways; camper supplies at Spring Creek, 0.8 mile northwest; adequate+ supplies and services are available in McCook.

Activities & Attractions: Reportedly excellent fishing for largemouth and smallmouth bass, crappie; boating; boat launch and swimming beach at Spring Creek area; new Museum of the High Plains in McCook.

Natural Features: Located on a bluff above the east shore of Hugh Butler Lake (Red Willow Reservoir); vegetation consists of crunchgrass, plus a few small hardwoods, cedars and pines; elevation 2700'.

Season, Fees & Phone: Open all year, with limited services November to April; please see Appendix for standard Nebraska state park fees; 14 day limit; phone c/o Nebraska Game & Parks Commission District IV Office, North Platte, (308) 535-8025.

Camp Notes: Although the parking pads themselves aren't overly long, there's actually plenty of overhang room behind most of them for a longer outfit. The areas available for tents, likewise, are sizable. (Bring long tent pegs or plenty of weighty gear in order to keep the canvas in Nebraska.) The views from this elevated, windblown vantage point are striking.

SHADY BAY
Medicine Creek State Recreation Area

Location: Southwest Nebraska east of McCook.

Access: From U.S. Highways 6 & 34 at milepost 109 +.4 (2 miles west of Cambridge, 5 miles east of Bartley), turn north onto a paved road and travel 8.3 miles; turn west (left) onto the campground access road and proceed 0.8 mile to the campground.

Facilities: 76 campsites, including 30 with electrical hookups; sites are generally small, with limited separation; parking pads are paved, short to medium-length straight-ins; some pads may require a little additional leveling; adequate space for a medium-sized, possibly large, tent; barbecue grills; b-y-o firewood; water at central faucets; restrooms with showers, plus auxiliary vaults; holding tank disposal station; paved driveways; camper supplies at the southwest end of the dam; limited+ supplies and services are available in Cambridge.

Activities & Attractions: Swimming beach; playground; fishing for walleye, crappie, white bass; boating; boat launch.

Natural Features: Located on the east shore of Harry D. Strunk Lake (Medicine Creek Reservoir); large hardwoods provide the majority of sites with wind shelter and light to ample midday shade; most sites have some sort of lake view; tree-dotted hills surround the lake; elevation 2500'.

Season, Fees & Phone: Open all year, with limited services mid-November to April; please see Appendix for standard Nebraska state park fees; 14 day limit; phone c/o Nebraska Game & Parks Commission District IV Office, North Platte, (308) 535-8025.

Camp Notes: If you arrive at night, take a good look around for a campsite--one group of sites at the northeast corner of the campground could be overlooked in the dark. (Who was Harry D. Strunk, you ask? Strunk was longtime publisher of the McCook *Daily Gazette* who gained national prominence as an advocate of water conservation and reclamation during the dust bowl days of the 30's and 40's.)

METHODIST COVE
Harlan County Lake/Corps of Engineers Park

Location: South-central Nebraska east of McCook.

Access: From U.S. Highway 183 at milepost 6 +.5 (on the south edge of Alma, at the north end of the causeway across the west end of Harlan County Lake), turn east onto South Street and proceed 2.4 miles; turn south (right) onto a paved access road for 0.25 mile, then turn east (left) into the campground. (Note: access is also possible from U.S. 136 near milepost 32 +.5, 3 miles east of Alma, south via a 1.2-mile gravel road, then west 1 mile.)

Facilities: 155 campsites, including 32 with electrical hookups, in a main loop and a secondary-loop; sites are medium-sized, mostly level, with minimal to fair separation; parking pads are gravel, medium-length straight-ins; excellent tent-pitching opportunities; fire rings; b-y-o firewood; water at central faucets; restrooms (H) with showers, plus auxiliary vault facilities; holding tank disposal station; paved or gravel driveways; gas and groceries in Alma and nearby Republican City.

Activities & Attractions: Fishing principally for walleye, white bass, channel catfish and northern pike; boating; boat launch; fish cleaning station; small playground.

Natural Features: Located on a large, grassy flat dotted with small hardwoods (main loop), and on a tree-sheltered, slight slope (secondary loop) on the north shore of Harlan County Lake on the Republican River; the lake is bound by low, grassy hills garnished with stands of trees; elevation 2100'.

Season, Fees & Phone: May to October; $7.00 for a standard site, $9.00 for an electrical hookup unit; 14 day limit; Harlan County Lake CoE Project Office (308) 799-2105.

Camp Notes: Methodist Cove has a number of unsheltered sites with excellent views within inches of the lake. In addition to Methodist Cove and Hunter Cove (see separate info), another north shore area is North Cove, 2 miles east of Methodist Cove. North Cove has water, vaults, no fee, and open camping on a small, tree-dotted point.

HUNTER COVE
Harlan County Lake/Corps of Engineers Park

Location: South-central Nebraska east of McCook.

Access: From U.S. Highway 136 in Republican City, turn south onto Republican Road and proceed 1.2 miles south, then southeast (becomes Berrigan Road), then south again to a 3-way intersection; turn west (right, at the water tower) onto a paved road and proceed 1 mile; turn south (left) onto the campground access road and continue for 0.3 mile to the campground.

Facilities: 142 campsites, including 84 with electrical hookups; sites are small to small+, with fair to excellent separation; parking pads are gravel, short to medium-length straight-ins; a little additional leveling may be required in some sites; adequate space for small to medium-sized tents; barbecue grills or fire rings; b-y-o firewood is recommended; water at central faucets; restrooms with showers; holding tank disposal station; paved or gravel driveways; gas and groceries are available in Republican City and in nearby Alma.

Activities & Attractions: Playgrounds; fishing; boating; boat launch; marina nearby.

Natural Features: Located at the northeast corner of Harlan County Lake, a flood control and irrigation impoundment on the Republican River; most sites are well sheltered/shaded by rows of hardwoods and evergreens; elevation 2100'.

Season, Fees & Phone: May to November; $7.00 for a standard site, $9.00 for an electrical hookup unit; 14 day limit; Harlan County Lake CoE Project Office (308) 799-2105.

Camp Notes: Many of the campsites here are small, but quite private, since they're in their own little wooded cubicles. It might take a while to select a site--the campground stretches for a half-mile along or near the lake shore. Hunter Cove is one of a pair of large, full service campgrounds on this lake. Smaller camping areas with water, vault facilities, and a nominal price tag are located on the east side of the lake below the dam, and on the southeast shore.

BOWMAN LAKE
Bowman Lake State Recreation Area

Location: Central Nebraska northwest of Grand Island.

Access: From Nebraska State Highway 92 at milepost 319 +.9 (1 mile west of the junction of Nebraska State Highways 92 & 58 & 10 at midtown Loup City, 21 miles east of Ansley), turn south onto a gravel road and proceed 0.2 mile to the campground.

Facilities: Approximately 12 campsites in a semi-open camping arrangement, in 2 sections; sites are level, with nominal to good separation; parking surfaces are grass or gravel, straight-ins or pull-offs; good to excellent tent-pitching possibilities; barbecue grills, plus a few fire rings; a limited amount of firewood may be available for gathering in the area, b-y-o is suggested; water at a hand pump; vault facilities; gravel driveways; limited supplies and services are available in Loup City.

Activities & Attractions: Canoeing, boating, floating; some fishing for catfish, bass, carp; playsets.

Natural Features: Located on a large, grassy flat along the Middle Loup River; most sites receive light shelter/shade from large hardwoods, cedars and pines; tiny, weedy/reedy Bowman Lake adjoins the camping area; surrounding countryside is level prairie and farmland; elevation 2100'.

Season, Fees & Phone: Open all year, subject to weather conditions; please see Appendix for standard Nebraska state park fees; 14 day limit; c/o Sherman Reservoir SRA, Loup City, (308) 745-0230.

Camp Notes: Alright, so the place is about as small and basic as they come. There are some great places for pitching a tent, but the self-contained camper probably is a little better suited to stay here. It does make a very pleasantly green, very handy, highway stop. It might also serve well as a camp for river floaters. Bowman Lake rarely receives a mention because the big local hangout is Sherman Reservoir, northeast of Loup City (see separate info). Bowman Lake itself is actually a big pond just off the highway.

SHERMAN RESERVOIR
Sherman Reservoir State Recreation Area

Location: Central Nebraska northwest of Grand Island.

Access: From the junction of Nebraska State Highways 92, 58 & 10 in Loup City, turn east onto O Street for 0.2 mile, then north (left) onto 10th Street for 1 block; turn east (right) onto N Street; proceed east on N Street, (the courthouse should be on your right) and travel out of town for 4 miles to the end of the pavement; turn north (left) onto a paved road and continue for 0.6 mile to the recreation area; camping is available in 5 sections at the southwest corner of the lake; or continue northeast across the dam to a single area at southeast corner of the lake.

Facilities: Approximately 60 camp/picnic sites in 6 areas; sites vary in size, are generally somewhat sloped, with fair to good separation; parking surfaces are paved or grass, short straight-ins or long pull-offs; adequate space for large tents on a grassy surface; several ramadas (sun shelters); barbecue grills; b-y-o firewood is recommended; water at hand pumps; vault facilities; holding tank disposal station; paved driveways; limited supplies and services are available in Loup City.

Activities & Attractions: Fishing for walleye, crappie, white bass, catfish; boating; boat launches.

Natural Features: Located on a series of small ridges on points of land at the southwest corner and at the southeast corner of Sherman Reservoir; scattered hardwoods and evergreens provide limited shelter/shade for some sites; surrounded by low, grass-covered bluffs; elevation 2200'.

Season, Fees & Phone: Open all year, subject to weather conditions; please see Appendix for standard Nebraska state park fees; 14 day limit; park office (308) 745-0230.

Camp Notes: Almost all of the campsites provide a scenic, ten-mile sweep in several directions. If the view isn't quite perfect you can always just pack up and head for the next ridge to find a better spot.

RAVENNA LAKE
Ravenna Lake State Recreation Area

Location: Central Nebraska northwest of Grand Island.

Access: From Nebraska State Highway 2 at milepost 328 +.4 (1 mile southeast of Ravenna, 30 miles west of Grand Island), turn northeast onto a paved road and proceed 0.8 mile to the recreation area; sites are located on the left, upon entering the area; or turn west (left) onto a paved driveway at the north end of the first group of sites for another 0.2 mile to a second major section.

Facilities: Approximately 20 camp/picnic sites; sites are medium-sized, with minimal to fairly good separation; parking surfaces are grass or gravel, straight-ins or whatevers; ample space for large tents; fire rings; water at a hand pump; vault facilities; mostly paved driveways; limited supplies and services are available in Ravenna.

Activities & Attractions: Fishing (channel catfish, crappie, largemouth bass, northern pike); limited boating (electric or hand-powered craft); playset.

Natural Features: Located on the east shore of long, slender, winding Ravenna Lake, a spring-fed backwater originally a channel of the South Loup River; about half the sites are on a lakeside flat, remainder are in a roadside area; sites are nicely sheltered by medium to large hardwoods and a few cedars on a good grassy surface; surrounded by level farmland; elevation 2000'.

Season, Fees & Phone: Open all year, subject to weather conditions; please see Appendix for standard Nebraska state park fees; 14 day limit; phone c/o Sherman Reservoir SRA, Loup City, (308) 745-0230.

Camp Notes: Judging from the results obtained by the local hawks, and by the number and size of the fish rings on the lake's surface, fishing might be fairly good on this serpentine bayou. In addition to camping in the main areas, there are a few sites scattered around the lake.

Nebraska 39

FORT KEARNY
Fort Kearny State Recreation Area

Location: South-central Nebraska south of Kearney.

Access: From Nebraska State Highway 44 at a point 2 miles south of Interstate 80 Exit 272 at Kearney, turn east onto Nebraska Route 50-A Link (L-50-A, paved) and travel 5 miles; turn north onto a paved access road and proceed 0.75 mile to the recreation area entrance; continue ahead for 0.2 mile, then turn west (left) into the campground. **Alternate Access:** From I-80 Exit 279 east of Kearney, turn south on State Highway 10 and proceed 3 miles; turn west onto Route 50-A Link for 2 miles to the access road; turn north, continue as above.

Facilities: 112 campsites, including 80 with electrical hookups; sites are small+, level, with minimal to fair separation; parking pads are medium-length, gravel straight-ins; small tent spots; barbecue grills or fire rings; b-y-o firewood; water at central faucets; restrooms with showers; holding tank disposal station; paved driveways; nearly complete supplies and services are available in Kearney.

Activities & Attractions: Fitness trail; hiking/biking trail; sandy swimming beach; fishing; handicapped-access fishing dock; limited boating; cross-country skiing; Fort Kearny State Historical Park, with exhibits and programs, 1 mile west.

Natural Features: Located around the grassy shores of a half-dozen small lakes; sites receive light to moderate shelter/shade from large cottonwoods and scattered evergreens; surrounded by table-level agricultural land; elevation 2100'.

Season, Fees & Phone: Open all year, with limited services November to May; please see Appendix for standard Nebraska state park fees; 14 day limit; phone c/o Fort Kearny State Historical Park (308) 234-9513.

Camp Notes: Note the slight difference in the spelling of the name of the nearby city and the name of the fort. (Not unlike Casper and Fort Caspar in neighboring Wyoming.) However you spell it, this park is definitely n-i-c-e.

Nebraska 40

WINDMILL
Windmill State Recreation Area

Location: South-central Nebraska east of Kearney.

Access: From Interstate 80 Exit 285 for Gibbon (13 miles east of Kearney, 27 miles west of Grand Island), turn north onto Nebraska Route 10-C Link (L-10-C, paved) and proceed 0.35 mile; turn east into the recreation area entrance and continue for 0.3 mile to the campground.

Facilities: 69 electrical hookup campsites, plus a separate tent camping section; sites are small, level, with fair separation; parking pads are paved, short+ straight-ins or long pull-offs; ample space for large tents; barbecue grills; b-y-o firewood; water at central faucets; restrooms with showers; coin-op laundries; holding tank disposal station; paved driveways; gas and snacks at the Interstate.

Activities & Attractions: Exhibits of reconstructed windmills of various designs; swimming; fishing; limited boating.

Natural Features: Located on a grassy flat north of the Platte River; sites are lightly sheltered/shaded by hardwoods, pines and cedars on a surface of mown grass; several small lakes/ponds dot the recreation area; elevation 2000'.

Season, Fees & Phone: Open all year, with limited services November to April; please see Appendix for standard Nebraska state park fees; 3 day limit; park office (308) 468-5700.

Camp Notes: As it was originally discovered, the virtually treeless prairie around here was decidedly unlike the watered, farmed, planted, mown, wooded country it is today. The distinguished American historical novelist, Willa Cather, wrote of this region's endless grasslands, sod houses and windmills; and explorer Zebulon Pike is famous not only for the piece of the Rockies that bears his name, but also for his description of our ancestral plains as "The Great American Desert". (You might not recognize the territory now, Willa and Zeb. Ed.)

Nebraska 41

GEORGE H. CLAYTON
Hall County Park

Location: Central Nebraska at Grand Island.

Access: From U.S. Highways 281 & 34 at milepost 230 +.05 (3.7 miles north of Interstate 80 Exit 312, 1 mile south of midtown Grand Island), turn east onto Schimmer Road (paved) and drive 0.1 mile; turn north (left) into the park for 0.1 mile to a "T"; turn east (right) onto a one-way driveway and proceed 0.2 mile to the tent area; or continue around the driveway for another 0.4 mile, then turn right into the "trailer park".

Facilities: 25 campsites, including 11 units with electrical hookups and 12 tent sites; sites are small+ to medium-sized, level, with fair to good separation; parking pads are medium-length straight-ins, paved in the hookup area, gravel in the tent section; ample space for a large tent in most sites; barbecue grills; b-y-o firewood is recommended; water at central faucets; restrooms with showers; holding tank disposal station; paved or gravel driveways; complete supplies and services are available within 3 miles.

Activities & Attractions: Running and walking course; nature trail; playground; ball fields; day use area; county-operated Stuhr Museum of the Prairie Pioneer, just north of the park, has a first-rate collection of prairie art and artifacts, Indian lore, a model village (including the small Grand Island home where well-known actor Henry Fonda was born), and a train tour of the museum's extensive grounds.

Natural Features: Located in a woodland of medium to large, dense hardwoods mixed with cedars; elevation 1800'.

Season, Fees & Phone: May to October; $5.00 for a tent site, $7.00 for a hookup site; 3 day limit; park office (308) 381-5087.

Camp Notes: This 60-acre park is in a really neat, very woodsy setting. The camping areas are fairly well sequestered from most of the day use activity. Having the museum right next door is a real bonus.

Nebraska 42

MORMON ISLAND
Mormon Island State Recreation Area

Location: Central Nebraska at Grand Island.

Access: From Interstate 80 Exit 312 for Grand Island-Hastings, turn north onto U.S. Highways 281 & 34 and proceed 0.2 mile; turn east (right) into the recreation area and continue for 0.4 mile to the campground.

Facilities: 34 campsites with electrical hookups, plus a small tent camping area; sites are small+, level, with minimal to fair separation; parking pads are paved, short to medium-length straight-ins, plus several pull-offs; adequate space for a medium to large tent in most sites; barbecue grills; b-y-o firewood; water at central faucets; restrooms with showers; coin-op laundry; holding tank disposal station; paved driveways; complete supplies and services are available in Grand Island, 5 miles north.

Activities & Attractions: Designated swimming beach; day use area; very limited boating.

Natural Features: Located on a grassy flat along the Platte River; most sites receive light to moderate shelter/shade from large hardwoods and cedars; tent area is minimally sheltered; a somewhat marshy area borders the campground along the north side; a small lake is a few yards south of the camping area; elevation 1800'.

Season, Fees & Phone: Open all year, with limited services November to April; please see Appendix for standard Nebraska state park fees; 3 day limit; park office (308) 381-5649.

Camp Notes: Purely from the standpoint of trans-continental convenience, this spot is matched only by a trio of national forest campgrounds in California (and one of the forest camps is *under* Interstate 80). The freeway's presence can be seen and heard (and sometimes *felt*). The three-day-stay limit is an indication of Mormon Island's popularity. Grand Island's Clayton Park (see info) provides a somewhat more tranquil alternative to camping by the Old Interstate.

Nebraska 43

Hord Lake
Hord Lake State Recreation Area

Location: East-central Nebraska northeast of Grand Island.

Access: From Nebraska State Highway 14 (17th Avenue) on the south side of Central City, turn east onto 20th Street and proceed 2.5 miles; turn south (right) onto a gravel road for 0.1 mile to the recreation area. (Note: it's possible to get here directly, more or less, from U.S. 30 east of Central City--drive south 2 miles on gravel, then west across a scant one-lane, wooden-floored bridge which spans the Platte River to the rec area.)

Facilities: Approximately 25 campsites; sites are generally small, level, and closely spaced; parking pads are short to medium-length gravel straight-ins or pull-offs; small to medium-sized spaces for tents; barbecue grills, plus a few fire rings; a small amount of firewood may be available for gathering, b-y-o is suggested; water at a hand pump; vault facilities; gravel driveways; adequate supplies and services are available in Central City.

Activities & Attractions: Fishing for bass, walleye, crappie, blue-gill, channel cat; limited boating (electric motors).

Natural Features: Located on the shores of 2 small lakes (totaling about 20 acres); campground vegetation consists of sparse grass and light to medium-dense hardwoods; the north bank of the Platte River lies a few hundred yards south/east; surrounding countryside is primarily level cropland; elevation 1700'.

Season, Fees & Phone: Open all year, subject to weather conditions; please see Appendix for standard Nebraska state park fees; 14 day limit; phone c/o Mormon Island SRA, Doniphan, (308) 381-5649.

Camp Notes: It would be less than honest to allege that this was anything more than a simple fishing camp. But there are some nice lake shore sites. And, with a good arm, you can get a line out to the middle of the lakes without a boat.

Nebraska 44

Crystal Lake
Crystal Lake State Recreation Area

Location: South-central Nebraska south of Hastings.

Access: From Nebraska State Highway 74, in the hamlet of Ayr (10 miles south of Hastings, 30 miles east of Minden), turn north onto a gravel road and travel 1 mile to a "T" intersection; turn west (left) and proceed 0.2 mile; turn north (right) into the recreation area entrance for 0.2 mile to the camping area. (Note: Highway maps often depict Ayr as being precisely at a right-angle turn on U.S. 281; but the tiny burg is actually on State Route 74, 0.35 mile west of the junction of Route 74 & U.S. 281.)

Facilities: Approximately 30 campsites, including 8 with electrical hookups; sites are medium to large, level, with nominal separation; parking surfaces are grass, medium-length straight-ins; excellent tent-pitching possibilities; barbecue grills, plus a few fireplaces; a limited amount of firewood may be available for gathering in the vicinity, b-y-o to be sure; water at central faucets; vault facilities; gravel driveways; complete supplies and services are available in Hastings.

Activities & Attractions: Tennis courts; large, old, stone shelter buildings (WPA, circa 1936); fishing for bass, bluegill, channel cat; very limited boating (electric motors, hand-propelled).

Natural Features: Located on a large, grassy flat along the Little Blue River; tiny Crystal Lake lies a few yards from the camp area; sites receive light shelter/shade from large hardwoods and a few cedars; bordered by lush pasture and cropland; elevation 2000'.

Season, Fees & Phone: Open all year, subject to weather conditions; please see Appendix for standard Nebraska state park fees; 14 day limit; phone c/o Mormon Island SRA, Doniphan, (308) 381-5649.

Camp Notes: Simple, very pleasant, and surprisingly popular in the off-season. The tennis courts bring the Big Apple to the Backwoods. (If your plans include boating, bring a craft that runs on 'D' batteries.)

NEBRASKA
Northeast Prairie
Please refer to the Nebraska map in the Appendix

Nebraska 45

CHILVERS
Plainview City Park

Location: Northeast Nebraska northwest of Norfolk.

Access: From U.S. Highway 20 (Park Avenue) at milepost 355 (2 blocks east of Main Street) in midtown Plainview, proceed around to the north-central side of the park to the camping area.

Facilities: 4 campsites with electrical hookups, plus room for several additional park n' walk campers; hookup sites are small+ and closely spaced; parking pads are paved, level, medium+ straight-ins; adequate space for large tents; barbecue grills nearby; water at a central faucet; restrooms; nearly adequate supplies and services are available in Plainview.

Activities & Attractions: Swimming pool; tennis courts; huge playground; spacious day use area with shelters.

Natural Features: Located on the edge of several acres of watered and mown lawns well-dotted with large hardwoods; sites are very lightly shaded/sheltered; elevation 1600'.

Season, Fees & Phone: May to October; no fee (subject to change); 3 day limit; Plainview Parks Department (402) 582-4928.

Camp Notes: Ordinarily, small city parks, though agreeable in their simplicity, lack enough interest to warrant more than just a casual mention. Every so often, however, a really nice one like this comes along. The park grounds look like they've been planted and maintained by a manicurist with a degree in agronomy. (One thing, though: the campsites are directly across the street from the high school. But school isn't in session during the peak traveling season, anyway.) If you like the congenial atmosphere of a well-kept-up western farming community, try this one. A dozen other small towns in Nebraska's northeast also have campgrounds. Possibly the next-best to Plainview's is Carney Park in O'Neill. It's near the south edge of town, on the east side of U.S. 281. O'Neill's park offers 10 sites (with a little more privacy and shade than those in Plainview), hookups, a disposal station, and no fee unless your stay is longer than 7 days.

Nebraska 46

WILLOW CREEK
Willow Creek State Recreation Area

Location: Northeast Nebraska northwest of Norfolk.

Access: From Nebraska State Highway 13 at the southwest corner of midtown Pierce (13 miles northwest of Norfolk), turn west onto Willow Street and proceed 0.15 mile; turn south (left) onto 7th Street, which shortly curves to the west and becomes H & N Boulevard; continue for 0.6 mile, then turn south onto a paved road and travel 2 miles; turn west (right) onto a paved road for 1 mile, then turn north (right) onto pavement and proceed 0.7 mile; make a final westerly turn (left) into the campground.

Facilities: 83 campsites, including 64 with electrical hookups; sites are medium-sized, with minimal separation; parking pads are medium to long, reasonably level, gravel straight-ins; large tent areas; barbecue grills; b-y-o firewood; water at a central faucet and a hand pump; vault facilities; (showers are planned); gravel driveways; limited to adequate supplies and services are available in Pierce.

Activities & Attractions: Fishing; boating; boat launch; swimming beach; day use area; granite monument erected in recognition of the project's 1983 board of directors; elevation 1600'.

Natural Features: Located on an expansive, grassy, windswept, gentle slope on the south shore of 700-acre Willow Creek Reservoir; hundreds of planted hardwoods should provide adequate shelter/shade by the year 2010.

Season, Fees & Phone: Open all year, subject to weather conditions, with limited services October to May; please see Appendix for standard Nebraska state park fees; 14 day limit; c/o Nebraska Game & Parks Commission District III Office, Norfolk, (402) 370-3374.

Camp Notes: Unlike nearly all of the other (very sheltered and wooded) campgrounds in this corner of Nebraska, Willow Creek still retains the prairie environment in which it is located. It might not be necessary to have a boat to fish here. A small cove near the campground is a likely place to fish for crappie from shore. Try it.

Nebraska 47

NIOBRARA
Niobrara State Park

Location: Northeast Nebraska northeast of O'Neill.

Access: From Nebraska State Highway 12 at milepost 159 +.3 (1.3 miles west of the junction of State Highways 12 and 14 near Niobrara, 9 miles east of Verdel), turn north to the park entrance station, then east for 0.2 mile to the main campground.

Facilities: 69 campsites with electrical hookups; sites are small, acceptably level and closely spaced; parking pads are medium-length, gravel straight-ins; adequate space for a medium to large tent in most sites; fire rings; b-y-o firewood; water at several faucets; restrooms with showers; laundry facilities; holding tank disposal station; gravel driveways; gas, camper supplies and a few limited services are available in the town of Niobrara, 2 miles northeast.

Activities & Attractions: Hiking trails; scenic loop drive; swimming pool; boat launch for Niobrara River access, nearby; fishing for walleye, sauger, catfish.

Natural Features: Located on a grassy, gentle slope above the west bank of the Niobrara River, 1 mile above the confluence of the Niobrara and Missouri Rivers; small conifers and hardwoods have been recently planted in the campground, but most sites are virtually unsheltered; elevation 1300'.

Season, Fees & Phone: Open all year, with limited services November to May; please see Appendix for standard Nebraska state park fees; 14 day limit; park office (402) 857-3373.

Camp Notes: As an option to staying in the main campground, virtually unlimited backpack/walk-in camping is available just about anywhere in the park. Several nice little camping/picnicking sites near the ponds in the center of the scenic loop deserve special mention. And there are really fabulous views of the valleys of the two rivers from just about any hilltop.

Nebraska 48

BURBACH
Lewis and Clark Lake State Recreation Area

Location: Northeast Nebraska northwest of South Sioux City.

Access: From Nebraska State Highway 121 at milepost 73 +.8 (3 miles south of Gavins Point Dam, 7 miles north of Crofton), turn west onto Recreation Road 54-C (paved) and travel 4.4 miles; turn north (right) onto a paved access road for 0.6 mile to a "T"; turn west (left) onto a gravel road; the campground stretches for the next mile along the access road.

Facilities: Approximately 125 campsites; sites are small to medium-sized, level, closely spaced, but with good visual separation; parking surfaces are short to medium-length, grass straight-ins; enough space for a small to medium-sized tent; barbecue grills; a small amount of firewood may be available early in the season, b-y-o is recommended; water at central faucets; restrooms; holding tank disposal station; gravel driveways; gas and camper supplies at the marina, 0.4 mile east, and in Crofton.

Activities & Attractions: Fishing; boating; boat launch at the nearby marina.

Natural Features: Located close to the south shore of Lewis and Clark Lake on the Missouri River; campground vegetation consists of long, wide rows of tall hardwoods, evergreens and large bushes, plus extensive open, grassy areas; Weigand Creek enters the lake at the east edge of the campground; glimpses of the lake through the trees from some campsites; elevation 1200'.

Season, Fees & Phone: Available all year, subject to weather conditions, with limited services October to May; please see Appendix for standard Nebraska state park fees; 14 day limit; phone c/o Nebraska Game & Parks Commission District III Office, Norfolk, (402) 370-3374.

Camp Notes: More privacy than you would first believe possible is provided at this enormous campground. Most of the campsites are in their own little wooded cubbyholes.

Nebraska 49

WEIGAND
Lewis and Clark Lake State Recreation Area

Location: Northeast Nebraska northwest of South Sioux City.

Access: From Nebraska State Highway 121 at milepost 73 + .8 (3 miles south of Gavins Point Dam, 7 miles north of Crofton), turn west onto Recreation Road 54-C (paved) and travel 4 miles; turn north (right) onto a paved access road for 0.25 mile to the campground; continue ahead, or turn left or right to the various camp sections.

Facilities: Approximately 120 campsites, including about 30 with electrical hookups, in 9 short rows; sites are small, level, closely spaced, with fair visual separation; parking surfaces are short to medium-length, grass straight-ins; small to medium-sized areas for tents; fireplaces; b-y-o firewood is recommended; water at central faucets; rest-rooms; holding tank disposal station; gravel driveways; gas and camper supplies at the marina and in Crofton.

Activities & Attractions: Boating; boat launch, marina; fishing.

Natural Features: Located close to the south shore of Lewis and Clark Lake; rows of tall hardwoods and evergreens provide ample shelter/shade for most sites; Weigand Creek enters the lake at the west edge of the recreation area; a few sites are lake shore, some others have glimpses of the lake; elevation 1200'.

Season, Fees & Phone: Available all year, subject to weather conditions, with limited services October to May; please see Appendix for standard Nebraska state park fees; 14 day limit; phone c/o Nebraska Game & Parks Commission District III Office, Norfolk, (402) 370-3374.

Camp Notes: Given a choice, most campers would probably choose one of the two-dozen or so lake shore sites. But there are also a number of pleasant spots about 50 yards from the high tide mark, plus some near the mouth of the creek, that merit consideration. It might take a while to pick your way past the many rows of sites here. No matter. Great views are just a short walk from any spot.

Nebraska 50

TAILWATERS
Lewis & Clark Lake/Corps of Engineers Park

Location: Northeast Nebraska northwest of South Sioux City.

Access: From Nebraska State Highway 121 at milepost 75 (0.6 mile east of Gavins Point Dam, 0.4 mile northeast of the CoE Gavins Point Visitor Center, 7 miles north of Crofton), turn northwest onto a paved access road and proceed 0.4 mile down and around to the campground. (Note: The highway makes several turns in this area; it might be easiest to think of the campground turnoff as being at an angle off Nebraska 121 at an east-south "L" turn in the highway; at this "L" a paved local road leads west to the dam.)

Facilities: 52 campsites, most with electrical hookups; sites are small, slightly sloped, with very little separation; most parking pads are paved, medium to long straight-ins; small tent areas; handicapped-access unit; fireplaces; b-y-o firewood; water at central faucets; restrooms; holding tank disposal station on Highway 121, just above the campground; paved driveway; camper supplies, 0.5 mile east on Highway 121.

Activities & Attractions: Fishing; boating; boat launch.

Natural Features: Located on a slightly sloping flat on a short bench on the south bank of the Missouri River, just below Gavins Point Dam; large hardwoods provide limited wind shelter and some shade for most campsites; elevation 1200'.

Season, Fees & Phone: May to October; $7.00 for a standard site, $9.00 for an electrical hookup unit; 14 day limit; Lewis and Clark Lake/Gavins Point Dam CoE Project Office (402) 667-7873.

Camp Notes: Fishing from a boat is a popular (and productive) activity along the dam's outlet stream, and probably a major reason campers stay here. Because of the red tape relating to whether you need a Nebraska or South Dakota angling license to fish from a boat on a specific segment of the river here, it might be a good idea to carefully read the local regs before you embark.

PONCA
Ponca State Park

Location: Northeast corner of Nebraska northwest of South Sioux City.

Access: From Nebraska State Highway 12 in Ponca City (18 miles northwest of South Sioux City) turn north onto Nebraska Route 26-E Spur (S-26-E); take the grand tour through midtown Ponca, then north for 3 miles to the park entrance station; continue ahead for 0.1 mile, then take a left fork and continue northwesterly on a winding road, past the park office and up the hill, for 0.85 mile to the first camp loop, or another 0.2 mile to the second loop.

Facilities: 91 campsites, most with electrical hookups, in 2 loops; most sites are small, somewhat sloped, with minimal separation; parking pads are short, packed gravel straight-ins; small (some medium) tent spots; barbecue grills; b-y-o firewood; water at several faucets; restrooms with showers; holding tank disposal station; paved/gravel driveways; limited supplies and services are available in Ponca.

Activities & Attractions: Swimming pool (extra fee); hiking trails; trail rides; cross-country skiing; fishing; boat launch.

Natural Features: Located on a hilltop and hillside several hundred yards from the Missouri River; campsites receive light to dense shelter/shade; dense hardwoods and cedars border the campground; (the river is within a short drive or a long hike, but is not within view); elevation 1200'.

Season, Fees & Phone: Open all year, with limited services October to May; please see Appendix for standard Nebraska state park fees; 14 day limit; park office (402) 755-2284.

Camp Notes: You might be able to tuck a vehicle with a small trailer into some of the parking spaces here, but the campground really doesn't readily accommodate large outfits. Whoever designed the campground apparently decided that it was better to work with the terrain and the beautiful, dense forest rather than attempt to alter them.

SCENIC
South Sioux City Park

Location: Northeast corner of Nebraska in South Sioux City.

Access: From U.S. Highways 75 & 77 at the far north end of South Sioux City (0.1 mile south of the Missouri River bridge, at the intersection of Dakota Avenue & East 6th Street) turn east onto East 6th Street; proceed 0.4 mile to E Street; turn north (left) onto E Street and continue for 0.1 mile, then turn east (right) for a final 0.15 mile to the campground. (Note that Dakota Avenue, which is the main drag that runs north-south through midtown, merges with Highways 75 & 77 here at the far north end the city.)

Facilities: 25 campsites; sites are small to medium-sized, basically level, with fair separation; parking pads are gravel, medium to long straight-ins; adequate space for large tents; barbecue grills; b-y-o firewood; water at central faucets; restrooms with showers; holding tank disposal station; paved driveway; complete supplies and services are available in South Sioux City.

Activities & Attractions: Swimming pool; playground; tennis courts; picnic areas.

Natural Features: Located along the south bank of the Missouri River at the northeast corner of a large city park complex; sites are moderately sheltered/shaded by mature hardwoods on a mown lawn; elevation 1100'.

Season, Fees & Phone: May to October; $7.00 for a standard site, $8.00 for an electrical hookup unit; 10 day limit; South Sioux City Parks Department (402) 494-2452.

Camp Notes: Even if you're a confirmed, country campground devotee, this spot may prove to be a useful, even welcome, stop someday. The riverfront has been pretty nicely maintained in this locale. And while there may not be rocky bluffs or towering mountains to view from your campsite, looking out across the Wide Missouri to the nighttime skyline of Sioux City, Iowa and the East, may still prove to be visually satisfying.

DEAD TIMBER
Dead Timber State Recreation Area

Location: East-central Nebraska northwest of Omaha.

Access: From U.S. Highway 275 at milepost 125 +.1 (7 miles south of West Point, 5 miles north of Scribner), turn east onto a paved county road and proceed east for 1 mile, then south for 0.5 mile; turn west (right) into the recreation area; bear southwest (left) and continue for 0.5 mile (just past the end of the pavement) to the campground.

Facilities: 42 campsites, most with electrical hookups; sites are small to medium-sized, level, with minimal separation; parking pads are short to medium-length, gravel straight-ins; ample space for a large tent in most sites; large, stone shelter; fire rings or barbecue grills; some firewood may be available for gathering in surrounding woodlands; water at a hand pump; vault facilities; gravel driveways; snacks at a park concession; limited supplies in Scribner; adequate supplies and services are available in West Point.

Activities & Attractions: Boating (electric or people power); canoe rentals; limited fishing; museum with exhibits of native grasses.

Natural Features: Located on a grassy, tree-dotted flat along the Elkhorn River; most sites are lightly sheltered/shaded by large hardwoods and a few small pines; large sections of grass and very dense woodland adjoin the campground; elevation 1300'.

Season, Fees & Phone: Available all year, with limited services November to May; please see Appendix for standard Nebraska state park fees; 14 day limit; phone c/o Nebraska Game & Parks Commission District III Office, Norfolk, (402) 370-3374.

Camp Notes: As the crow flies, the main highway is only a few hundred yards west of the recreation area. But you'd almost never know it was there most of the time. This is a neat, woodsy place that's nice for just dinking around on sheltered water in a kayak or canoe.

SUMMIT LAKE
Summit Lake State Recreation Area

Location: East-central Nebraska north of Omaha.

Access: From U.S. Highway 75 at a point 1.5 miles south of Tekamah, 15 miles north of Blair, turn west onto a gravel road and proceed 3.2 miles; turn northwest (right), and proceed 1.2 miles around the south end of the lake to a point above the west side of the lake; turn north (right) into the recreation area and continue down a fairly steep hill for 0.25 mile, then left for a final 0.25 mile to the campground. (Note: access is also possible from Nebraska State Highway 32 west of Tekamah, on gravel road to the north shore, then via a winding route to the campground.)

Facilities: 26 campsites; sites are very small, with zip separation; parking pads are medium-length, gravel straight-ins which might require a little additional leveling; adequate space for a small to medium-sized tent in most sites; barbecue grills; b-y-o firewood; water at a hand pump; vault facilities; gravel driveways; limited to adequate supplies and services are available in Tekamah.

Activities & Attractions: Fishing for catfish, bluegills, walleye, northern pike and crappie; limited boating (max. 5 mph); boat launch; fish cleaning station (on the north shore); designated swimming beach; hiking trail; day use area.

Natural Features: Located on a small, grassy flat at the west end of 190-acre Summit lake, in a basin ringed by grassy bluffs dotted with a few trees; campsites lack shelter/shade; elevation 1100'.

Season, Fees & Phone: Open all year, subject to weather conditions; please see Appendix for standard Nebraska state park fees; phone c/o Nebraska Game & Parks Commission District III Office, Norfolk, (402) 370-3374.

Camp Notes: The hiking trail and swimming beach are welcome add-ons, but this is still primarily a simple fishing camp. (Dead trees have been left standing just offshore of the campground. While this feature is certainly important in attracting fish, it's not a visual enhancement.)

FREMONT LAKES
Fremont Lakes State Recreation Area

Location: East-central Nebraska northwest of Omaha.

Access: From U.S. Highway 30 at milepost 422 +.8 (3 miles west of Fremont, 12 miles east of North Bend), turn south onto a paved road and proceed 0.6 mile; turn east into the Main camp area. (Note: Additional, primitive camping is available at the North camping area, off the main highway just west of the turnoff; and at the South camping area, 0.1 mile south of the Main camp area.)

Facilities: 99 campsites, most with electrical hookups, in the Main camping area, plus open camping in the North and South areas; sites are mostly medium to large, basically level, with reasonable separation; parking pads are medium+, grass/sand straight-ins; lots of grassy space for tents; fire rings or barbecue grills; b-y-o firewood; water at several faucets; restrooms with showers, plus auxiliary vaults; holding tank disposal station; gravel driveways; snacks and fishing supplies at an area concession; complete supplies and services are available in Fremont.

Activities & Attractions: Fishing for nearly a dozen warm-water species; boating (some restrictions); boat launches; waterskiing; designated swimming areas; playground.

Natural Features: Located on the shores of 20 small, sandpit lakes; vegetation consists of light to medium-dense, large hardwoods and grass; elevation 1200'.

Season, Fees & Phone: Open all year, with limited services November to April; please see Appendix for standard Nebraska state park fees; 14 day limit; park office (402) 727-3290.

Camp Notes: If you'll be doing anything more than camping here, it might behoove you to check the local regs soon after arriving. Each lake has its own peculiarities. (If you're planning to fish, it'll help you determine what most likely will be lurking hungrily at the end of your line in any given lake.)

GLENN CUNNINGHAM LAKE
Omaha City Recreation Area

Location: Eastern border of Nebraska in Omaha.

Access: From Interstate 680 Exit 9 for 72nd Street (on the north-central edge of Omaha), turn north onto 72nd Street and proceed 0.6 mile; turn west (left) onto Rainwood Road and continue for 0.8 mile; turn southwest (left) onto the campground access road (paved) and proceed 0.5 mile to the campground.

Facilities: 58 campsites; sites are medium-sized with fair spacing and minimal visual separation; parking pads are sandy gravel straight-ins; about half of the pads may require a little additional leveling; large tent areas, may be slightly sloped; barbecue grills; b-y-o firewood; water at several faucets; restrooms with showers; holding tank disposal station; gravel driveways; complete supplies and services are available within 3 miles.

Activities & Attractions: Fishing; boating; boat launch; playground; Fort Atkinson State Historical Park, with rebuilt structures and a top-notch visitor center, is a short drive away--take I-680 Exit 12 for 48th Street/U.S. 75 (3 miles east of Exit 9), then north on U.S. 75 for 8 miles.

Natural Features: Located on a semi-open, gentle slope on a small bay on the east shore of Glenn Cunningham Lake, an impoundment on Little Papillion Creek; campground vegetation consists of mown lawns and hardwoods and pines which provide limited shelter/shade for some sites; elevation 1000'.

Season, Fees & Phone: Mid-May to mid-October; $6.00; 14 day limit; park office (402) 444-4627.

Camp Notes: Freeway *swoooosh* is slightly audible, and the neighbors in the subdivision on the hill overlooking the campground may drop in for tea, but otherwise it's not evident that this is a city park. This is a fairly new campground with very good facilities. For a more woodsy setting, check out Omaha's N. P. Dodge Park (see listing).

N.P. DODGE
Omaha City Park

Location: Eastern border of Nebraska in Omaha.

Access: From Interstate 680 Exit 13 for 30th Street (on the northeast tip of Omaha, 0.4 mile west of the Missouri River bridge), turn south off the freeway for 0.05 mile, then east (left) onto Dick Collins Road for 0.25 mile to a "T" intersection; turn north (left), pass under the freeway, and travel north on John J. Pershing Drive for 1.1 miles; turn east (right) into the park for 0.5 mile, then south (right) for a final 0.2 mile to the campground. (Whew!)

Facilities: 46 campsites, most with electrical hookups, in 2 loops; sites are small to medium-sized, with fair separation overall; parking pads are gravel, medium straight-ins or long pull-throughs; medium to large tent areas; barbecue grills; b-y-o firewood; water at central faucets; restrooms with showers; holding tank disposal station; gravel driveways; complete supplies and services are available within 3 miles.

Activities & Attractions: Paved bikeways and walkways; horse trails; boating; boat launches and moorings; fishing; tennis courts; soccer and baseball fields; playgrounds; Neale Woods Nature Center.

Natural Features: Located on a wooded flat within a very short walk of the west bank of the Missouri River; sites are nicely-sheltered/shaded by large hardwoods; expanses of grass adjoin the campground; elevation 1000'.

Season, Fees & Phone: Mid-May to mid-October; $3.00 for a tent in the tent area, $6.00 for a standard site, $7.00 for an electrical hookup site, $2.00 for disposal station use; 14 day limit; park office (402) 444-4673.

Camp Notes: It goes without saying that it's often pretty busy in here. But Dodge is probably one of the nicest big city parks you'll encounter--and one of the largest at that. (Just the half-dozen or more soccer fields cover acres of turf). Lots of room to roam.

NEBRASKA
Southeast Prairie
Please refer to the Nebraska map in the Appendix

Nebraska 58

HAWORTH
Bellevue City Park

Location: Eastern border of Nebraska south of Omaha.

Access: From Nebraska State Highway 370 at milepost 19 (at the far east edge of the city of Bellevue, at the west end of the Missouri River toll bridge to Iowa), turn south onto Payne Drive and proceed 0.2 mile, then east (left) for 0.1 mile; turn north (left) into the campground entrance.

Facilities: 111 campsites, including 14 standard sites, 30 electrical hookup sites, and 67 partial hookup units, in 3 loops; sites are small to medium-sized, with minimal to fair separation; parking pads are reasonably level, medium to long, paved straight-ins; adequate room for medium to large tents; barbecue grills, plus some fire rings; b-y-o firewood; water at sites and at central faucets; restrooms with showers; holding tank disposal station; community shelters; paved driveways; complete supplies and services are available in Bellevue.

Activities & Attractions: Playground; marina nearby; river tour boat in summer; athletic fields, adjacent; Strategic Air Command Museum and SAC base in Bellevue.

Natural Features: Located on a large flat near the west bank of the Missouri River; campground vegetation consists of patches of grass, and large hardwoods which provide ample to excellent shelter/shade for most sites; elevation 1000'.

Season, Fees & Phone: Open all year, with limited services November to April; $4.00 for a tent, $5.00 for campers, plus $2.00 for electric use, $2.00 for disposal station use; 14 day limit; park manager (402) 291-3122.

Camp Notes: There are no really big attractions in the area that would explain this pleasantly nice camp's surprising popularity--it's just the most economical camp around here.

Nebraska 59

COTTONWOOD
Two Rivers State Recreation Area

Location: East-central Nebraska west of Omaha.

Access: From Nebraska State Highway 92 at milepost 464 +.4 (8 miles east of Mead, 14 miles west of Omaha), turn south onto County Road 96 (paved) and proceed 1 mile; turn west onto the park access road for 1.1 miles to the park entrance; turn north (right) and proceed 0.6 mile (around to the northwest side of the main loop roadway) to the campground, on the right side of the road.

Facilities: 50 campsites with electrical hookups; sites are good-sized, essentially level, with fairly good separation; parking pads are medium to long, sandy gravel pull-offs; adequate space for large tents; fire rings; b-y-o firewood; water at central faucets; restrooms with showers; holding tank disposal station near Fawn Meadow Campground, 0.5 mile south; sandy gravel driveways; gas and camper supplies on the main highway.

Activities & Attractions: Lake fishing for small trout (extra fee), plus lake and river fishing for warm-water species; handicapped-access fishing dock; lake swimming beach; playground.

Natural Features: Located in a grove of enormous cottonwoods on a flat along the bank of the Platte River; sites are well sheltered/shaded; a half-dozen small, sandpit lakes lie within the recreation area; surrounding countryside is level farmland; elevation 1100'.

Season, Fees & Phone: Open all year, with limited services November to April; please see Appendix for standard Nebraska state park fees; 14 day limit; park office (402) 359-5165.

Camp Notes: Two Rivers tends to fill up on most summer weekends, and Cottonwood is its most-favored campground. It seems to combine some of the more desirable attributes of the rec area's other principal campgrounds, Goldenrod and Fawn Meadows (see separate listing). Having a lot of riverfront real estate helps too. Three other campgrounds on the north side of the park in Cottonwood's vicinity offer basic (primitive) camping. Goldenrod, Riverside, and Oak Grove Campgrounds all have drinking water and vaults, parking, ample space for tents, pleasant surroundings, and bargain prices.

Nebraska 60

GOLDENROD & FAWN MEADOWS
Two Rivers State Recreation Area

Location: East-central Nebraska west of Omaha.

Access: From Nebraska State Highway 92 at milepost 464 +.4 (8 miles east of Mead, 14 miles west of Omaha), turn south onto County Road 96 (paved) and proceed 1 mile; turn west onto the park access road for 1.1 miles to the park entrance; turn *north* (right) and proceed 0.5 mile to *Goldenrod*; or drive ahead for 100 yards, then turn *south* (left) and continue past the caboose park for 0.2 mile to *Fawn Meadows*.

Facilities: *Goldenrod:* approximately 50 standard ('primitive') campsites; sites are medium-sized, level, with moderate separation; parking pads are medium-length, sandy gravel straight-ins; large, grassy tent areas; fire rings; water at a hand pump; vault facilities; gravel driveways. *Fawn Meadows:* 23 full hookup units in a paved parking lot arrangement; sites are very small, level, with nearly nil separation; parking pads are medium-length, paved straight-ins; water at sites; restrooms with showers; holding tank disposal station; b-y-o firewood; gas and camper supplies on the main highway.

Activities & Attractions: Lake fishing for small trout (extra fee), also for typical warm-water species; handicapped-access fishing dock; lake swimming beach; playground.

Natural Features: Goldenrod: located on a grassy flat dotted with hardwoods by Lake No. 4; sites are moderately shaded. **Fawn Meadows:** located on the edge of a meadow by Lake No.1; sites are lightly shaded; several other small lakes in the area; elevation 1100'.

Season, Fees & Phone: Open all year, with limited services November to April; please see Appendix for standard Nebraska state park fees; 14-day limit; park office (402) 359-5165.

Camp Notes: Ten bright yellow cabooses were contributed to the park by the Union Pacific Railroad. They're lined up single file on their own rail 'siding' just across from Fawn Meadows.

Nebraska 61

MEMPHIS LAKE
Memphis Lake State Recreation Area

Location: East-central Nebraska southwest of Omaha.

Access: From Nebraska State Highway 63 at milepost 26 +.4 (7 miles northwest of Ashland, 18 miles southeast of Wahoo), turn west onto Nebraska Route 78-C Spur (paved); proceed 0.6 mile to the west edge of the small community of Memphis, where the road curves north for another 0.1 mile to the recreation area; continue along the east side of the lake for 0.3 mile to the campground.

Facilities: Approximately 60 campsites; sites are small to medium-sized, with minimal to fair separation; parking pads are medium-length, gravel/grass straight-ins which may require a little additional leveling; big, grassy, tent areas, may be slightly sloped; barbecue grills and fire rings; b-y-o firewood; water at a central faucet and at hand pumps; vault facilities; holding tank disposal station; gravel driveways, paved main roadway; snacks at a park concession; nearest source of supplies and services (adequate) is Ashland.

Activities & Attractions: Fishing (catfish, bass, crappie, bluegill); limited boating (OK for electric motors, sail, hand and foot propulsion); playground.

Natural Features: Located on a gentle slope which ends at a level shoreline on the north shore of Memphis Lake; campsites receive ample shade and light wind shelter from rows of large hardwoods and a few pines and cedars on a thick carpet of grass; elevation 1100'.

Season, Fees & Phone: Open all year, subject to weather conditions; please see Appendix for standard Nebraska state park fees; 14 day limit; c/o Nebraska Game & Parks Commission District V Office, Lincoln, (402) 471-0641.

Camp Notes: Pretty lake. Small, tidy, nice. Very nice, actually. Several edgewater campsites provide some of the best tent spots you'll find anywhere. (Keep the flaps closed when the wind picks up!) Excellent lake views throughout.

Nebraska 62

EUGENE T. MAHONEY
Eugene T. Mahoney State Park

Location: Eastern Nebraska southwest of Omaha.

Access: From Interstate 80 Exit 426 for Ashland (25 miles southwest of Omaha, 25 miles northwest of Lincoln), from the north side of the freeway head north on a paved local road for 0.5 mile to the park. **Alternate Access:** From U.S. Highway 6 in midtown Ashland, travel south, then east for 4 miles to the park.

Overnight Facilities: 149 campsites with electrical hookups in 2 areas; ('primitive' tent sites are also available); sites are small+, with nominal separation; parking pads are paved; adequate space or tents; fire rings; b-y-o firewood; water at several faucets; restrooms with showers; holding tank disposal station; paved driveways; adequate supplies and services are available in Ashland.

Activities & Attractions: Large day use areas, swimming pool, waterslide, sports fields, hiking trails, equestrian trails, miniature golf, 70-foot observation tower, nature conservatory, marina, x-c skiing, sled runs, ice skating, etc, etc, etc.

Natural Features: Located on densely wooded hills and bluffs interspersed with open grassy areas, along and above the south bank of the Platte River; elevation 1100'.

Season & Fees: Open all year, with limited services November to May; please see Appendix for standard Nebraska state park fees; 14-day limit; park office (402) 944-2523; fax (402) 944-7604.

Park Notes: This park was named for the state parks director who was the prime mover behind the rejuvenation of the Nebraska state parks system. The Platte River views from atop the observation tower are inspirational.

Nebraska 63

LOUISVILLE
Louisville State Recreation Area

Location: East-central Nebraska southwest of Omaha.

Access: From Nebraska State Highway 50 at milepost 76 +.4 (abeam of midtown Louisville), turn west/north-west onto the park access road and proceed 0.1 mile to the entrance station; continue ahead 0.1 mile, then northeast (right) or southwest (left) to the camping areas.

Facilities: 229 campsites, including 145 with electrical hookups, plus park n' walk tent sites and open camping, in a half-dozen areas; sites are small to medium-sized, most are level, with nominal to fair separation; parking pads are medium-length straight-ins; medium to large tent areas; barbecue grills or fire rings; b-y-o firewood; water at central faucets; restrooms with showers; holding tank disposal station; gravel loop driveways, paved main roadways; limited supplies and services are available in Louisville.

Activities & Attractions: Swimming beach; fishing; limited boating (electric motors, sail, human effort); x-c skiing.

Natural Features: Located along the shores of 5 small lakes and within a few yards of the Platte River; campground vegetation consists of light to medium-dense hardwoods and lots of grass; lake views from the majority of campsites; low, wooded hills lie in the surrounding area; elevation 1100'.

Season, Fees & Phone: Open all year, with limited services November to May; please see Appendix for standard Nebraska state park fees; 14 day limit; park office (402) 234-6855.

Camp Notes: The three hookup loops are also referred to as the A.C. Nelsen camping areas as an acknowledgement of a grant by the Omaha company which funded much of the construction. Tent campers didn't get short-changed, though--there are some dandy lakeside tent sites as well. In some respects, this place looks more like a state park than "just" a state recreation area.

MIDDLE OAK CREEK
Branched Oak State Recreation Area

Location: Southeast Nebraska northwest of Lincoln.

Access: From U.S. Highway 34 at milepost 312 +.3 (midway between Lincoln & Seward), turn north onto NW 112th Street and proceed 1.8 miles to a "T" intersection (just west of Malcolm); turn left and travel 3.1 miles to a second "T" on the south shore of the lake; turn west (left) and proceed 2.2 miles west, then 0.6 mile north; turn east (right) onto West Branched Oak Road and continue for 1.4 miles to the campground. **Alternate Access:** From Nebraska State Highway 79 at milepost 5 (just west of Raymond), turn west onto West Raymond Road and travel 4.3 miles to the second "T"; continue west, as above.

Facilities: 197 campsites, including 114 electrical hookups and 11 tent sites; sites are small+, with minimal to fair separation; parking pads are gravel, medium-length straight-ins; pads are tolerably level, considering the slope; space for small to medium-sized tents; fire rings; b-y-o firewood; water at central faucets; restrooms with solar showers; holding tank disposal station; gravel driveways; gas and groceries in Malcolm and Raymond.

Activities & Attractions: Swimming beach; arboretum; fishing for a dozen warm water species; boating; boat launches and docks; playground.

Natural Features: Located on an open, south slope on a large peninsula separating the 2 major "arms" or "branches" of Branched Oak Lake; sites are very lightly sheltered/shaded by small hardwoods and evergreens; elevation 1500'.

Season, Fees & Phone: Open all year, with limited services November to April; please see Appendix for standard Nebraska state park fees; phone c/o Nebraska Game & Parks Maintenance District, Lincoln, (402) 471-5545.

Camp Notes: Although this is the principal campground on Branched Oak Lake, it is only one of 14 recreation areas on this forked, multi-bayed lake. Have a great time!

LAKE VIEW
Pawnee State Recreation Area

Location: Southeast Nebraska west of Lincoln.

Access: From U.S. Highway 6 at milepost 307 +.2 in the hamlet of Emerald (8 miles west of Lincoln), turn north onto NW 84th Street and proceed 2 miles; turn west onto West Adams Street and continue west then north for 3 miles; turn sharply south (left) onto the campground access road for 0.4 mile to the campground. **Alternate Access:** From U.S. 34 at milepost 312 +.3 (midway between Lincoln and Seward), turn south onto NW 112th St. and proceed 1.8 miles to the campground access road.

Facilities: Approximately 95 campsites, including 67 with electrical hookups, and 7 tent-only units, in 3 areas; sites are small+, with nil to fair separation; parking pads are gravel, short to medium-length straight-ins; some pads probably will require a little additional leveling; enough space for medium to large tents; fire rings; b-y-o firewood; water at several faucets; restrooms with showers, plus auxiliary vault facilities; holding tank disposal station; gravel driveways; gas and snacks in Emerald.

Activities & Attractions: Swimming beach; small playground; fishing; boating; boat launches and docks.

Natural Features: Located on a grassy hilltop and hillside above the north shore of Pawnee Lake; hookup and tent sites are quite unsheltered; a small group of standard sites in a grove of hardwoods have ample shade; surrounded by wooded hills and some agricultural land; elevation 1500'.

Season, Fees & Phone: Open all year, with limited services November to April; please see Appendix for standard Nebraska state park fees; 14 day limit; phone c/o Nebraska Game & Parks Maintenance District, Lincoln, (402) 471-5545.

Camp Notes: In addition to the main campground, primitive camping is available at the northwest tip of the lake. Lake View is quite aptly named--the views of this pretty lake from the perch on the hill are prime.

Nebraska 66

CONESTOGA
Conestoga State Recreation Area

Location: Southeast Nebraska southwest of Lincoln.

Access: From U.S. Highway 6 at milepost 307 +.2 in the hamlet of Emerald (8 miles west of Lincoln), turn south onto Nebraska Route 55-A Spur (S-55-A, paved) and proceed 3 miles; turn west onto West Pioneers Boulevard and continue for 1.1 miles; turn south into the recreation area; campsites are located along the shore and in a small loop on the east side of the area.

Facilities: Approximately 12 campsites, including 6 tent-camping units; sites are small and closely spaced; parking pads are short, gravel straight-ins which will probably require additional leveling; adequate space for medium to large tents in all sites; barbecue grills or fire rings; water at a hand pump; vault facilities; holding tank disposal station; paved main driveway, gravel loop drive; gas and snacks in Emerald and in Denton, 2 miles south on S-55-A.

Activities & Attractions: Fishing for bass, crappie, walleye, sunfish, etc; boating; boat launch and small dock.

Natural Features: Located on the north shore of Conestoga Lake; the small, standard loop is on a sloping hilltop overlooking the lake; tent camping area is on a grassy, edgewater slope; standard sites are moderately sheltered/shaded by large hardwoods, tent sites have limited shelter; in a shallow basin ringed by grassy hills with patches of woods; elevation 1400'.

Season, Fees & Phone: Open all year, subject to weather conditions; please see Appendix for standard Nebraska state park fees; phone c/o Nebraska Game & Parks Maintenance District, Lincoln, (402) 471-5545.

Camp Notes: Conestoga is the smallest and least developed of the trio of horse-or-oxen-drawn recreation areas in the Lincoln area. (Also see information for Stagecoach and Wagon Train State Recreation Areas.) The facilities are very basic and the surrounding countryside is likable.

Nebraska 67

BLUESTEM
Bluestem State Recreation Area

Location: Southeast Nebraska southwest of Lincoln.

Access: From U.S. Highway 77 at milepost 48 +.9 (2 miles south of the junction of U.S. 77 and Nebraska Highway 33, 14 miles south of Lincoln), turn west onto Sprague Road and proceed 2.1 miles to Sprague; continue west on West Sprague Road for 3 miles to Area 3; turn north (right) onto a paved road for 0.3 mile, then north (left, this time) on gravel for 0.4 mile to the camp area. **Alternate Access:** From Nebraska State Highway 33 at milepost 23 +.3 (14 miles east of Crete, 2 miles west of the junction of Highway 33 and U.S. 77 south of Lincoln), turn south onto Nebraska Route 55-B Spur (S-55-B), and proceed 2 miles to Sprague; continue as above.

Facilities: Approximately 12 campsites, plus semi-open camping; sites are small, vary from level to sloped, with no separation; parking pads are short to medium-length, gravel straight-ins; small tent areas; fire rings or barbecue grills; ; b-y-o firewood; water at a central faucet and at a hand pump; vault facilities; holding tank disposal station; gravel driveways; gas and camper supplies in Sprague; adequate supplies and services in Crete.

Activities & Attractions: Fishing for most major warm water species; boating; boat launch; playground.

Natural Features: Located on the west shore of Bluestem Lake; shelter/shade from hardwoods varies from none to moderate; low hills encircle the lake; elevation 1400'.

Season, Fees & Phone: Available all year, subject to weather conditions; please see Appendix for standard Nebraska state park fees; 14 day limit; phone c/o Nebraska Game & Parks Maintenance District, Lincoln, (402) 471-5545.

Camp Notes: A second state recreation area in this vicinity is Olive Creek SRA. Olive Creek Lake is about half the size of Bluestem Lake, and has roughly similar facilities, fishing, and 5 mph boating. To reach it, turn south off Highway 33 at milepost 16 +.3 (5 miles east of Crete) and proceed 5 miles on pavement, then 1 mile on gravel.

Nebraska 68

WAGON TRAIN
Wagon Train State Recreation Area

Location: Southeast Nebraska south of Lincoln.

Access: From U.S. Highway 77 at milepost 48 +.9 (2 miles south of the junction of U.S. 77 and Nebraska State Highway 33, 14 miles south of Lincoln), turn east onto Nebraska Route 55-G Spur (S-55-G) and proceed 4.1 miles to Hickman; continue straight east on East 7th St./Hickman Road for 2 miles, then south for 0.5 mile, east for 1 mile, then north for 0.5 mile to the main camping areas. (Note: Perhaps a simpler way of describing the access is to drive east for 6 miles from U.S. 77, then continue for 2 miles on paved roads around the south end of the lake to the east shore. Take your pick.)

Facilities: Approximately 60 campsites, including a designated tent camping area; sites are small+, slightly to somewhat sloped, with minimal to fair separation; parking surfaces are grass any-which-way-you-cans; ample space for large tents in most sites; barbecue grills or fire rings; b-y-o firewood; water at a central faucet; vault facilities; holding tank disposal station; gravel or paved driveways; limited supplies and services are available in Hickman.

Activities & Attractions: Swimming beach; angling for most major warm water fish; boating (5 mph); boat launch; playground.

Natural Features: Located on both sides of a large bay on grassy, hardwood and pine dotted slopes above the east shore of Wagon Train Lake; elevation 1400'.

Season, Fees & Phone: Open all year, subject to weather conditions; please see Appendix for standard Nebraska state park fees; 14 day limit; phone c/o Nebraska Game & Parks Maintenance District, Lincoln, (402) 471-5545.

Camp Notes: Wagon Train is probably the nicest of the cluster of five major sra's south/southwest of Lincoln. Another nearby area is Stagecoach, reached by turning south off 55-G Spur onto South 68th Street in Hickman for 2 miles, then west on Panama Road for 1.2 miles. Semi-open camping is available on the west shore of Stagecoach Lake.

Nebraska 69

ALEXANDRIA LAKES
Alexandria Lakes State Recreation Area

Location: Southeast Nebraska southwest of Beatrice.

Access: From Nebraska State Highway 53 at milepost 7 at the northeast corner of the small community of Alexandria (7 miles north of the junction of Highway 53 and U.S. 136), turn east onto a paved road and travel 3.1 miles; turn south (right), continuing on pavement for 1 mile; jog east then south into the recreation area; hookup sites are near the entrance; a second large camp area is reached via a gravel road across an embankment between the lakes, to the south shore then to the west shore.

Facilities: Approximately 35 campsites, including several with electrical hookups; sites are medium-sized, level to sloped depending upon camp area, with minimal to fair separation; parking surfaces are grass or gravel straight-ins/pull-offs; plenty of tent space; barbecue grills; some firewood may be available for gathering; water at a hand pump; vault facilities; gravel driveways; gas and groceries are available in Alexandria.

Activities & Attractions: Fishing (channel and flathead catfish, bass, crappie, bluegill); limited boating (electric/manual).

Natural Features: Located along the level north shore and on a hillside above the west shore of Alexandria Lakes; majority of sites are moderately sheltered/shaded by large hardwoods; some sites are on an open hillside; elevation 1500'.

Season, Fees & Phone: Open all year, subject to weather conditions, with limited services November to May; please see Appendix for standard Nebraska state park fees; 14 day limit; c/o Rock Creek Station State Historical Park, Fairbury, (402) 729-5777.

Camp Notes: No doubt this is mainly a fishing camp, but the setting is pleasantly blue and green and gold enough for a casual stay by any camper. If you don't fish, or if you become bored with angling, time can be passed away by watching for trains on the tracks along the south shore; or by pondering occasional B-52's as they execute their low-and-slow bomb runs over the plains.

Nebraska 70

ROCK CREEK STATION
Rock Creek Station State Historical Park

Location: Southeast Nebraska southwest of Beatrice.

Access: From Nebraska State Highway 15 (South K St.) at milepost 8 +.9 on the south edge of Fairbury, turn east onto a paved road and travel 5.6 miles; turn south onto a gravel road and proceed 1 mile; turn east (left) for 0.2 mile, then south (right) into the park entrance; proceed 0.1 mile, then turn west (left) onto the campground access road and continue for 0.35 mile to the campground. **Alternate Access:** From Nebraska Highway 103 near milepost 6 (1 mile north of Diller), turn west onto a paved road and proceed 7 miles; turn south, continue as above.

Facilities: 24 campsites with electrical hookups, plus a small tent camping area; sites are medium-sized, with fair to good separation; parking pads are medium-length, reasonably level, straight-ins; enough space for medium-sized, possibly large, tents; several ramadas (sun shelters); barbecue grills, plus a few fire rings; some gatherable firewood may be available in the surrounding area, b-y-o to be sure; water at central faucets; restrooms with showers; holding tank disposal station; gravel driveways; adequate+ supplies and services are available in Fairbury.

Activities & Attractions: Impressive, new visitor center; interpretive and nature trails; remnants of log buildings.

Natural Features: Located on a gently rolling plain above Rock Creek; cedars and hardwoods provide moderate wind shelter but limited shade for most sites; elevation 1500'.

Season, Fees & Phone: Open all year, subject to weather, with limited services mid-November to April; please see Appendix for standard Nebraska state park fees; 14 day limit; park office (402) 729-5777.

Camp Notes: This was a stop along the Oregon Trail as well as the Pony Express and Overland Stage routes. An incident here in 1861 figures prominently in the life of western gunfighter, lawman and folk hero, Wild Bill Hickok.

Nebraska 71

CHAUTAUQUA
Beatrice City Park

Location: Southeast Nebraska in Beatrice.

Access: From U.S. Highway 77 (South 6th Street) at a point 0.1 mile south of the Big Blue River bridge on the south side of Beatrice, turn east onto Grable Avenue and proceed 0.4 mile to the campground.

Facilities: 11 campsites with electrical hookups, plus room for several tent campers; sites are small, level, and closely spaced; parking pads are short+, gravel straight-ins; excellent tent-pitching possibilities; large, gazebo-type shelter; central barbecue grill and tables; b-y-o firewood or charcoal; water at central faucets; restrooms (H) with showers; holding tank disposal station; gravel driveway; virtually complete supplies and services are available in Beatrice.

Activities & Attractions: Traditional city park atmosphere.

Natural Features: Located in a very large city park within a short walk of the south bank of the Big Blue River; sites receive light to moderate shelter/shade from large hardwoods on expansive, watered and mown lawns; elevation 1300'.

Season, Fees & Phone: May to mid-October; $4.00; 10 day limit; Beatrice City Parks and Recreation Department (402) 228-3649.

Camp Notes: Although the campground is small and the sites little, with acres of lawns and trees surrounding them, probably no one except a confirmed hermit has ever been claustrophobic here. The daily rate (at current prices) is certainly very reasonable. A second city park, Riverside, also has camping.

From U.S. 136 (Court St.) on the west side of town, turn north onto Sumner St. for 0.35 mile to River St., then a short jog left and right into the park. The half-dozen small, grassy campsites are squarely in the middle of the heavy traffic zone, but it's super handy to the swimming pool and tennis courts. One more thing: this *must* be the West; the folks in town typically respond to a "Thank You" with a cordial "You Bet!".

Nebraska 72

ROCKFORD LAKE
Rockford Lake State Recreation Area

Location: Southeast Nebraska east of Beatrice.

Access: From U.S. Highway 136 & Nebraska State Highway 4 (combined highway) at milepost 185 +.7 (8 miles east of Beatrice, 2 miles west of the junction of Highways 136 & 4 near Filley), turn south onto a paved road and proceed 2 miles to a 3-way intersection; continue south on gravel for 1 mile; turn east (left) onto a gravel road for 0.55 mile, then north (left) onto the campground access road for 0.25 mile to the campground.

Facilities: Approximately 20 campsites in somewhat of a "park 'em and pitch 'em wherever" situation; sites are basically small, sloped, and closely spaced; parking surfaces are grass or gravel; ample space for large tents on a grassy surface; barbecue grills or fire rings; some collectable firewood is available in the vicinity; water at a hand pump; vault facilities; gravel driveways; virtually complete supplies and services are available in Beatrice.

Activities & Attractions: Fishing for bass, crappie, bluegill, catfish, some walleye; boating; boat launch; playset.

Natural Features: Located on a grassy slope on the southwest shore of Rockford Lake; a few large hardwoods and smaller cedars and pines dot the slope, but the majority of sites have minimal shelter/shade; elevation 1300'.

Season, Fees & Phone: Open all year, subject to weather conditions; please see Appendix for standard Nebraska state park fees; 14 day limit; phone c/o Nebraska Game & Parks Commission District V Office, Lincoln NE, (402) 471-0641.

Camp Notes: Because of the semi-open layout here, if the camp area wasn't busy, the site size could be expanded to some degree. Nothing really fancy here, but the surroundings are nice, and there are a half-dozen lake shore sites. For more in the way of creature comforts, but less solitude, try the city park in Beatrice.

Nebraska 73

VERDON LAKE
Verdon Lake State Recreation Area

Location: Southeast corner of Nebraska northwest of Falls City.

Access: From U.S. Highway 73 at milepost 16 +.4 (0.8 mile west of the town of Verdon, 6 miles east of the junction of U.S. Highways 73 & 75 north of Dawson), turn north into the recreation area. (There's a short, steepish dropoff from the highway onto the gravel driveway, so 'easy does it' with a larger vehicle.)

Facilities: Approximately 20 camp/picnic sites in 2 areas; sites are small, most are level, with minimal to fair separation; parking pads are gravel/grass, short to medium-length straight-ins or pull-offs; space for small to medium-sized tents in most sites; small, concrete pads for some table areas; barbecue grills; b-y-o firewood; water at a hand pump; vault facilities; gravel driveways; gas and limited groceries in Verdon; adequate supplies and services are available in Falls City, 12 miles southeast.

Activities & Attractions: Fishing for crappie, bluegill, largemouth bass, catfish; limited boating (electric, hand-propelled).

Natural Features: Located on the west and east shores of 30-acre Verdon Lake; most sites are along the lightly sheltered/shaded lake shore; a few sites are on a well sheltered hillside a few yards from the west shore; gently rolling hills lie in the surrounding area; elevation 1000'.

Season, Fees & Phone: Open all year, subject to weather conditions; please see Appendix for standard Nebraska state park fees; 14 day limit; phone c/o Nebraska Game & Parks Commission District V Office, Lincoln NE, (402) 471-0641.

Camp Notes: This is the only highwayside stop in Nebraska's southeast corner. Although it probably serves principally as a day use area, one of the sites a little farther from the highway certainly would suffice for a short term stay. Simple, but very agreeable, setting.

Nebraska 74

RIVERVIEW MARINA
Riverview Marina State Recreation Area

Location: Eastern border of Nebraska in Nebraska City.

Access: From U.S. Highway 75 (11th Street) on the north edge of Nebraska City, turn east onto 5th Avenue for 1 block to 10th Street; turn north (left) onto 10th Street for 2 blocks to 7th Avenue; turn east (right) onto 7th Avenue for 6 blocks to 4th Street; turn north (left) onto 4th Street and continue for 0.4 mile down the hill, then right for 0.2 mile to the recreation area. (Note: if you arrive at night, it's all too easy to launch your camper into the Missouri at the end of the parking lot. Get the drift?)

Facilities: Approximately 20 campsites in a paved, semi-parking-lot arrangement, plus several park n' walks; sites are small, level, and closely spaced; parking spots are long straight-ins or pull-offs; medium to large, grassy tent spots; barbecue grills in some sites; b-y-o firewood; water at central faucets; restrooms; paved driveways; adequate supplies and services are available in Nebraska City.

Activities & Attractions: Boating; boat launch; fishing; Arbor Lodge State Historical Park in Nebraska City, featuring a 52-room mansion built by the Morton family (you know, "When It Rains It...").

Natural Features: Located on several wooded acres on the west bank of the Missouri River; elevation 1000'.

Season, Fees & Phone: Open all year, subject to weather conditions; please see Appendix for standard Nebraska state park fees; 14 day limit; phone c/o Nebraska Game & Parks Commission District V Office, Lincoln NE, (402) 471-0641.

Camp Notes: Well...it's like this: although camping is permitted here, it really is more of a boating/fishing access and day use area than a campground. The place does get pretty busy. But consider these points: (a) it's the only public camping area for many miles; (b) the charge for camping is only the cost of admission; (c) it still beats getting a room at the Shake N' Rattle Inn in Nebraska City, then listening to four 18-wheelers per minute rumble by all night long.

Nebraska 75

BROWNVILLE
Brownville State Recreation Area

Location: Eastern border of Nebraska southeast of Nebraska City.

Access: From U.S. Highway 136 in midtown Brownville, at the west end of the Missouri River bridge to Iowa, turn south onto a paved local road; proceed 0.4 mile south, east, and south (past the day use area entrance); turn east (left) onto a paved driveway to the campground.

Facilities: 14 campsites; sites are medium-sized, level, with nominal to fair separation; parking pads are medium-length, paved straight-ins; good tent-pitching possibilities; some sites lack tables; barbecue grills in most units; b-y-o firewood; water at a central faucet in the adjoining day use area; vault facilities in the day use area; paved driveways; gas and very limited groceries in Brownville.

Activities & Attractions: Missouri River History Museum and tours aboard the sidewheeler *Captain Meriwether Lewis*, a riverboat formerly with the Corps of Engineers, moored alongside the day use area; boating; small boat launch.

Natural Features: Located on a flat along the west bank of the Missouri River; shelter/shade from large hardwoods varies from none to light; a heavily wooded, steep hill forms the western backdrop for the area; elevation 900'.

Season, Fees & Phone: Open all year, subject to weather conditions; please see Appendix for standard Nebraska state park fees; 14 day limit; phone c/o Nebraska Game & Parks Commission District V Office, Lincoln NE, (402) 471-0641.

Camp Notes: This campground has real potential. Currently, it's probably better-suited to self-contained campers (or tent campers who like a lot of exercise). The *Captain Meriwether Lewis* is one of the largest and neatest inland crafts most people might have an opportunity to examine--and it's berthed right in its original environment. A bit of history is associated with Brownville: the nation's first homestead claim was filed here after Abraham Lincoln signed the Homestead Act in 1862.

INDIAN CAVE
Indian Cave State Park

Location: Southeast corner of Nebraska north of Falls City.

Access: From Nebraska State Highway 67 at milepost 8 (18 miles north of Falls City), turn east onto Nebraska Route 64-E Spur (S-64-E) and travel 5.1 miles to the park entrance; proceed 0.2 mile to the tent area, or continue for another 0.4 mile to the main campground.

Facilities: 134 campsites, including 104 with electrical hookups in the main campground, plus a small tent camping area, and a score of backpack camps (some with shelters); sites are small+, with fair separation; parking pads are mostly medium-length, paved, respectably level (considering the terrain), straight-ins; adequate space for small to medium-sized tents; barbecue grills or fire rings; b-y-o firewood; water at central faucets; restrooms with showers; holding tank disposal station; paved driveways; camper supplies near the park; adequate supplies and services are available in Falls City.

Activities & Attractions: Miles and miles of hiking trails; river access (foot traffic); historical sites; interpretive programs.

Natural Features: Located on a steep hillside (main campground) and on a ridgetop (tent area) among the densely wooded hills along the Missouri River; elevation 1200'.

Season, Fees & Phone: Open all year, subject to weather, with limited services November to April; please see Appendix for standard Nebraska state park fees; 14 day limit; park office (402) 883-2575.

Camp Notes: Tell you what: Nebraska has a number of really nice state parks; a few of them are a trifle glitzy; but this one is for real, so to speak. True, Indian Cave does have a small share of programmed catfish frys and proposed swimming pools. But the park's main orientation seems to be, and hopefully will remain, in harmony with the philosophy of the individual who finds simple satisfaction in hills, trails, woodlands, and river lore. A fine place.

Kansas

Public Campgrounds

The Kansas map is located in the Appendix on page 157.

Kansas 1

PRAIRIE DOG
Prairie Dog State Park

Location: Northwest Kansas west of Norton.

Access: From the junction of U.S. Highway 36 & Kansas State Highway 261 (at milepost 112 +.5 on U.S. 36, 5 miles west of Norton, 30 miles east of Oberlin), turn south onto State Highway 261; proceed 1.3 miles to a 3-way intersection; continue straight ahead for 0.5 mile to the standard camping area; or turn east (left) and proceed 0.85 mile; turn southeast (right) and continue for a final 0.35 mile to the hookup area.

Facilities: 62 campsites, including 30 with partial hookups, 12 with electrical hookups, and 20 standard sites; most sites are level, medium-sized, with minimal separation; parking pads are mostly medium-length, gravel straight-ins; (electrical-only sites are tightly spaced, short straight-ins); medium to large tent areas; small sun/wind shelters for many sites; barbecue grills; b-y-o firewood; water at some sites and at central faucets; restrooms with showers; holding tank disposal station; gravel driveways; adequate supplies and services are available in Norton.

Activities & Attractions: Fishing (especially for crappie, channel cats, and wiper); boating; boat launch; swimming beach; an original adobe prairie home is on display as a museum.

Natural Features: Located on a short bluff at the head of Leota Cove on the north shore of Keith Sebelius Lake, a reservoir on Prairie Dog Creek; campground vegetation consists of sparse grass and primarily planted hardwoods; larger hardwoods and a few cedars border the camp areas; dry, gently rolling prairie surrounds the park; elevation 2300'.

Season, Fees & Phone: Open all year, with limited services mid-October to April; please see Appendix for standard Kansas state park fees and reservation information; 14-day limit; park office (913) 877-2953.

Camp Notes: OK, so this isn't the Ritz. But the high plains hold a certain fascination that transcends the importance of mere camping appliances. Prairie Dog is about as far away from Kansas' centers of civilization as you can get, Toto.

Kansas 2

WEBSTER
Webster State Park

Location: Northwest Kansas north of Hays.

Access: From U.S. Highway 24 at milepost 143 +.8 (9 miles west of Stockton, 26 miles east of Hill City), turn south onto the main park road; proceed 2 miles in a general southwesterly direction along the lakeshore to the park office; turn south (left) for a final 0.4 mile to the campground; turn east (left) into the principal hookup area and the standard camping area, just beyond.

Facilities: 26 electrical hookup campsites, plus a number of standard sites; hookup sites are level, small+, with nil separation; standard sites are large, level, with fair to good separation; parking pads are gravel/grass, medium to long straight-ins; adequate space for a large tent in most sites; a few sites have ramadas (sun shelters); barbecue grills; limited firewood may be available for gathering in adjacent woodland, b-y-o is recommended; water at central faucets; restrooms with showers; holding tank disposal station; paved or gravel driveways; limited+ supplies and services are available in Stockton.

Activities & Attractions: Fishing (reportedly excellent for walleye and crappie); boating; boat launch; prairie baseball field.

Natural Features: Located on a crunchgrass flat on a point along the north shore of Webster; most hookup sites lack natural shade/shelter; standard sites are in a grove of large hardwoods; surrounded by fairly dry, very gently rolling prairie and agricultural land; elevation 2000'.

Season, Fees & Phone: Open all year, with limited services mid-October to mid-April; please see Appendix for standard Kansas state park fees and reservation information; 14 day limit; park office (913) 425-6558.

Camp Notes: A surprising number of campers stay here in the off-season. Good fishing and fairly mild weather bring people here well into November. Some maps and signs also refer to this area as "North Shore" or "Rock Point".

Kansas 3

CEDAR BLUFF
Cedar Bluff State Park

Location: Central Kansas southwest of Hays.

Access: From Kansas State Highway 147 at milepost 12 +.2 (13 miles south of Interstate 70 Exit 135 east of WaKeeney, 12 miles north of Brownell), turn west onto the park road; proceed 0.4 miles to the park office; turn south (left) for 0.2 mile to the 'trailer park'; or continue ahead for an additional 0.7 mile to an electrical hookup area.

Facilities: 81 campsites, including 10 with full hookups and 78 with electrical hookups, in 2 sections, plus standard ('open') camping; sites are medium-sized, level, with minimal separation; parking pads are long, paved straight-ins in the 'trailer park', or long, gravel/grass straight-ins in the electrical area; good-sized, grassy tent spots; barbecue grills; b-y-o firewood; water at central faucets; restrooms with showers; holding tank disposal station; paved driveways; gas and snacks at the Interstate; adequate supplies in WaKeeney, 20 miles; nearest complete supplies and services are in Hays, 37 highway miles northeast.

Activities & Attractions: Boating; boat launches; fishing; swimming beach.

Natural Features: Located on a large, level plain above the north shore of Cedar Bluff Reservoir; a few medium-height hardwoods render minimal shelter/shade in the trailer park; slightly more shelter is provided by larger hardwoods in the electrical hookup area; elevation 2400'.

Season, Fees & Phone: Available all year, with limited services October to May; please see Appendix for standard Kansas state park fees and reservation information; 14 day limit; park office (913) 726-3212.

Camp Notes: This camping area is also called "North Shore". But you'll have to hoof it for a way to get to the water's edge (particularly in a dry year). Although the campsites are tightly spaced, there's plenty of open country adjacent to them. The reservoir is very big with local boaters.

Kansas 4

SCOTT
Scott State Park

Location: Western Kansas south of Oakley.

Access: From U.S. Highway 83 at milepost 121 +.3 (16 miles north of Scott City, 29 miles south of Oakley), turn southwest onto Kansas State Highway 95 and proceed 3.5 miles to the park entrance, on the right; continue northwest beyond the entrance station to the "modern" camping areas and standard ("primitive") areas, or to the right, to the standard "Big Grove" area. **Alternate Access:** From U.S. 83 at milepost 116 +.3, turn northwest onto Kansas 95 and proceed 3.1 miles to the park entrance.

Facilities: 61 campsites with electrical hookups in two areas, plus numerous standard sites in several other locations; sites are generally small, with minimal separation; parking pads are medium to long, gravel straight-ins which may require additional leveling; many good, grassy tent sites; barbecue grills; b-y-o firewood; water at several faucets; restrooms with showers; holding tank disposal station; gravel/dirt loop driveways; limited to adequate supplies and services are available in Scott City.

Natural Features: Located along the shore of Lake Scott, a small impoundment on Ladder Creek on the high plains; most sites have a grassy surface; acres of large hardwoods and a few pine provide shelter/shade in most standard sites; limited natural shade in the hookup areas; bordered by rocky/grassy hills and bluffs; elevation 2900'.

Activities & Attractions: Fishing; sailing; swimming beach; Big Springs nature trail; El Cuartelejo Pueblo ruins.

Season, Fees & Phone: May to mid-October; please see Appendix for standard Kansas state park fees and reservation information; 14 day limit; park office (316) 872-2061.

Camp Notes: A bit of all right, considering this *is* western Kansas. The vegetation and the bluffs provide interesting topographical relief from the rest of the region's level landscape. Usually nice and breezy, too.

Kansas 5

MEADE
Meade State Park

Location: Southwest Kansas northeast of Liberal.

Access: From Kansas State Highway 23 at milepost 13 +.1 (14 miles southwest of Meade, 13 miles north of the Kansas-Oklahoma border), turn north into the state park entrance and proceed 0.1 mile to the first of a half-dozen camping areas around Lake Meade.

Facilities: 32 electrical hookup campsites in 3 areas on the west and north shores, plus a couple-dozen standard ("tent" or "primitive") campsites; sites are basically small, with little to some separation; parking pads are mostly level, short to long, gravel straight-ins; adequate space for a large tent in most sites; barbecue grills, plus a few fireplaces; b-y-o firewood; water at several faucets, plus auxiliary hand pumps; restrooms with showers; holding tank disposal station on the north side of the lake; gravel loop driveways, paved roadway; limited supplies and services are available in Meade.

Activities & Attractions: Fishing; limited boating (electric motors OK); small boat launch; swimming beach; hiking trail along the west/northwest side of the lake.

Natural Features: Located on the high plains on the shore of Lake Meade, a small impoundment of a few acres in a very shallow basin surrounded by grassy slopes; most campsites are very well sheltered/shaded by large hardwoods; several lakeshore campsites; the park covers about 450 acres; elevation 2900'.

Season, Fees & Phone: Open all year, with limited services mid-October to April; please see Appendix for standard Kansas state park fees and reservation information; 14-day limit; park office (316) 873-2572.

Camp Notes: Sure, this small, simple spot isn't like the posh parks in eastern Kansas. But it is well shaded, and, like all Kansas state parks, has waterfront property.

KANSAS
Central Plains
Please refer to the Kansas map in the Appendix

Kansas 6

LOVEWELL
Lovewell State Park

Location: North-central Kansas north of Beloit.

Access: From Kansas State Highway 14 at milepost 249 + 50 yards (41 miles north of Beloit, 7 miles south of Superior, Nebraska), turn east onto a gravel road and travel 4.1 miles; turn south onto another gravel road and proceed 1 mile on gravel and another 0.9 mile on pavement to the park office (on the left); turn west (right) and continue for 0.4 mile to the campground.

Facilities: 30 campsites with electrical hookups, plus numerous standard campsites; hookup sites are small to medium-sized, with little separation; parking pads are long, gravel/grass pull-throughs; some additional leveling will probably be required; adequate space for a large tent in most units, but may be sloped; barbecue grills; b-y-o firewood; water at central faucets; restrooms with showers; holding tank disposal station; gravel driveways; gas and camper supplies at the marina; nearest source of adequate supplies and services is Superior, Nebraska.

Activities & Attractions: Swimming beach; fishing; boating, boat launch, marina; playground.

Natural Features: Located on a knoll on a large point along the northeast shore of Lovewell Lake; most sites have minimal to fair shelter/shade provided by small hardwoods; surrounding area is primarily rolling or hilly, tree-dotted grassland; views of the west and south sections of the lake from most campsites; elevation 1500'.

114

Season, Fees & Phone: Open all year, with limited services mid-October to April; please see Appendix for standard Kansas state park fees and reservation information; 14-day limit; park office (913) 753-4305.

Camp Notes: As the northernmost (and, in some respects, least accessible) of the state park campgrounds, this out-of-the-way spot doesn't experience the high traffic count of many others in the state. The facilities may not be four star, but the Western atmosphere and the local scenery are good.

Kansas 7

GLEN ELDER
Glen Elder State Park

Location: North-central Kansas west of Beloit.

Access: From the junction of U.S. Highway 24 & Kansas State Highway 128, (at milepost 207 +.6 on U.S. 24, 2 miles west of Glen Elder, 6 miles east of Cawker City), turn south onto the park access road and proceed 0.5 mile to an intersection; continue straight to Camp 2, or turn left or right to Camps 1 or 3, each within 0.4 mile. **Alternate Access:** From U.S. 24 at milepost 208 +.6 (1 mile west of Glen Elder), turn southwest/west and proceed west on the main park road, (past the park office); turn south (left) into the 3 camp areas, all within 1.5 miles of the highway.

Facilities: 139 partial-hookup campsites, plus dozens of standard sites, in 3 loops; sites are level, small to medium-sized and closely spaced; parking pads are sandy gravel, short or medium straight-ins or long pull-throughs; small to large tent spaces on a sand or grass surface; barbecue grills; b-y-o firewood; water at sites and at central faucets; restrooms with showers; holding tank disposal station; paved driveways; camper supplies at a park store; limited supplies and services in Glen Elder and Cawker City.

Activities & Attractions: Fishing; boating; boat launch; marina; baseball field; amphitheater; information center.

Natural Features: Located on 3 points of land along the northeast shore of Waconda Lake; hardwoods provide light shade/shelter for many campsites; elevation 1500'.

Season, Fees & Phone: Open all year, with limited services October to mid-April; please see Appendix for standard Kansas state park fees and reservation information; 14-day limit; park office (913) 545-3345.

Camp Notes: The Waconda Lake area has achieved quite a far-reaching reputation for top-notch fishing and hunting. (If even just a fraction of the 'fishtales' told by the locals and the park people were accurate, the fish and game action would still receive an "A" grade.) The best campsites are probably those in Camp 3, at the west end of the park.

Kansas 8

MINOOKA
Wilson Lake/Corps of Engineers Park

Location: Central Kansas between Salina and Hays.

Access: From Interstate 70 Exit 199 for Dorrance, proceed north on Dorrance Road for 5.2 miles to an "L" intersection at the bottom of a steep hill; turn east (right) and proceed east for 0.4 mile, north 0.5 mile, then east again 0.2 mile to the entrance station; continue east for 0.2 mile beyond the entrance, then turn north (left) into the primary camping area, or continue east for 1 mile to the tent area. **Alternate Access:** From Kansas State Highway 232 at milepost 7 south of Wilson Dam, proceed west on South Shore Drive for 7.3 miles to Dorrance Road; turn north onto Dorrance Road, and continue as above.

Facilities: 183 campsites, including about 60 with electrical hookups, in 6 loops; sites are medium-sized, with minimal separation; parking pads are gravel, medium-length straight-ins; additional leveling will probably be required; adequate, though sloped, space for a large tent in most sites; fire rings in some sites; b-y-o firewood; water at central faucets; central restrooms with showers; holding tank disposal station; paved/oiled gravel driveways; nearest supplies (limited) in Wilson, 11 miles southeast.

Activities & Attractions: Boating; boat ramps; fishing; fish cleaning stations; swimming beach, 2 miles west.

Natural Features: Located along both sides of a ridge on a point on the south shore of Wilson Lake in the Smoky Hills region; vegetation consists of sparse grass, a few hardwoods, cedars (junipers) and pines; most sites lack natural shelter/shade; surrounding hills have patches of hardwoods and evergreens; some sites are lakeside; elevation 1600'.

Season, Fees & Phone: May to October; $7.00 for a standard site, $9.00 for an electrical hookup site; 14 day limit; Wilson Lake CoE Project Office (913) 658-2551.

Camp Notes: Beaucoups bucks were recently spent in order to refurbish and modernize this remote, windswept camp. Enjoy!

Kansas 9

LUCAS
Wilson Lake/Corps of Engineers Park

Location: Central Kansas between Salina and Hays.

Access: From Kansas State Highway 232 at milepost 11 (at the north end of Wilson Dam, 9 miles north of Interstate 70 Exit 206 at Wilson, 7 miles south of Lucas), turn southwest onto a paved access road; proceed 1.4 miles to a "T" intersection; turn south (left) and continue for 0.75 mile, almost to the bottom of the hill; turn east (left) to the primary camping areas, along the next 0.75 mile.

Facilities: 30 campsites in 2 sections; sites are generally large, with fair to fairly good separation; parking pads are mostly long, gravel straight-ins; additional leveling will probably be required in most sites; large tent areas, may be sloped; barbecue grills; b-y-o firewood; water at several faucets; vault facilities; gravel driveways; nearest source of supplies (limited) is in Lucas.

Activities & Attractions: Hang glider area; 3-mile hiking trail through 300-acre Rocktown Natural Area, adjacent; playground; fishing; swimming beach, boat launch, about a dozen scattered additional individual campsites, and a group camp, near Lucas Point, 2 miles southwest.

Natural Features: Located on a grassy slope on the north shore of Wilson Lake; scattered hardwoods and a few evergreens provide minimal to light shelter/shade for most campsites; the lake is surrounded by nearly treeless, grass-covered hills and bluffs; comparatively dry climate; elevation 1600'.

Season, Fees & Phone: Open all year, with limited services October to May; no fee (subject to change); 14 day limit; Wilson Lake CoE Project Office (913) 658-2551.

Camp Notes: As you travel the back roads in this region, note the thousands of stone fence posts which serve to support the barbed wire. The quarried stone columns, averaging some 350 pounds apiece, were pressed into service by the resourceful pioneers as a substitute for wooden posts. Timber is still not found in abundance here, but it was a *very* scarce commodity on the high plains of frontier days.

Kansas 10

SYLVAN
Wilson Lake/Corps of Engineers Park

Location: Central Kansas between Salina and Hays.

Access: From Kansas State Highway 232 at milepost 10 (8 miles north of Interstate 70 Exit 206 at Wilson, 8 miles south of Lucas), turn southeast onto Kansas State Highway 181 for 0.1 mile, then turn northwest (a sharp left) onto the paved project access road; continue down the hill, past the project office and across the outlet stream for 0.7 mile to the campground.

Facilities: 18 campsites; sites are small to medium-sized, level, with minimal separation; parking pads are long, gravel straight-ins; adequate space for large tents on a grassy surface; barbecue grills; b-y-o firewood; water at central faucets; vault facilities; gravel driveways; gas and snacks at the I-70 interchange; limited supplies and services are available in Wilson, Lucas, and Sylvan Grove, (all are within 9 miles of this point).

Activities & Attractions: Bur Oak Nature Trail; lake fishing for walleye, white bass, smallmouth bass and striped bass; boating; boat launch on the lake, 0.5 mile south.

Natural Features: Located on a grassy flat along the north bank of the Saline River, the outlet stream for Wilson Lake, in the Smoky Hills; about half the sites are lightly shaded/sheltered by hardwoods and a few evergreens, remainder are in the open; elevation 1400'.

Season, Fees & Phone: Open all year, with limited services October to May; no fee (subject to change); 14 day limit; Wilson Lake CoE Project Office (913) 658-2551.

Camp Notes: If you have an interest in Western Plains history and ecology, a stop at the small visitor information center in the project office should be very worthwhile. In addition to viewing exhibits about prairie life, you can pick up a nature trail guide, plus pamphlets and maps which provide details of the local flora and fauna. There's reportedly very good fishing here--the lake's high salinity produces stripers that can weigh as much as their seagoing ancestors.

116

HELL CREEK
Wilson State Park

Location: Central Kansas between Salina and Hays.

Access: From Kansas State Highway 232 at milepost 7 (5 miles north of Interstate 70 Exit 206 at Wilson, 11 miles south of Lucas), turn west onto South Shore Drive; proceed west then south for 1.6 miles; turn west (right) into the park entrance and continue west, then north, for 0.9 mile to a "Y"; turn right, proceed down the hill for 0.2 mile; turn northwest (left) for 0.5 mile to the primary camping area, or continue ahead for 0.2 mile to the small camping area at the marina.

Facilities: 54 electrical hookup campsites, plus a number of standard sites; sites vary from small to medium+, with minimal to fair separation; parking pads are gravel, primarily medium-length straight-ins, plus a few pull-throughs; medium-sized tent areas; barbecue grills; b-y-o firewood; water at several faucets; restrooms with showers; holding tank disposal station; paved driveways; gas and camper supplies at the marina; limited supplies and services are available in Wilson, Lucas, and Sylvan Grove, (all within 11 miles).

Activities & Attractions: Boating; boat launch, marina; fishing.

Natural Features: Located on several small points at the mouth of Hell Creek Inlet on the southeast corner of Wilson Lake; campground vegetation consists of a few hardwoods, cedars and pines on a surface of sparse grass; surrounded by high hills flecked with a few trees; elevation 1600'.

Season, Fees & Phone: Open all year, with limited services mid-October to April; please see Appendix for standard Kansas state park fees and reservation information; 14 day limit; park office (913) 658-2465.

Camp Notes: This is a surprisingly popular place, considering the comparatively rigorous surroundings. (Compared, that is, to the much more verdant parks east of here.)

OTOE
Wilson State Park

Location: Central Kansas between Salina and Hays.

Access: From Kansas State Highway 232 at milepost 7 (5 miles north of Interstate 70 Exit 206 at Wilson, 11 miles south of Lucas), turn west onto South Shore Drive; proceed west for 0.5 mile; turn south (left), then west, then swing around to the north and pass under the bridge; continue north/northwest for 0.65 mile to the campground entrance station; proceed straight ahead for 0.15 mile to the main camp loop.

Facilities: 27 partial hookup campsites in the main loop, plus a number of scattered standard sites; hookup sites are level, small to small+, and closely spaced; parking pads are gravel, medium-length straight-ins; adequate space for a medium to large tent in standard and hookup units; barbecue grills; b-y-o firewood; water at sites and at central faucets; restrooms with showers (H); holding tank disposal station; paved main roadways, gravel loop driveways; limited supplies and services are available in Wilson, Lucas, and Sylvan Grove, (all within 10 miles).

Activities & Attractions: Swimming beach; boating; boat launch; fishing.

Natural Features: Located on a hilltop on a small point along the east shore of Wilson Lake in the Smoky Hills region; campground vegetation consists primarily of short grass and a few small hardwoods; the recreation area's several small hills are dotted by larger hardwoods; nearly treeless hills and bluffs, some with eroded rock formations, surround the lake; elevation 1600'.

Season, Fees & Phone: Open all year, with limited services mid-October to April; please see Appendix for standard Kansas state park fees and reservation information; 14 day limit; park office (913) 658-2465.

Camp Notes: This is the smaller, and in some respects nicer, of the two camping areas in the state park. Several of the standard campsites offer very good tenting possibilities.

EAST SHORE
Kanopolis State Park

Location: Central Kansas southwest of Salina.

Access: From Kansas State Highway 141 at milepost 5 +.2 (5 miles north of the junction of Kansas Highways 141 & 4 west of Lindsborg, 8 miles south of the junction of Kansas Highways 141 & 140 east of Ellsworth), turn west onto a paved access road; proceed west, north, west (past the park office), then north again for 2.1 miles to a "T" intersection; turn left to the main camping areas, or right to the small Horsethief Canyon area; **Alternate Access:** From Kansas State Highway 141 at milepost 7 +.2, turn west onto the park road (the first few yards are actually Kansas State Highway 241) and proceed west, then south for 0.3 mile or 0.9 mile to the camp areas.

Facilities: 46 campsites with electrical hookups; sites are basically level, small and closely spaced; parking pads are medium to long, gravel/grass straight-ins; adequate tent space in most sites; fireplaces; b-y-o firewood; water at central faucets; restrooms with showers; holding tank disposal station; gravel driveways; gas and camper supplies, 3 miles south; limited to adequate supplies and services are available in Ellsworth or Lindsborg.

Activities & Attractions: Swimming beach; nature trail at Horsethief Canyon; fishing; boating.

Natural Features: Located on a short bluff above the east shore of Kanopolis Lake; large hardwoods provide shelter for some sites; surrounded by gently rolling terrain; elevation 1500'.

Season, Fees & Phone: Open all year, with limited services mid-October to April; please see Appendix for standard Kansas state park fees and reservation information; 14-day limit; park office (913) 546-2565.

Camp Notes: In addition to the usual summertime recreational activities, park officials report that the surrounding area offers "some of the best hunting in Kansas...for just about anything you can name". Kansas 241 must be one of the shortest state highways in the country.

SOUTH SHORE
Kanopolis State Park

Location: Central Kansas southwest of Salina.

Access: From Kansas State Highway 141 at milepost 2 +.7 (2.7 miles north of the junction of Kansas Highways 141 & 4 west of Lindsborg, 10 miles south of the junction of Kansas Highways 141 & 140 east of Ellsworth), turn west onto the paved park access road; proceed 0.5 mile to the trailer park, or 0.8 mile to the main camping area; or 1.1 miles to a third small area, all on the north (right) side of the park road.

Facilities: 88 campsites, including 16 with full hookups in the trailer park, and 72 with electrical hookups (20 with water) in the other areas, plus numerous standard sites; sites are generally small+, level and closely spaced; parking pads are gravel, medium to long straight-ins or pull-throughs in the main area; paved, medium to long straight-ins in the trailer park; medium to large tent spots; fireplaces or barbecue grills; b-y-o firewood is recommended; water at sites and at central faucets; central restrooms with showers; disposal stations; paved or gravel driveways; gas and camper supplies, 0.5 mile south; limited to adequate supplies and services are available in Lindsborg or Ellsworth.

Activities & Attractions: Swimming beach; fishing; boating; boat launch, marina; ball field; amphitheater.

Natural Features: Located on grassy flats on the south shore of Kanopolis Lake; most sites have adequate shelter provided by large hardwoods, (except campsites in the small section at the far west end, which are basically unsheltered); elevation 1500'.

Season, Fees & Phone: Open all year, with limited services mid-October to April; please see Appendix for standard Kansas state park fees and reservation information; 14 day limit; park office (913) 546-2565.

Camp Notes: The South Shore area of the park is also known as Langley Point.

VENANGO
Kanopolis Lake/Corps of Engineers Park

Location: Central Kansas southwest of Salina.

Access: From Kansas State Highway 141 at milepost 5 +.2 (5 miles north of the junction of Kansas Highways 141 & 4 west of Lindsborg, 8 miles south of the junction of Kansas Highways 141 & 140 east of Ellsworth), turn west onto a paved access road; proceed 0.6 miles (after 0.2 mile the road curves toward the southwest), to the campground pay station; turn southeast (left) just after the pay station and continue southeast, then east, for 0.5 mile to the campground, on both sides of the access road.

Facilities: 35 campsites, including 25 with electrical hookups; sites are average in size, level, with scant separation; parking pads are gravel/grass, mostly medium to long straight-ins; good-sized tent spots; barbecue grills; some firewood may be available for gathering in the area; water at central faucets; restrooms (about 100 yards east); showers (0.15 mile west); holding tank disposal station; paved/gravel driveways; gas and camper supplies, 3 miles south; limited to adequate supplies and services are available in Ellsworth or Lindsborg.

Activities & Attractions: Swimming beach; motorcycle trail; fishing; boating; boat launch; day use areas.

Natural Features: Located near the east shore of Kanopolis Lake, an impoundment on the Smoky Hill River; campground vegetation consists of a grassy surface dotted with large cottonwoods that provide light to moderate shelter/shade for most campsites; elevation 1500'.

Season, Fees & Phone: April to October; $7.00 for a standard site, $9.00 for an electrical hookup site; 14 day limit; Kanopolis Lake CoE Project Office (913) 546-2294.

Camp Notes: Although no lake views are afforded from the campground, a short walk or drive will bring you to any of a dozen points along the shore. This campground is sometimes called "Cottonwood Grove".

RIVERSIDE
Kanopolis Lake/Corps of Engineers Park

Location: Central Kansas southwest of Salina.

Access: From Kansas State Highway 141 at milepost 2 +.7 (2.7 miles north of the junction of Kansas Highways 141 & 4 west of Lindsborg, 10 miles south of the junction of Kansas Highways 141 & 140 east of Ells-worth), turn east onto a paved access road and proceed 0.3 mile to a point just beyond the project office; turn left, then right, and continue down the hill to the campground.

Facilities: 25 campsites; sites are medium-sized, level, with fairly good spacing; parking pads are grass/gravel medium to long straight-ins; large, grassy tent areas; barbecue grills, plus a few fire rings; a small amount of firewood may be available for gathering in the vicinity; water at central faucets; restrooms with showers; holding tank disposal station; paved driveways; gas and camper supplies, 0.5 mile south; limited to adequate supplies and services are available in Lindsborg or Ellsworth.

Activities & Attractions: Playground; fishing, particularly for walleye and white bass, also crappie and cats; local interest exhibits at the project office.

Natural Features: Located on a grassy flat in a narrow valley along the south bank of the Smoky Hill River, the outlet stream for Kanopolis Lake; most campsites have light to moderate shelter/shade provided by large hardwoods; elevation 1500'.

Season, Fees & Phone: April to October; no fee (subject to change); 14 day limit; Kanopolis Lake CoE Project Office (913) 546-2294.

Camp Notes: If you see a reference to "Outlet" campground in some literature, it's the same place as Riverside. Whatever you prefer to call it, its a real deal, if not a steal. How many places provide you with restrooms, showers, and lots of trees and grass for as long as a fortnight, yet ring up a "No Charge" at the end of your stay?

WEST SHORE
Cheney State Park

Location: South-central Kansas west of Wichita.

Access: From U.S. Highway 54 at milepost 190 +.7 (18 miles east of Kingman, 24 miles west of Wichita), turn north onto Kansas State Highway 251 (391st West) and proceed 3.6 miles to 21st North; turn west (left) onto 21st North and continue for 2.6 miles; turn north (right) for 0.15 mile to the park entrance; hookup areas are to the left; standard camping areas are left and right.

Facilities: 110 partial hookup campsites, plus uncounted standard sites, in 7 areas; sites are medium+ and close together; parking pads are long, level, gravel/grass straight-ins or pull-throughs; large, grassy areas for tents; barbecue grills; b-y-o firewood; water at central faucets; restrooms with showers; holding tank disposal station; paved driveways; camp host; camper supplies at a small store just outside the park; adequate supplies in Kingman; complete supplies and services are available in Wichita.

Activities & Attractions: Boating; boat launches; waterskiing; sailboat cove; fishing; swimming beaches; bathhouse; Geifer Creek Trail; several playgrounds.

Natural Features: Located on the southwest corner of Cheney Lake, a major reservoir on the Ninnescah River; most hookup sites have minimal to limited shelter/shade; other campsites tend to be well sheltered by large hardwoods, plus some cedars (junipers) and pine; expansive sections of mown lawns throughout the park; elevation 1400'.

Season, Fees & Phone: Open all year, with limited services from mid-October to April; please see Appendix for standard Kansas state park fees and reservation information; 14 day limit; park office (316) 542-3664.

Camp Notes: This is a biggie--and a nice one at that. Like several other Kansas state parks, this area is under the auspices of a "Green Thumb Project" sponsored by a farmers' organization. It's exceptionally well-landscaped.

EAST SHORE
Cheney State Park

Location: South-central Kansas west of Wichita.

Access: From U.S. Highway 54 at milepost 190 +.7 (18 miles east of Kingman, 24 miles west of Wichita), turn north onto Kansas State Highway 251 (391st West) and proceed 3.8 miles to the end of Highway 251; continue ahead on the paved road for another 1.8 miles; turn west (left) into the park entrance; proceed straight ahead 0.1 mile to a hookup area, or turn north (right) and follow the road around for 1 mile to the other hookup area at Heimerman Point; standard camping is also available at M & M Point, 1 mile farther west.

Facilities: 75 partial hookup campsites, plus numerous standard sites, in 3 areas; sites tend to be small, with minimal separation; most parking pads are gravel/dirt, short to medium-length, fairly level straight-ins; medium-sized tent areas; barbecue grills; b-y-o firewood; water at several faucets; restrooms with showers; holding tank disposal station; paved driveways; camper supplies at nearby small stores; adequate supplies in Kingman; complete supplies and services are available in Wichita.

Activities & Attractions: Boating; boat launch; fishing for crappie, white and striped bass, catfish, and some walleye; marina.

Natural Features: Located on a pair of coves on the east shore of Cheney Lake, a 1700-acre reservoir with 67 miles of shoreline, on the Ninnescah River; shelter/shade varies from minimal to moderate; bordered by woodlands; elevation 1400'.

Season, Fees & Phone: Open all year, with limited services from mid-October to April; please see Appendix for standard Kansas state park fees and reservation information; 14 day limit; park office (316) 542-3664.

Camp Notes: East Shore provides a more remote and natural alternative to the park's excellent facility at West Shore. Many standard campsites are right along the water's edge. Good lake views from most other sites as well.

Kansas 19

WAKEFIELD
Clay County Park

Location: Northeast Kansas northwest of Junction City.

Access: From Kansas State Highway 82 in the community of Wakefield at a point 0.1 mile west of the Milford Lake causeway, turn south onto Birch St. and proceed 2 blocks to the campground.

Facilities: Approximately 80 campsites, many with electrical hookups; sites are generally small to medium-sized, basically level, with minimal to fair separation; parking pads are gravel, mostly short to medium straight-ins, plus a few longer pads; large, grassy tent areas; barbecue grills; b-y-o firewood; water at faucets throughout; restrooms, shower building; holding tank disposal station; paved main driveway, other drives are gravel; gas, groceries and laundromat are available in Wakefield.

Activities & Attractions: Large, fenced playground; ball field; swimming pool; Kansas Landscape Arboretum, a mile south of town, has several self-guiding nature trails; fishing; boating; boat launch.

Natural Features: Located on the gently sloping west shore of Milford Lake, an impoundment on the Republican River; campground vegetation consists of expanses of grass and moderately dense hardwoods; terrain bordering the lake is generally quite low; elevation 1200'.

Season, Fees & Phone: May to October; $4.00 for a standard site, $7.00 for an electrical hookup site.

Camp Notes: There are few places in these parts where you can get an electrical connection for less than ten bucks, or a tent spot for half of that, and have a morning shower to boot. From the objective description, the campsites may seem a little small and close together. But the place ordinarily doesn't overflow with campers, so chances are you won't be close enough to the next outfit to have to entertain questions or comments about what you're having for dinner.

Kansas 20

TIMBER CREEK
Milford Lake/Corps of Engineers Park

Location: Northeast Kansas north of Junction City.

Access: From Kansas State Highway 18 at milepost 8 +.6 (2 miles west of the junction of Highway 18 & U.S. 77 north of Junction City, 3 miles east of Wakefield), turn north for 0.6 mile, or south for 0.4 mile, to the two camping areas.

Facilities: 75 campsites in 2 areas; sites are medium-sized, essentially level, with fairly good separation in the north unit; sites in the south unit tend to be smaller, with less separation, and are more sloped; parking pads are gravel, medium to long straight-ins; good to very good tent-pitching possibilities; barbecue grills; some firewood is available for gathering in the vicinity; water at central faucets; vault facilities (H); holding tank disposal station; paved driveways; gas and groceries are available in Wakefield.

Activities & Attractions: Nature trail (accessible from the south unit); small playgrounds; fishing for several varieties of bass, plus walleye, crappie, and channel catfish; boating; boat launch and dock (at the far end of the south unit).

Natural Features: Located on the east shore of Milford Lake; mown grass, quite a variety of large hardwoods and medium-sized evergreens comprise the campground vegetation; the lake has a somewhat marshy shoreline in this area; elevation 1200'.

Season, Fees & Phone: May to October; $6.00; 14 day limit; Milford Lake CoE Project Office (913) 238-5714.

Camp Notes: The majority of the sites have at least a good glimpse of the lake through the trees, some have full views. Reportedly, this campground has not had capacity crowds in the past few years, so you'll *probably* be assured of a site, even on Fourth of July weekend. For a site with hookups, a shower and flush facilities, trip on over to the county park in Wakefield.

FARNUM CREEK
Milford Lake/Corps of Engineers Park

Location: Northeast Kansas north of Junction City.

Access: From U.S. Highway 77 at milepost 163 +.4 (11 miles north of Junction City, 1.5 miles south of the community of Milford), turn west onto a paved access road and proceed 0.25 mile; turn south (left) and continue for 0.4 mile to the campground.

Facilities: 88 campsites, including 49 with electrical hookups, in 3 loops; sites are small to a scant medium in size, with minimal to fair separation; parking pads are gravel, mostly medium-length straight-ins which will probably require additional leveling; large, though slightly sloped, grassy tent areas; 8 park n' walk sites on a grassy slope in Loop C; barbecue grills; b-y-o firewood is recommended; water at central faucets; vault facilities; holding tank disposal station; paved driveways; nearly complete supplies and services are available in Junction City.

Activities & Attractions: Model airplane field; fishing; boating; boat launch; nearby group camp; day use area.

Natural Features: Located on the sloping west shore of Milford Lake; campground vegetation consists of mown grass, and medium to tall hardwoods which provide light to moderate shelter/shade for most sites; a number of sites are lakeside; Loop C is situated along the south shore of a small bay; elevation 1200'.

Season, Fees & Phone: May to October; $6.00 for a standard site, $8.00 for an electrical hookup site, $1.00 surcharge for so-called "premium" or "prime" sites; 14 day limit; Milford Lake CoE Project Office (913) 238-5714.

Camp Notes: This campground is somewhat of a compromise between the (subjectively) nicer Corps camps at the south end of the lake and the more "basic" camping area several miles north of here at Timber Creek. (But why the extra *dinero* for the "prime" sites? Perhaps for a better grade of electricity, or greener grass? Ed.)

MILFORD
Milford State Park

Location: Northeast Kansas north of Junction City.

Access: From U.S. Highway 77 near milepost 157 (5 miles north of Interstate 70 Exit 295 at Junction City, 8 miles south of the community of Milford), turn northwest onto Kansas State Highway 57 and proceed 4 miles; turn northwest (left) into the park entrance; continue ahead, left, or right to the camping areas, all within 1 mile of the entrance. **Alternate Access:** If southbound on U.S. 77 from Milford, turn southwest onto Kansas State Highway 57 at U.S 77 milepost 160 +.3; proceed 1.2 miles to the park entrance and continue as above.

Facilities: 156 designated campsites, including 126 with electrical hookups and 30 with full hookups, plus numerous standard sites, in 5 areas; sites are small to medium-sized, and vary from level to sloped; majority of parking pads are gravel/grass, about half are pull-throughs, remainder are straight-ins; large tent spots; tent camping permitted in the standard areas or in hookup area 1; barbecue grills; b-y-o firewood; water at some sites and at central faucets; central restrooms with showers; holding tank disposal station; paved driveways; nearly complete supplies and services are available in Junction City.

Activities & Attractions: Swimming beach; fishing; boating; boat launches; playgrounds; amphitheater.

Natural Features: Located on several points of land along the east shore of Milford Lake; campground vegetation consists of light to medium dense hardwoods and some evergreens on a grassy surface; elevation 1200'.

Season, Fees & Phone: Open all year, with limited services mid-October to April; please see Appendix for standard Kansas state park fees and reservation information; 14-day limit; park office (913) 238-3014.

Camp Notes: The access to the park is a little tricky since high-way signs in the area are a bit unclear. Note that Kansas 57 is a half-loop that connects to U.S. 77 at two points.

ROLLING HILLS
Milford Lake/Corps of Engineers Park

Location: Northeast Kansas northwest of Junction City.

Access: From Interstate 70 Exit 290 (9 miles west of Junction City, 15 miles east of Abilene), turn north onto a paved local road and proceed 4.3 miles to Kansas State Highway 244; turn east (right) onto Highway 244 for 0.25 mile; turn north onto the Rolling Hills access road and proceed 0.2 mile to Loop C, 0.7 mile to Loop B, or 1.5 miles to the main camping area in Loop A.

Facilities: 228 campsites, including 36 with electrical hookups, in 3 loops; sites are small to medium-sized, with nominal to fairly good separation; parking pads are primarily medium to long, gravel straight-ins; additional leveling may be needed in some sites; good-sized, grassy tent spots in most units; also separate tent camping area; fire rings or barbecue grills; b-y-o firewood is recommended; water at central faucets; restrooms with showers; holding tank disposal station; paved driveways; nearly complete supplies and services are available in Junction City.

Activities & Attractions: Fishing; boating; boat launch; playground; swimming beach in day use area, 2 miles east.

Natural Features: Located on a point of land on the south shore of Milford Lake; most sites are along, or very near, the lakeshore; vegetation consists of grass and light to medium-dense hardwoods; elevation 1200'.

Season, Fees & Phone: Open all year, with limited services and no fee, November to April; $7.00 for a standard site, $9.00 for an electrical hookup site, add $1.00 for a "prime" site; portions of Loops B & C are free use areas; 14-day limit; Milford Lake CoE Project Office (913) 238-5714.

Camp Notes: There are some really dandy campsites here. (The better ones will cost you an extra dollar.) Incidentally, there is a nice group of exhibits (small, but comprehensive) at the Milford Lake CoE information center, less than 3 miles northeast of here, at the dam.

CURTIS CREEK
Milford Lake/Corps of Engineers Park

Location: Northeast Kansas northwest of Junction City.

Access: From Interstate 70 Exit 290 (9 miles west of Junction City, 15 miles east of Abilene), turn north onto a paved local road and proceed 4.3 miles to Kansas State Highway 244; turn west, and proceed west, north, then east for 5.2 miles; as the main road turns north once again, turn southeast onto the campground access road and continue for 0.4 mile to the campground entrance; the principal camp area lies just beyond the entrance; secondary areas are located midway on the point and at the tip of the point.

Facilities: 105 campsites, including 30 with electrical hookups; sites are small to medium-sized, with nominal to fairly good separation; parking pads are gravel, mostly medium to long straight-ins; additional leveling may be needed in some units; good-sized, grassy tent spots in most sites; fire rings or barbecue grills; b-y-o firewood is suggested; water at central faucets; restrooms with showers (H); disposal station; paved driveways; nearly complete supplies and services are available in Junction City.

Activities & Attractions: Fishing; boat launch; playground.

Natural Features: Located on a long point (which almost could be termed a peninsula) at the southwest corner of Milford Lake, a flood control impoundment on the Republican River; campground vegetation consists of light to moderately dense hardwoods on a grassy surface; a number of sites are lakeside; elevation 1200'.

Season, Fees & Phone: Open all year, with limited services and no fee, October to April; $7.00 for a standard site, $9.00 for an electrical hookup site, add $1.00 for a "prime" site; 14-day limit; Milford Lake CoE Project Office (913) 238-5714.

Camp Notes: If the notion of hookups and 'prime' sites wrinkles your plaid flannel shirt, try School Creek, another CoE area, 4 miles north of here. School Creek has relatively cheap 'primitive' sites and not-so-good drinking water from a hand pump.

FANCY CREEK
Tuttle Creek State Park

Location: Northeast Kansas northwest of Manhattan.

Access: From Kansas State Highway 16 at milepost 1 + .6 (1.6 miles east of the junction of U.S. 77 and Kansas State Highways 16 & 378 near the community of Randolph, 0.1 mile west of the Highway 16/Blue River Bridge), turn north onto the paved park access road and continue for 1.2 miles; continue ahead 0.3 mile to the electrical hookup section, or turn right for 0.25 mile to the full hookup ("trailer park") and standard camping areas.

Facilities: 36 designated campsites, including 12 with full hookups and 24 with electrical hookups, plus standard camping, in 3 areas; sites vary from small to medium+, with minimal to fairly good separation; parking pads are paved or gravel, medium-length, wide straight-ins; a little additional leveling may be required; good-sized, grassy tent areas; fireplaces or barbecue grills; some firewood is available for gathering nearby; water at some sites and at several faucets; restrooms with showers; holding tank disposal station; gas and camper supplies in Randolph.

Activities & Attractions: Swimming beach; hiking trail; fishing; boating; boat launch.

Natural Features: Located along the west shore of Tuttle Creek Lake, an impoundment on the Big Blue River; campground vegetation consists of grass and moderately dense, large hardwoods; elevation 1200'.

Season, Fees & Phone: Mid-April to October; please see Appendix for standard Kansas state park fees and reservation information; 14 day limit; park office (913) 539-7941.

Camp Notes: Camping (of sorts) is also available in the Randolph area of the state park, at the *east* end of the Blue River Bridge. But unless you're a hermit on the lam, (or if by some chance the facilities have been significantly improved in recent months) you probably won't want to spend much time over there. Fancy Creek is fine.

STOCKDALE
Tuttle Creek Lake/Corps of Engineers Park

Location: Northeast Kansas northwest of Manhattan.

Access: From U.S. Highway 24 at milepost 305 + .2 (11 miles north of Manhattan, 3 miles southeast of the junction of U.S. Highways 24 & 77 and Kansas State Highway 177 east of Riley), turn north onto Riley County Road 895 and proceed 1.6 miles to Riley County Road 396; turn east (right) onto County Road 396 and continue for 2.7 miles, then turn left into the campground. **Alternate Access:** From the junction of U.S. 24 & 77, Kansas Highway 177 and County Road 396, proceed east on County Road 396 for 6.3 miles to the campground.

Facilities: 10 campsites; sites are small, with little in the way of separation; parking pads are short, gravel straight-ins which will probably require additional leveling; medium-sized, sloped tent areas; fire rings, plus several barbecue grills; some firewood may be available for gathering in the vicinity; water at a central faucet; restrooms with showers, (accessible via steps at the upper end of the campground, or by driving up the hill); auxiliary vaults; holding tank disposal station; gravel driveway; limited supplies in Riley.

Activities & Attractions: Fishing; boating; paved boat launch.

Natural Features: Located on a hillside near the mouth of Mill Creek inlet on the west shore of Tuttle Creek Lake; the campground is ringed by medium to tall hardwoods and a few bushy pines and junipers; elevation 1200'.

Season, Fees & Phone: April to October; no fee (subject to change); 14 day limit; Tuttle Creek Lake CoE Project Office (913) 539-8511.

Camp Notes: Where else around here can you get a free campsite with showers? (Knock on wood!). The first of the above access instructions will get you here faster from Manhattan; the alternate method is quicker if approaching from the north or west. This inlet--bordered by hills covered with tall grass, flowers, trees, and teeming with waterfowl--is really scenic.

TUTTLE CREEK COVE
Tuttle Creek Lake/Corps of Engineers Park

Location: Northeast Kansas northwest of Manhattan.

Access: From U.S. Highway 24 at milepost 311 +.3 (5 miles north of Manhattan, 10 miles southeast of the junction of U.S. Highways 24 & 77 near Riley), turn north onto Riley County Road 897S (paved), proceed 0.15 mile, then turn west/northwest (left) and continue for 3.5 miles to the campground; sites are situated along the next 0.6 mile of roadway (turnaround loop at the far end).

Facilities: 24 campsites; sites are medium to large, with fair to very good separation; parking pads are gravel, short to medium-length straight-ins, plus a couple of long pull-throughs; most pads will probably require additional leveling; large, but generally sloped, tent areas; fire rings; some collectable firewood may be available in the area; water at a central faucet; restrooms, plus auxiliary vault facilities; paved roadway, gravel driveways; complete supplies and services are available in Manhattan.

Activities & Attractions: Swimming beach; fishing; boat launch.

Natural Features: Located along the south and west shores of Tuttle Creek Cove on the west side of Tuttle Creek Lake, in the northern Flint Hills region; most sites are fairly well sheltered by large hardwoods, others are in the open; dead trees left standing in the water as fish attractors fill a portion of the cove; bordered by grass-covered, partly timbered hills; elevation 1200'.

Season, Fees & Phone: April to October; no fee (subject to change); 14 day limit; Tuttle Creek Lake CoE Project Office (913) 539-8511.

Camp Notes: The camping here is pretty basic; but it's fairly remote, there's elbow room, the vistas of the main body of the lake from the hilltops are quite good, and it's free. If you like sailboats, the marina across the cove has lots of them to watch. (Judging by the signs posted along the road, Tuttle Creek Cove might be a popular area for keggers and other entertainment sponsored by the local college crowd from KSU in Manhattan.)

RIVER POND
Tuttle Creek State Park

Location: Northeast Kansas north of Manhattan.

Access: From U.S. Highway 24 at milepost 311 +.9 (5 miles north of Manhattan, 10 miles southeast of the junction of U.S. Highways 24 & 77 east of Riley), turn east, then jog north onto a local access road; proceed north to the base of the dam, then east across the outlet, for a total of 1.2 miles; turn south (right) into the campground.

Facilities: 104 partial hookup campsites, plus a small, standard (tent camping) area; sites are medium-sized, level, with nominal to fairly good separation; most parking pads are medium to long, gravel pull-throughs; excellent tent-pitching possibilities in most sites; fire rings, plus barbecue grills in some units; b-y-o firewood; water at sites and at central faucets; restrooms with showers; holding tank disposal station; paved driveways; complete supplies and services are available in Manhattan.

Activities & Attractions: Swimming beach on River Pond (Tuttle Puddle?); boating and fishing on the river and on the lake.

Natural Features: Located on a huge, grass-covered, tree-dotted flat along the outlet channel for Tuttle Creek Lake; a large, backwater pond with an island lies just south of the campground; many sites are only lightly sheltered/shaded; the tent area is in a stand of large hardwoods at the southwest corner of the campground; elevation 1000'.

Season, Fees & Phone: Open all year, with limited services mid-October to mid-April; please see Appendix for standard Kansas state park fees and reservation information; 14 day limit; park office (913) 539-7941.

Camp Notes: Tent campers get a little break here because the tenting area is not only better-shaded, but it is the section that's closest to the shower building. (Are they trying to tell us canvasbacks something? Ed.) A few camp/picnic sites are also available at Spillway, an area just northeast of River Pond, at the southeast corner of the lake itself.

CANNING CREEK
Council Grove Lake/Corps of Engineers Park

Location: East-central Kansas northwest of Emporia.

Access: From Kansas State Highways 57 & 177 at a point 1.8 miles north of Council Grove, 27 miles south of Interstate 70 Exit 313 at Manhattan), turn west/southwest onto the main project access road; proceed 1.4 miles (across the dam) to a point just west of the project office; continue around the south end of the lake for 2 miles to a point just west of the Canning Creek bridge; turn north (right), and continue for 0.9 mile to the campground. **Alternate Access:** From U.S. Highway 56 (Main Street) at a point 0.2 mile west of midtown Council Grove, turn north onto North Mission Street and proceed 1.4 miles north/northwest to the project office; continue as above.

Facilities: 55 campsites, including 16 with electrical hookups, in 2, figure-8 loops; sites are medium-sized, basically level, with nominal to fairly good separation; parking pads are gravel, short straight-ins or long pull-throughs; adequate tent space; ramadas (sun shelters) in most units; barbecue grills; b-y-o firewood is suggested; water at central faucets; restrooms with showers; holding tank disposal station; paved driveways; adequate supplies and services are available in Council Grove.

Activities & Attractions: Tallgrass Day Trail, 2.2 mile loop; swimming beach; fishing; boating; amphitheater.

Natural Features: Located on the west shore of Council Grove Lake at the mouth of long, narrow, Canning Creek Inlet; most sites have light to ample natural shelter/shade provided by an assortment of evergreens and hardwoods; elevation 1300'.

Season, Fees & Phone: May to October; $7.00 for a standard site, $9.00 for an electrical hookup site; 14 day limit; Council Grove Lake CoE Project Office (316) 767-6612.

Camp Notes: There are plenty of nice lakeside sites here, and plenty of natural shelter--although most campsites have a ramada for good measure, anyway. Try the trail.

NEOSHO
Council Grove Lake/Corps of Engineers Park

Location: East-central Kansas northwest of Emporia.

Access: From Kansas State Highways 57 & 177 at a point 1.8 miles north of Council Grove, 27 miles south of Interstate 70 Exit 313 at Manhattan), turn west/southwest onto the main project access road; proceed 1.4 miles (across the dam) to a point just west of the project office; turn north (right) into Neosho #1, or continue west for 0.5 mile to Neosho #2 or 0.8 mile to Neosho #4. **Alternate Access:** From U.S. Highway 56 (Main Street) at a point 0.2 mile west of midtown Council Grove, turn north onto North Mission Street and proceed 1.4 miles north/north-west to the project office; continue as above.

Facilities: 30 campsites in 3 sections; sites are generally medium-sized, slightly sloped, with nominal to good spacing and visual separation; parking pads are mostly short to medium-length, gravel straight-ins; medium to large tent areas; barbecue grills; b-y-o firewood is recommended; water at central faucets; vault facilities; paved/gravel driveways; adequate supplies and services are available in Council Grove; elevation .

Activities & Attractions: Boating; boat launch; fishing; nature trail.

Natural Features: Located on the southwest shore of Council Grove Lake; campground vegetation consists primarily of grass and medium-dense hardwoods; elevation 1300'.

Season, Fees & Phone: Open all year, with reduced services and no fee, October to April; $4.00; 14 day limit; Council Grove Lake CoE Project Office (316) 767-6612.

Camp Notes: This camp was named for the great river whose course has been idled by the dam. Note that the lake is basically V-shaped, the result of the damming action on a pair of streams--the Neosho River from the northwest and Munkers Creek from the north. A 3-mile-long peninsula intervenes between the two arms of the V. Council Grove claims the title of "Birthplace of the Santa Fe Trail".

RICHEY COVE SOUTH
Council Grove Lake/Corps of Engineers Park

Location: East-central Kansas northwest of Emporia.

Access: From Kansas State Highways 57 & 177 at a point 2.8 miles north of Council Grove, 26 miles south of Interstate 70 Exit 313 at Manhattan), turn west into Richey Cove South #2 (the primary camping area); or at a point 0.2 mile south of #2, turn west into Richey Cove South #1.

Facilities: 62 campsites, including 48 sites with electrical hookups in Unit #2, and 14 semi-developed sites (a few with electrical hookups) in Unit #1; sites are medium-sized, reasonably level, with fair to fairly good separation; most parking pads are long, gravel straight-ins; adequate space for a large tent in most sites; some sites have small ramadas (sun shelters); barbecue grills; b-y-o firewood; water at central faucets; restrooms with showers, plus auxiliary vaults in Unit #2; vaults only in Unit #1; holding tank disposal station; paved driveways; adequate supplies and services are available in Council Grove.

Activities & Attractions: Swimming beach; nature trail; boating; boat launch; fishing.

Natural Features: Located on the east shore of Council Grove Lake; campground vegetation consists of light to moderately dense hardwoods on a grassy surface; the lake is rimmed by gently sloping hills; elevation 1300'.

Season, Fees & Phone: May to October; $4.00 for a standard site, $6.00-$9.00 for an electrical hookup site; 14 day limit; Council Grove Lake CoE Project Office (316) 767-6612.

Camp Notes: If your camping hardware consists of a maxi motorhome towing a triple-axle trailer, chances are the combo will fit into some of the parking spaces here, no sweat. The majority of the campsites have a lake view, and there are some neat spots out at the end of a long, level, wooded point.

HILLSBORO COVE
Marion Lake/Corps of Engineers Park

Location: Central Kansas southeast of Salina.

Access: From U.S. Highway 56 at milepost 296 +.8 (5 miles west of Marion, 31 miles east of McPherson), turn north then immediately east (right) onto a paved access road; continue east, parallel to the highway, for 0.5 mile to the campground entrance.

Facilities: 51 campsites in 2 sections; sites are medium to large, level, with fair to fairly good separation; most parking pads are gravel, medium to super long, straight-ins; several units have long pull-throughs; good-sized, grassy tent spots; ramadas (sun shelters) in some sites; barbecue grills and fire rings; b-y-o firewood; water at several faucets; vault facilities; holding tank disposal station; paved main driveways, gravel sub-drives; gas and groceries in Marion; quite adequate supplies and services are available in McPherson.

Activities & Attractions: Fishing for crappie, bass, catfish, and some walleye; boating; boat launch.

Natural Features: Located at the southwest corner of Marion Lake, a flood control impoundment on the Cottonwood River; campground vegetation consists of expanses of grass dotted with large hardwoods and evergreens; elevation 1400'.

Season, Fees & Phone: Mid-April to mid-October; $7.00; 14 day limit; Marion Lake CoE Project Office (316) 382-2114.

Camp Notes: The overall atmosphere here is one of space and openness, and there are good views in several directions from most campsites. Although you can see many of your neighbors, there's still enough elbow room between sites. For a little more in the way of natural shade (but also more company) the CoE camp on the east shore, Cottonwood Point, may be worth considering. Hillsboro Cove is rarely more than half-filled.

COTTONWOOD POINT
Marion Lake/Corps of Engineers Park

Location: Central Kansas southeast of Salina.

Access: From U.S. Highway 56 at milepost 297 +.9 (4.5 miles west of Marion, 32 miles east of McPherson), turn north onto the (paved) project access road and proceed north 0.4 mile; continue northeast across the dam to the project office for 1.6 miles; bear north at the project office for another 0.95 mile, then turn west onto a gravel/paved access road for a final 0.5 mile to the entrance station and the campground. (Note: the final westerly turnoff to Cottonwood Point may not be clearly signed, and could be overshot, particularly in dim light.

Facilities: 92 electrical hookup campsites; sites are medium to large, basically level, with nominal to good separation; parking pads are gravel, short to very long straight-ins; large tent areas; most sites have ramadas (sun shelters); concrete pads for table areas in some units; barbecue grills or fire rings; b-y-o firewood; water at central faucets; restrooms with showers; holding tank disposal station; paved or gravel driveways; gas and groceries in Marion; quite ad-equate supplies and services are available in McPherson.

Activities & Attractions: Swimming beach; fishing; boating; boating launch.

Natural Features: Located on the east shore of Marion Lake; campground vegetation consists of mown lawns, light to moderately dense hardwoods and some evergreens; many nice waterfront sites; elevation 1400'.

Season, Fees & Phone: Mid-April to mid-October; $9.00; 14 day limit; Marion Lake CoE Project Office (316) 382-2114.

Camp Notes: Some of the campsites which are farther from the water's edge may only have a glimpse of the lake through the trees--but they are among the roomiest to be found anywhere in the region's CoE campgrounds.

Kansas 34

BOULDER BLUFF
El Dorado State Park

Location: Southeast Kansas northeast of Wichita.

Access: From the junction of U.S. Highways 54 & 77 in midtown El Dorado, travel north on U.S. 77 for 1 mile to 12th Avenue; turn east and proceed 2.1 mile to the park entrance; turn north (left) and drive 2.9 miles to the first pair of loops (Camping Area 2) and the restroom/shower building, on the right side of the roadway; or continue ahead for 0.9 mile to the northernmost loop (Camping Area 1). **Alternate Access:** From Interstate 35 (Kansas Turnpike) Exit 76, proceed southeast on a paved access road 1.7 miles to a secondary park entrance, then drive north 1.3 miles to the first loops and proceed as above.

Facilities: 150 campsites in 3 loops, plus several other areas for open camping; sites are small to medium-sized, with nil to fair separation; parking pads are medium to long, framed, gravel straight-ins which may require a little additional leveling; adequate space for a large tent in most units; barbecue grills; b-y-o firewood; water at several faucets; central restrooms with showers, plus auxiliary vault facilities; holding tank disposal station, 3 miles south; paved driveways; quite adequate supplies and services are available in El Dorado.

Activities & Attractions: Fishing; boating; boat launch and dock adjacent to the northernmost loop; playground.

Natural Features: Located on several points of land along the west shore of El Dorado Lake; 2 loops are on open, grassy flats or gentle slopes, but the middle loop is in a grove of large hardwoods; breezy; elevation 1400'.

Season, Fees & Phone: April to October; please see Appendix for standard Kansas state park fees; 14 day limit; park office (316) 321-7180.

Camp Notes: Many of the campsites provide distant views for several miles in almost every direction. Since many sites are right along the edge of the water, boating up to within arm's reach of your tent flap is possible.

Kansas 35

WALNUT RIVER
El Dorado State Park

Location: Southeast Kansas northeast of Wichita.

Access: From the junction of U.S. Highways 54 & 77 in midtown El Dorado, travel north on U.S. 77 for 1 mile to 12th Avenue; turn east and proceed 2.1 mile to the park entrance; turn north (left) and continue for 0.7 mile; turn northwest (left) and drive 0.2 mile to Loop 3; Loops 1 and 2 are within 0.4 mile "around the corner" beyond Loop 3.

Facilities: 176 campsites, including 50 with full hookups and 102 with partial hookups, in 3 loops; sites are medium-sized with minimal to nominal separation; most parking pads are long, gravel straight-ins, and some are double-wide; a small amount of additional leveling may be required in some sites; large, grassy tent areas; barbecue grills; b-y-o firewood; water at faucets throughout; restrooms with showers; holding tank disposal station; paved driveways; quite adequate supplies and services are available in El Dorado.

Activities & Attractions: Fishing, boating on the lake; large swimming beach on the lagoon; playground; footbridges to the beach; amphitheater.

Natural Features: Located around the perimeter of large, grassy flats along Walnut River, the outlet stream for El Dorado Lake; most campsites are a few yards from the water's edge; a lagoon lies between Loops 1 & 2; quite a few sites are in the open, but many have adequate to excellent shelter/shade provided by large hardwoods; the campground area is bordered by very dense woods; elevation 1400'.

Season, Fees & Phone: Open all year, with limited services mid-October to April; please see Appendix for standard Kansas state park fees and reservation information; 14-day limit; park office (316) 321-7180.

Camp Notes: Even though the immense dam looms over the campground, it's so well "camouflaged" by well-maintained, mown grass that you'll barely notice it. Loop 3, with the full-hookups, is usually open to some extent all year.

Kansas 36

BLUESTEM POINT
El Dorado State Park

Location: Southeast Kansas northeast of Wichita.

Access: From U.S. Highway 54 at milepost 257 +.5 (5 miles east of El Dorado, 25 miles west of Eureka), turn north onto Kansas State Highway 177 and proceed 4.5 miles; turn west onto a paved access road to the entrance station and continue for 0.2 mile to the 7 camping areas.

Facilities: 468 campsites, including 203 with partial hookups and 50 with full hookups, in 7 loops; sites are generally small and closely spaced; parking pads are gravel, medium to long straight-ins or pull-throughs, and may require some additional leveling; large, grassy tent spots; designated backpack camping area near the tip of the point; barbecue grills; b-y-o firewood; water at many sites and at central faucets; restrooms with showers; holding tank disposal stations; paved driveways; quite adequate supplies and services are available in El Dorado.

Activities & Attractions: Boating; fishing; swimming beach; bathhouse; playgrounds; foot trails.

Natural Features: Located along grassy, tree-dotted slopes on Bluestem point, a major promontory on the east shore of El Dorado Lake; scattered hardwoods and pines provide shelter/shade for some campsites, particularly in the backpacking area; hundreds of (deceased) trees have been left standing in the lake near this shore to improve the fish habitat; elevation 1400'.

Season, Fees & Phone: April to October; please see Appendix for standard Kansas state park fees and reservation information; 14 day limit; park office (316) 321-7180.

Camp Notes: Bluestem Point's campsites are, for the most part, quite exposed to the elements. But there's an advantage to that: in the heat of midsummer, the prevailing breeze off the lake helps keep things a little cooler here than at the park's other campgrounds.

KANSAS
Bluestem Prairie Northeast
Please refer to the Kansas map in the Appendix

Kansas 37

PERRY
Perry State Park

Location: Northeast Kansas northeast of Topeka.

Access: From U.S. Highway 24 at milepost 378 +.6 (6 miles west of Perry, 8 miles east of Topeka), turn north onto Kansas State Highway 237 and proceed 5.7 miles to a point just past the park office; turn right and continue for 0.1 mile to 1 mile southeast to the 5 principal camping areas, all on the left side or at the end of the campground access road.

Facilities: 205 campsites, including 78 with partial hookups, in 5 areas, plus open camping; sites are generally small and close together; parking pads are mostly gravel, medium to long pull-throughs or short to medium-length straight-ins; additional leveling will be required in most units; adequate, though sloped, tent spaces; barbecue grills; b-y-o firewood; water at sites and at central faucets; restrooms with showers; holding tank disposal stations; gravel or paved driveways; limited to adequate supplies in Perry; complete supplies and services are available in Topeka.

Activities & Attractions: Fishing; boating; boat launch; swimming beach & bathhouse; equestrian trails.

Natural Features: Located on the west shore of Perry Lake; densely wooded hills and ravines border most of the camping areas; majority of the standard sites and about half of the hookup sites have lake views; elevation 1000'.

Season, Fees & Phone: Available all year, with limited services mid-October to April; please see Appendix for standard Kansas state park fees and reservation information; 14 day limit; park office (913) 289-3449.

Camp Notes: Inasmuch as it's so close to the state capitol, this is a predictably well-used (well-worn) park. If you don't need a lake view, but just want the water within walking distance, a secluded tent camping area with restrooms and showers is located on the northwest corner of the park. Take a *left* just *before* the park office. (See above access.)

Kansas 38

OLD TOWN
Perry Lake/Corps of Engineers Park

Location: Northeast Kansas northeast of Topeka.

Access: From U.S. Highway 24 at milepost 383 +.1 (on the east edge of the community of Perry, 3 miles west of the junction of U.S. 24 & 59 northwest of Lawrence, 18 miles east of Topeka), turn north onto a paved road and travel 12 miles to Kansas State Highway 92; turn west onto Highway 92 and proceed 1 mile; turn south (left) for 0.15 mile to the main camping area.

Facilities: 147 campsites; sites are small to medium-sized, with nominal separation; parking pads are medium to long, gravel straight-ins; a little additional leveling may be required; adequate space for large tents; barbecue grills; some firewood is available for gathering in the surrounding area; water at central faucets; restrooms with showers; holding tank disposal station; paved driveways; limited to adequate supplies and services are available in Perry.

Activities & Attractions: Fishing primarily for crappie and catfish, also bass, and walleye (best in spring); boating; boat launch; playground; closest campground to the north trailhead for Perry Lake Trail, a designated National Recreational Trail, 2 miles southwest.

Natural Features: Located at the mouth of a bay on the east shore of Perry Lake; most sites have at least some shelter/shade provided by scattered large hardwoods on a grassy surface; elevation 1000'.

Season, Fees & Phone: May to October; $7.00; 14 day limit; Perry Lake CoE Project Office (913) 597-5144.

Camp Notes: The shoreline of Perry Lake provides a little more in the way of scenic interest than some of the other lakes in eastern Kansas. The hills and bluffs seem a little higher and more forested. For a good view of the surroundings, you might check out the simple secondary camping area on a hill just north of the principal camp, on the opposite side of Highway 92. There are showers up there as well.

Kansas 39

SLOUGH CREEK
Perry Lake/Corps of Engineers Park

Location: Northeast Kansas northeast of Topeka.

Access: From U.S. Highway 24 at milepost 383 +.1 (on the east edge of the community of Perry, 3 miles west of the junction of U.S. 24 & 59 northwest of Lawrence, 18 miles east of Topeka), turn north onto a paved road and travel 7.5 miles; turn south/southwest onto a paved access road for 1.7 miles; turn left and continue for 0.4 mile to the first loop; the others are along the next mile, all on the left.

Facilities: 270 campsites in 5 loops; sites are medium-sized, with minimal to fair separation; parking pads are short to medium-length, gravel straight-ins, and many are extra wide; additional leveling will be required for about half of the pads; adequate space for a tent on a grassy surface or on parking pad extensions; fire rings; limited firewood is available for gathering in the general vicinity, b-y-o to be sure; restrooms with showers, plus auxiliary vault facilities; holding tank disposal station; paved driveways; limited to adequate supplies and services are available in Perry.

Activities & Attractions: Fishing; boating; boat launches; hiking trail along the shore; day use area.

Natural Features: Located at the mouth of a long, narrow inlet (Big Slough Creek) on the east shore of Perry Lake; campsites are situated along a level shore or on the slope above the shore; campground vegetation consists of grass and scattered hardwoods; many sites are unsheltered; elevation 1000'.

Season, Fees & Phone: May to October; $7.00 for a standard site, $9.00 for an electrical hookup site, add $1.00 for a "prime" site; 14 day limit; Perry Lake CoE Project Office (913) 597-5144.

Camp Notes: There are some really nice campsites here, particularly in the Limestone Cove Loop (the one farthest from the entrance). However, you also get a great shot of the bare rock face of the dam. An extra buck is extracted for the "prime" sites--generally the ones closest to the lake. (Maybe it cost more to build these campsites? Ed.)

Kansas 40

SHAWNEE LAKE
Shawnee County Park

Location: Northeast Kansas southeast of Topeka.

Access: From Kansas Turnpike Exit 182 (the East Topeka Exit), proceed east on SE 21st Street for 0.1 mile to Croco Road; turn south (right) onto Croco Road and continue for 2.8 miles (past the huge water tower, to the second park access road); turn west/southwest (right) to the Eastedge Road-Croco Road entrance for a final 0.75 mile to the campground. **Alternate Access:** From Interstate 70 (non-toll segment) enroute from West Topeka, take the Rice Road-SE 21st Street Exit, just east of milepost 365.

Facilities: 157 campsites with partial hookups in a long-term area and a short-term area, plus a dozen tent sites; sites are basically level, small and close together; most parking pads are gravel, short, extra-wide straight-ins; tents are permitted only in a somewhat sloped, grassy section at the northeast corner; b-y-o barbecue grill and charcoal; water at sites and at central faucets; restrooms with showers; holding tank disposal station; paved driveways; complete supplies and services are available within a mile.

Activities & Attractions: Small swimming beach; playground; golf course; fishing; limited boating.

Natural Features: Located along the east shore of Shawnee Lake; most sites receive some shelter/shade from large hardwoods; expansive, mown grass 'infield'; elevation 1000'.

Season, Fees & Phone: Open all year, with limited services and fees October to May; $5.00 for a tent site, $6.00 for a hookup site; 30-day rates are available; (note that fees include a $1.00 surcharge for non-county residents; county residents subtract $1.00); Shawnee County Parks and Recreation Department, Topeka, (913) 267-2000.

Camp Notes: For a park located so close to a major city, this one is entitled to good grades. Access is one-way-in-one-way-out, so there's no through traffic. A handy place to camp when you come to town to confer with the governor.

Kansas 41

CLINTON
Clinton State Park

Location: East-central Kansas west of Lawrence.

Access: From the junction of U.S. Highway 59 and Clinton Parkway in midtown Lawrence, travel west on Clinton Parkway (4-lane, divided) for 4.2 miles to a "T" intersection; turn north (right) onto a paved road for 0.2 mile; turn west (left) onto the state park road and proceed 0.9 mile to the park entrance station; continue for 0.9 mile to Camp 1, 1.1 mile to Camp 2, or 1.7 miles to Camp 3.

Facilities: 398 designated campsites, including about half with partial hookups, plus open camping, in 3 loops; sites are small to medium-sized, with minimal separation; parking pads are gravel or grass straight-ins; a little additional leveling will be required in some units; excellent tent areas; walk-in sites at the east end of Camp 1; barbecue grills; b-y-o firewood; water at sites and at central faucets; restrooms with showers; holding tank disposal stations; paved driveways; complete supplies and services are available in Lawrence.

Activities & Attractions: Swimming beach; fishing; boat launches and docks; marina; playgrounds; cross-country ski trail.

Natural Features: Located on expansive, gently rolling flats on the north shore of Clinton Lake; campground vegetation consists of acres of tree-dotted grass bordered by large hardwoods; some sites have lake views; elevation 900'.

Season, Fees & Phone: Available all year, with limited services November to April; please see Appendix for standard Kansas state park fees and reservation information; 14 day limit; park office (913) 842-8562.

Camp Notes: Camps 1 & 3 are very similar "full service" campgrounds, while Camp 2 has open camping with limited services. Although the campsites themselves aren't the most spacious units in Kansas, there's still plenty of room to roam in this park. (No, the lake and state park weren't named for Bill C. from Arkansas.)

Kansas 42

OUTLET
Clinton Lake/Corps of Engineers Park

Location: East-central Kansas west of Lawrence.

Access: From the junction of U.S. Highway 59 and Clinton Parkway in midtown Lawrence, travel west on Clinton Parkway (4-lane, divided) for 4.2 miles to a "T" intersection; turn south (left) onto a paved road and proceed 0.45 mile to a point just at the north end of the dam; turn east (left) and continue for 0.2 mile down to the campground.

Facilities: 30 campsites; sites are medium to large, level, with a little visual separation; parking pads are gravel, mostly medium to long straight-ins; plenty of tent space; barbecue grills; b-y-o firewood; water at a central faucet; vault facilities; gravel driveway; complete supplies and services are available in Lawrence.

Activities & Attractions: Fishing for walleye, northern pike, largemouth and smallmouth bass, striped bass, crappie, bluegill and channel cats; boating; nearest boat launch on the lake is in Clinton State Park, 2 miles northwest.

Natural Features: Located on a plain along the outlet channel just below Clinton Dam on the Wakarusa River; campground vegetation consists of mown grass dotted with small hardwoods and evergreens; surrounded by tallgrass fields and patches of woods; elevation 900'.

Season, Fees & Phone: Open all year, with limited services October to April; no fee (subject to change); 14 day limit; Clinton Lake CoE Project Office and Information Center(913) 843-7665.

Camp Notes: Clinton Lake is the result of one of the newer flood control projects in Kansas. A lot of campers say it's one of the prettier lakes as well. Of all the Kansas lakes which offer camping, Clinton is the one which is handiest to the services of a major community. (If you're a confirmed and conditioned walker or a jogger, you may prefer to get to town via the paved sidewalk which parallels Clinton Parkway all the way to Lawrence.)

Kansas 43

ROCKHAVEN
Clinton Lake/Corps of Engineers Park

Location: East-central Kansas southwest of Lawrence.

Access: From U.S. Highway 56 at milepost 420 +.3 (8 miles east of Overbrook, 12 miles west of Baldwin), turn north onto Douglas County Road 1029 (paved) and travel 6.5 miles to a "T" intersection; turn east (right) onto Douglas County Road 458 and proceed 1.5 miles; turn north (left) onto a gravel road (700E) and continue for 1.1 miles to the campground. **Alternate Access:** From U.S. Highway 59 at a point 3.5 miles south of midtown Lawrence, turn west onto County Road 458 and proceed west, then south, then west again for 9 miles to the Rochkaven turnoff; turn north, as above.

Facilities: 15 campsites; sites are medium-sized, level, with no visual separation; parking pads are medium-length, gravel straight-ins; large, grassy tent areas; barbecue grills; some firewood may be available for gathering in the surrounding area, b-y-o to be sure; water at central faucets; vault facilities; gravel driveway; gas and camper supplies in Clinton, 7 miles northwest; complete supplies in Lawrence.

Activities & Attractions: Hiking trail and equestrian trail (parallel to each other) along the shoreline; hitching rails; fishing.

Natural Features: Located on a grassy flat bordered by woodland; sites are situated around the perimeter of the flat and most have some shelter/shade provided by large hardwoods; the south shore of Clinton Lake is a couple-hundred yards north of the campground, but not in view; elevation 900'.

Season, Fees & Phone: Open all year, with limited services, October to May; no fee (subject to change); 14 day limit; Clinton Lake CoE Project Office and Information Center(913) 843-7665.

Camp Notes: Although the stock-handling facilities aren't elaborate, this is still a favorite spot with horse owners. It is also a good area if your requirements are simple and you want a somewhat secluded, free place to camp.

Kansas 44

BLOOMINGTON
Clinton Lake/Corps of Engineers Park

Location: East-central Kansas southwest of Lawrence.

Access: From U.S. Highway 56 at milepost 420 + .3 (8 miles east of Overbrook, 12 miles west of Baldwin), turn north onto Douglas County Road 1029 (paved) and travel 6.5 miles to a "T" intersection; turn west (left) onto Douglas County Road 458 and proceed 1.7 miles to Douglas County Road 6; turn northeast (right) onto Road 6 and continue for 3.6 miles (through the hamlet of Clinton) to Bloomington; turn left to the Cedar Ridge area; turn right to the Hickory, Walnut and Oak areas.

Facilities: 384 campsites, majority with electrical or electrical & water hookups; sites are small to medium-sized, with minimal to fair separation; parking pads vary from long, level, pull-throughs in Cedar Ridge, to sloped, medium-length straight-ins in Hickory & Walnut; large, grassy tent areas, but may be sloped; barbecue grills; b-y-o firewood; water at sites and at central faucets; restrooms with showers; holding tank disposal station; paved or gravel driveways; gas and camper supplies in Clinton.

Activities & Attractions: Fishing for crappie, northern pike, walleye, largemouth and smallmouth bass, etc; boat launches; swimming beach; playground; camping museum.

Natural Features: Located at the tip of a peninsula on the southwest shore of Clinton Lake; Cedar Ridge is level, grassy and dotted with small hardwoods; Hickory and Walnut are sloped, grassy, with somewhat larger trees; shelter/shade varies from very little to fairly good; dense woodlands in the surrounding area; elevation 900'.

Season, Fees & Phone: May to October; $7.00 for a standard site, $9.00 for a hookup site; 14 day limit; Clinton Lake CoE Project Office and Information Center(913) 843-7665.

Camp Notes: This recreation complex may very well be the CoE showplace of eastern Kansas. There's *lots* of room to wander on acres and acres of grassy slopes.

Kansas 45

WOLF CREEK
Pomona Lake/Corps of Engineers Park

Location: East-central Kansas south of Topeka.

Access: From Kansas State Highway 268 at milepost 6 + .05 (6 miles east of the junction of Highway 268, State Highway 31 and U.S. 75 just north of Lyndon, 11 miles west of Pomona, 17 miles west of Ottawa), turn north onto a paved local road and travel 2.3 miles (across the dam) to a point just at the north end the dam; turn west (left) and proceed on a paved road that winds around the north side of a small bay and across a causeway for 1.6 miles (the last 0.2 mile is gravel); turn west (left) into the main camping area, 0.3 mile beyond the entrance.

Facilities: 83 campsites, including 31 with electrical hookups, in the main area, plus another 50 in an adjacent free use area; sites are fairly small, basically level, with nominal to fair separation; parking pads are medium-length, gravel straight-ins; large, grassy tent spots; fire rings and barbecue grills; b-y-o firewood is recommended; water at central faucets; restrooms with showers, plus auxiliary vaults; holding tank disposal station; paved main driveway, gravel driveways; nearest supplies are in Lyndon or Pomona.

Activities & Attractions: Fishing; boating; boat launch; huge, grassy baseball field; playground.

Natural Features: Located on the northeast shore of Pomona Lake near the mouth of a large 'arm'; campground vegetation consists of expanses of mown grass dotted with large hardwoods and evergreens; most sites are sheltered, others are on a semi-open, grassy beach; elevation 1000'.

Season, Fees & Phone: Open all year, with limited services, October to May; $7.00 for a standard site, $9.00 for a hookup site; 14 day limit; Pomona Lake CoE Project Office (913) 453-2202.

Camp Notes: If this spot (which rarely is more than half full) isn't remote enough for you, try the 110-Mile Campground, on a forested point on the west side of the arm, 4 gravel miles west. 110-Mile has 25 sites and an equestrian trail.

MICHIGAN VALLEY
Pomona Lake/Corps of Engineers Park

Location: East-central Kansas south of Topeka.

Access: From Kansas State Highway 268 at milepost 6 +.05 (6 miles east of the junction of Highway 268, State Highway 31 and U.S. 75 just north of Lyndon, 11 miles west of Pomona, 17 miles west of Ottawa), turn north onto a paved local road and proceed 2.3 miles (across the dam) to a point just at the north end the dam; turn west (left) then jog south and go down a paved access for 0.2 mile to the campground entrance.

Facilities: 96 campsites, including 60 with partial hookups, in 7 loops; sites are basically small to medium in size, level, with limited to fair visual separation; parking pads are gravel, medium to long straight-ins; enough space for a large tent in all sites; fire rings or barbecue grills; b-y-o firewood; water at sites and at central faucets; restrooms with showers; holding tank disposal station; paved main driveway, gravel loop driveways; limited supplies and services are available in Lyndon, also in Pomona.

Activities & Attractions: Fishing; boating; boat launch at a nearby marina; swimming beach; large playgrounds; short trail; amphitheater.

Natural Features: Located on the northeast shore of Pomona Lake; campground vegetation consists of expanses of mown grass dotted with small to medium-sized hardwoods that provide limited to moderate shelter/shade for nearly all sites; elevation 1000'.

Season, Fees & Phone: Open all year, with limited services, October to May; $7.00 for a standard site, $9.00 for a partial hookup site; 14 day limit; Pomona Lake CoE Project Office (913) 453-2202.

Camp Notes: Most campsites have at least a glimpse of this large lake, and the shore is within a few minutes' stroll from anywhere. The standard sites generally enjoy somewhat better views. Of the campgrounds on Pomona Lake, Michigan Valley has the most "open" natural environment.

OUTLET
Pomona Lake/Corps of Engineers Park

Location: East-central Kansas south of Topeka.

Access: From Kansas State Highway 268 at milepost 6 +.05 (6 miles east of the junction of Highway 268 with State Highway 31 and U.S. 75 just north of Lyndon, 11 miles west of Pomona, 17 miles west of Ottawa), turn north onto a paved local road and proceed 0.75 mile to a point just past the information center and just before the dam; turn southeast (right) and go down a paved access road for 0.25 mile, then turn right into the campground.

Facilities: 36 campsites with partial hookups, in 3 small sections; sites tend to be small and closely spaced; parking pads are gravel, medium to long, straight-ins; about half of the pads will require a little additional leveling; good-sized, grassy tent areas, though they may be slightly sloped; fire rings; b-y-o firewood is recommended; water at sites; restrooms with showers; holding tank disposal station; paved driveways; limited supplies and services are available in Lyndon, also in Pomona.

Activities & Attractions: Fishing; boating; boat launch on the lake; large playground; information center.

Natural Features: Located on a densely wooded hillside above the south bank of 110-Mile Creek (the outlet stream for Pomona Lake) below Pomona Dam; campground vegetation consists of lots of grass and a variety of mature hardwoods that provide ample to excellent shelter/shade for most sites; elevation 900'.

Season, Fees & Phone: Open all year, with limited services November to April; $9.00 for a hookup site; 14 day limit; Pomona Lake CoE Project Office (913) 453-2202.

Camp Notes: A number of campsites here overlook the river, but otherwise the views are somewhat restricted. If you travel to Pomona Lake early or late in the season, Outlet, and nearby Pomona State Park, offer your best chance of having a campsite with the tap water turned on.

Kansas 48

POMONA
Pomona State Park

Location: East-central Kansas south of Topeka.

Access: From Kansas State Highway 268 at milepost 4 +.5 (4.5 miles east of the junction of Highway 268, State Highway 31 and U.S. 75 just north of Lyndon, 9 miles west of Pomona, 19 miles west Of Ottawa), turn north onto Kansas State Highway 368 and proceed 1.2 miles to the park entrance station; the camping areas are left, right, and straight ahead from the entrance.

Facilities: 137 electrical hookup or full hookup campsites, in 7 "trailer courts", plus 2 standard camp loops; sites are generally medium-sized, with minimal to fair separation; parking pads are gravel, mostly long straight-ins, plus some long to super long pull-throughs; additional leveling will probably be required in most units; large, grassy, but usually sloped, tent spots; barbecue grills; b-y-o firewood; water at some sites and at central faucets; restrooms with showers; holding tank disposal stations; paved driveways; limited supplies and services in Lyndon, also Pomona.

Activities & Attractions: Boating; boat launches; marina; fishing for crappie, channel catfish, white bass, walleye, and the elusive 'wiper'; small swimming beach; playground.

Natural Features: Situated on the slightly sloping south shore of Pomona Lake; most sites are fairly well sheltered/shaded by large hardwoods, plus some bushy pines for variety; some lake views; elevation 1000'.

Season, Fees & Phone: Open all year, with limited services November to April; please see Appendix for standard Kansas state park fees and reservation information; 14 day limit; park office (913) 828-4933.

Camp Notes: If your camping vehicle is an 18-wheeler, one of the several super long (paved) parking pads in trailer court 1 should serve you well. Subjectively, the better campsites are on the east side of the park. This area is also called "Vassar" in some literature that's in current distribution.

Kansas 49

CARBOLYN
Pomona Lake/Corps of Engineers Park

Location: East-central Kansas south of Topeka.

Access: From U.S. Highway 75 at milepost 130 +.7 (4 miles north of Lyndon, 10 miles south of Carbondale, 21 miles south of Topeka), turn east onto a paved access road, then immediately jog north and continue north 0.3 mile, then east again for 0.1 mile to the campground entrance station, on the left side of the road; the first sites are 0.25 mile beyond the entrance.

Facilities: 31 campsites, most with electrical hookups; sites are generally small, level, and closely spaced; parking pads are medium-length, gravel straight-ins; adequate space for a large tent in most sites; fire rings; some firewood may be available for gathering, b-y-o is recommended; water at central faucets; restrooms with showers; holding tank disposal station; paved/gravel driveway; limited supplies and services are available in Lyndon and Carbondale.

Activities & Attractions: Boating; boat launch; fishing; weekend evening interpretive programs in summer; playground.

Natural Features: Located on a grassy, flat-topped, low ridge along the south bank of Dragoon Creek at the west tip of Pomona Lake; most sites have moderate to ample shelter/shade provided by a variety of hardwoods and a few pine; the campground is flanked by densely wooded ravines north and south; elevation 1000'.

Season, Fees & Phone: Open all year, with limited services, October to April; $7.00 for a standard site, $9.00 for an electrical hookup site; 14 day limit; Pomona Lake CoE Project Office (913) 453-2202.

Camp Notes: Carbolyn is the handiest to Topeka of the Pomona Lake camps. But, since it doesn't have lake views like the others in the area, it is often overlooked. Interestingly, in an apparent effort to maintain the spirit of local service, the Corps has coined the name of the campground from the two nearby communities.

TURKEY POINT
Melvern Lake/Corps of Engineers Park

Location: East-central Kansas east of Emporia.

Access: From U.S. Highway 75 at milepost 121 (8 miles north of Interstate 35 Exit 155, 5 miles south of Lyndon), turn west onto Kansas State Highway 278 and travel 3 miles to the end of 278 at the end of the pavement; continue on gravel for 3.7 miles, then another 0.15 mile on pavement; turn south (left) onto a paved access road and proceed south, then east, for 1.3 miles; turn south again (right turn this time) and continue for a final 0.7 mile to the west area; or continue ahead 0.6 mile to the east area.

Facilities: 69 campsites, including 15 with electrical hookups, in 2 sections; sites are small to medium-sized, with limited to fairly good separation; parking pads are medium-length, gravel straight-ins which will probably require some additional leveling; large, grassy, somewhat sloped tent areas; fire rings and barbecue grills; b-y-o firewood; water at central faucets; restrooms (H) with showers, plus auxiliary vaults; disposal stations; paved driveways; limited supplies and services in Melvern, 11 miles east, and in Lyndon.

Activities & Attractions: Fishing; boating; boat launch; small playgrounds.

Natural Features: Located on a hillside on the north shore of Melvern Lake; campground vegetation consists of mown grass, plus small to medium-sized hardwoods and evergreens which provide at least some shelter/shade in most sites; elevation 1100'.

Season, Fees & Phone: Available all year, with limited services October to May; $7.00 for a standard site, $9.00 for an electrical hookup site; 14 day limit; Melvern Lake CoE Project Office (913) 549-3414.

Camp Notes: There are many nice edgewater sites throughout this campground, (particularly the low-numbered sites in the east area) and the views are excellent. Turkey Point is the campground of choice at Melvern Lake if you prefer to leave civilization behind and still have a morning shower.

MELVERN
Melvern State Park

Location: East-central Kansas east of Emporia.

Access: From U.S. Highway 75 at milepost 121 (8 miles north of Interstate 35 Exit 155, 5 miles south of Lyndon), turn west onto Kansas State Highway 278 and travel 3 miles to the end of 278 at the end of the pavement; turn south (left) into the park entrance and continue for 1 mile on the main park road; turn west (right) and proceed 0.2 mile to the 5 camping areas.

Facilities: 202 designated campsites, including 127 with electrical-only hookups, and 75 with partial hookups, plus numerous other sites, in 5 loops; sites are generally smallish, with very little separation; parking pads are mostly medium to very long, gravel pull-throughs, plus some straight-ins; a little additional leveling will be required in most units; adequate space for a large tent in most sites; fire rings; b-y-o firewood; water at sites and at central faucets; restrooms with showers; holding tank disposal station; paved driveways; limited supplies and services in Melvern, 8 miles east, and in Lyndon.

Activities & Attractions: Fishing; boating; boat launches; swimming beach and bathhouse; amphitheater.

Natural Features: Located on a series of small ridges/hills on a point of land along the north shore of Melvern Lake; most campsites have minimal to nominal natural shelter/shade, except for those in a grove of large hardwoods in camp area 4; lake views from most sites; elevation 1100'.

Season, Fees & Phone: Open all year, with limited services mid-October to April; please see Appendix for standard Kansas state park fees and reservation information; 14-day limit; park office (913) 528-4900.

Camp Notes: If you don't need hookups and don't mind being some distance from the showers, there are several really nice, big camping/picnicking units along the east side of the park that can be camped-in, provided they're not reserved for day-trippers.

OUTLET
Melvern Lake/Corps of Engineers Park

Location: East-central Kansas east of Emporia.

Access: From the junction of U.S. Highway 75 at milepost 119 +.1 and Kansas State Highway 31 (6 miles north of Interstate 35 Exit 155, 7 miles south of Lyndon, 3 miles west of Melvern), turn west onto the recreation area access road; proceed 0.2 mile, turn right, proceed another 0.2 mile, turn right again, and continue for 0.4 mile (across the outlet of the lake) to the campground entrance.

Facilities: 150 campsites, including 61 with partial hookups and 89 with full hookups, in 3 loops; sites are small to medium-sized, with nominal to fair separation; parking pads are medium to long, level, gravel straight-ins or pull-throughs; terrific tenting opportunities; fire rings, plus barbecue grills in many units; b-y-o firewood; restrooms with showers; laundry rooms; water at sites and at central faucets; holding tank disposal station; paved driveways; limited supplies and services are available in Melvern and Lyndon.

Activities & Attractions: Boating, boat launch, fishing on Melvern Lake; designated swimming area; interpretive trail; primitive trail; small amphitheater; information center.

Natural Features: Located on a very large, grassy flat around the perimeter of a small lake along the Marais de Cygnes River just below Melvern Dam; most sites have some shelter/shade provided by hardwoods and a few evergreens; partially bordered by dense woodland; elevation 900'.

Season, Fees & Phone: Open all year, with limited services November to April; $10.00 for a partial hookup site, $11.00 for a full hookup site; 14 day limit; Melvern Lake CoE Project Office (913) 549-3414.

Camp Notes: Choice of campsites here is subjective at best, but you might want to check the C Loop (the one farthest from the entrance) first. The presence of the dam is relatively unobtrusive, once you get used to it. The entire campground is quite a showplace. *Very* impressive.

COEUR D' ALENE
Melvern Lake/Corps of Engineers Park

Location: East-central Kansas east of Emporia.

Access: From the junction of U.S. Highway 75 at milepost 119 +.1 and Kansas State Highway 31 (6 miles north of Interstate 35 Exit 155, 7 miles south of Lyndon, 3 miles west of Melvern), turn west onto the recreation area access road; proceed 0.2 mile, then turn south (left) and continue for 1.3 miles (past the administration office and the marina access road); turn west (right) onto the campground access road and proceed 0.6 mile to the campground entrance, then 0.1 mile farther to the campground.

Facilities: 60 campsites, half with electrical hookups; sites are small to medium-sized, with nominal to fairly good separation; parking pads are gravel, medium to long straight-ins which may require additional leveling; large, grassy tent spots, may be sloped; fire rings and barbecue grills at most sites; b-y-o firewood; water at central faucets; restrooms with showers; holding tank disposal station; paved driveways; limited supplies and services are available in Melvern and Lyndon.

Activities & Attractions: Fishing; boating; boat launch and marina nearby; designated swimming beach nearby; nice playground in day use area, 1 mile north.

Natural Features: Located on a grassy, tree-covered hillside on the south shore of Melvern Lake, a flood-control impoundment on the Marais de Cygnes River; vegetation consists of large hardwoods and evergreens that provide ample to very good shelter/shade in most sites; elevation 1100'.

Season, Fees & Phone: Open all year, with limited services October to May; $7.00 for a standard site, $9.00 for an electrical hookup site; 14 day limit; Melvern Lake CoE Project Office (913) 549-3414.

Camp Notes: The nearby big, beautiful, dee-lux campground at Outlet may very well be the camp spot of choice for most visitors. But Coeur d' Alene provides a good option for those who prefer a breezier, more remote environment.

ARROW ROCK
Melvern Lake/Corps of Engineers Park

Location: East-central Kansas east of Emporia.

Access: From U.S. Highway 75 at milepost 116 +.9 (4 miles north of Interstate 35 Exit 155, 9 miles south of Lyndon), turn west onto Kansas State Highway 276 and proceed 1.2 miles to the end of 276; turn north (right) onto a paved access road and continue for 0.8 mile; turn west (left) onto the campground access road for a final 0.6 mile to the campground.

Facilities: 45 campsites; sites are small to medium-sized, with minimal to fair separation; parking pads are gravel, mostly straight-ins, plus a few pull-throughs; additional leveling will be required in most sites; large, though somewhat sloped, grassy tent spots; fire rings in all sites, also barbecue grills in some; b-y-o firewood; water at central faucets; restrooms (H) with showers; holding tank disposal station; gravel/paved driveways; limited supplies and services are available in Melvern, 6 miles east, or in Lyndon.

Activities & Attractions: Boating; boat launch nearby; fishing; large playground; 12-mile long equestrian trail follows the lake shore from here west to Sundance recreation area.

Natural Features: Located on a grassy, tree-dotted, westward-facing slope overlooking a small bay on the south shore of Melvern Lake; most sites have at least a little shelter/shade, but are basically in the open; elevation 1100'.

Season, Fees & Phone: April to October; $7.00 for a standard site, $9.00 for an electrical hookup site; 14 day limit; Melvern Lake CoE Project Office (913) 549-3414.

Camp Notes: Although many campers might not consider this to be the "best" of the campgrounds on the lake, it has a couple of things going for it. A dozen or so nice sites are situated along the edge of the small bay a few feet above water level. And there are excellent views of the lake and its surroundings from atop the hill within a short walk of the campground.

SUNDANCE
Melvern Lake/Corps of Engineers Park

Location: East-central Kansas east of Emporia.

Access: From Interstate 35 Exit 148 for Lebo (18 miles east of Emporia, 35 miles southwest of Ottawa), turn north onto a paved road (a northerly extension of Kansas State Highway 131) and proceed 3.6 miles; turn east (right) and continue for 0.2 mile to the campground.

Facilities: 29 campsites; sites are small to medium-sized, with minimal to nominal visual separation; parking pads are medium-length, level, gravel straight-ins; large, grassy tent areas; tables in most sites; barbecue grills in many sites; b-y-o firewood; water at a central faucet; vault facilities; paved driveway; gas and snacks at the freeway; complete supplies and services are available in Emporia.

Activities & Attractions: Boating; boat launch; fishing; a 12-mile-long equestrian trail follows the shoreline from here east to Arrow Rock Campground.

Natural Features: Located on a very large, grassy, tree-dotted flat on the west edge of a cove on the south shore of Melvern Lake; the lake is the result of a major flood-control project on the Marais des Cygnes River (French for "Marsh of the Swans"); campground vegetation consists of expanses of grass and a few small hardwoods and pines; surrounded by wooded, grassy hills; elevation 1100'.

Season, Fees & Phone: Open all year, with limited services October to April; no fee (subject to change); 14 day limit; Melvern Lake CoE Project Office (913) 549-3414.

Camp Notes: It's quite possible to pull a boat right up to several of the campsites located along the shore of the cove. Even though the camp spots themselves aren't all that big, you'll normally not have much company, and therefore there'll still be plenty of elbow room. If you find yourself traveling the freeway and need a really handy place to pull into, and if you like the wide open spaces, check it out. For a freebie, it's a deal.

Kansas 56

DAM SITE
John Redmond Reservoir/Corps of Engineers Park

Location: Southeast Kansas Southeast of Emporia.

Access: From U.S. Highway 75 at milepost 101 (4.5 miles north of Burlington, 12 miles south of Interstate 35 Exit 155 east of Emporia), turn west onto a paved access road and proceed 1.3 miles; (note that the road curves to the southwest, i.e., left, at a point 0.3 mile from U.S. 75); turn west (right) into the recreation area; campsites are in several sections, left and right from the entrance.

Facilities: 16 campsites with electrical hookups, in 3 small sections; sites are medium-sized, with nominal separation; parking pads are basically level, medium to very long, gravel straight-ins; adequate space for a large tent in most sites; most sites have ramadas (small sun shelters) over table areas; fire rings and barbecue grills; b-y-o firewood; water at central faucets; restrooms with showers; holding tank disposal station; paved driveways; adequate supplies and services are available in Burlington.

Activities & Attractions: Boating; boat launch; fishing; deluxe playground; day use area; information center nearby.

Natural Features: Located at the east end of John Redmond Reservoir, an impoundment on the on the Neosho River; campground vegetation consists of mown lawns, junipers (cedars) and hardwoods; lake views from most sites; waterfowl and bobwhites are frequent visitors; elevation 1100'.

Season, Fees & Phone: Open all year, with limited services October to April; $7.00 for a standard site, $9.00 for an electrical hookup site; 14 day limit; John Redmond Reservoir CoE Project Office (316) 364-2311.

Camp Notes: This is the only full-featured campground in the area which has lake views. It was the victim of floods and has been rebuilt. Another small camping area with lake views is Otter Creek--with 8 sites, drinking water, and no fee--at the opposite end of the dam. But the campground described on this page is a Dam Site better than Otter Creek.

Kansas 57

RIVERSIDE: EAST
John Redmond Reservoir/Corps of Engineers Park

Location: Southeast Kansas southeast of Emporia.

Access: From U.S. Highway 75 at milepost 101 (4.5 miles north of Burlington, 12 miles south of Interstate 35 Exit 155 east of Emporia), turn west onto a paved access road and proceed 1.3 miles; (the road curves/forks to the southwest, i.e., left, at a point 0.3 mile from U.S. 75); turn south/east (left) onto a paved access road and continue for 0.3 mile, then turn left into the campground entrance.

Facilities: 53 campsites with electrical hookups, in a large loop and a small loop; sites are medium-sized, with nominal to very good separation; parking pads are gravel, basically level, medium to very long straight-ins; adequate space for a large tent in most sites; fire rings; b-y-o firewood; water at faucets throughout; vault facilities; restrooms with showers and holding tank disposal station nearby); mostly gravel driveways; adequate supplies and services are available in Burlington.

Activities & Attractions: Boating; boat launch with access to the reservoir, across the road at Dam Site; fishing.

Natural Features: Located on a short shelf above the east bank of the Neosho River at the east end of John Redmond Reservoir; most sites have a river view; campground vegetation consists of mown lawns and large hardwoods; elevation 1000'.

Season, Fees & Phone: April to October; $6.00 for an electrical hookup site; 14 day limit; John Redmond Reservoir CoE Project Office (316) 364-2311.

Camp Notes: Of the trio of campgrounds in this immediate area (also see info for Riverside West and Dam Site), Riverside East has the least to offer, not only in terms of facilities but also in terms of fees and usage. You can save several bucks a day on the fees if you don't require a hot shower and a flush within walking distance.

Kansas 58

RIVERSIDE: WEST
John Redmond Reservoir/Corps of Engineers Park

Location: Southeast Kansas southeast of Emporia.

Access: From U.S. Highway 75 at milepost 101 (4.5 miles north of Burlington, 12 miles south of Interstate 35 Exit 155 east of Emporia), turn west onto a paved access road and proceed 2.7 miles; (the road curves/forks to the southwest, i.e., left, at a point 0.3 mile from U.S. 75); at approximately the center of the dam, turn southeast (left) onto a paved access road for 0.1 mile, then turn left and continue 0.3 mile to the campground; sites are straight ahead and to the right.

Facilities: 34 campsites with electrical hookups; sites vary from medium to large, with fair to excellent separation; parking pads are gravel, mainly long, level, straight-ins, plus several super-long pull-throughs; enough space for a large tent in most units; fire rings; b-y-o firewood; water at several faucets; restrooms with showers; holding tank disposal station; paved driveways; adequate supplies and services are available in Burlington.

Activities & Attractions: Boating; boat launch for lake access nearby; fishing; playground.

Natural Features: Located on the west bank of the Neosho River at the east end of John Redmond Reservoir; a few units are in the open, but most sites are very well-sheltered/shaded by large hardwoods; elevation 1000'.

Season, Fees & Phone: April to October; $9.00 for an electrical hookup site; 14 day limit; John Redmond Reservoir CoE Project Office (316) 364-2311.

Camp Notes: While some sites here do have river views, many are tucked away in dense vegetation several yards from the water. In fact, many of the campsites here are very secluded and quite private. It becomes rather still and steamy during midsummer, but spring and fall should be excellent times in the almost rain forest-like surroundings. Subjectively, Riverside West is the nicest of the several campgrounds in the John Redmond Reservoir area.

Kansas 59

NORTH ROCK RIDGE COVE
Fall River Lake/Corps of Engineers Park

Location: Southeast Kansas east of Wichita.

Access: From Kansas State Highway 96 at milepost 361 +.9 (7 miles east of Severy, 27 miles northwest of Fredonia), turn north on the paved access road to Fall River State Park and proceed 1.7 miles to the park entrance; turn west (left) and continue for 0.45 mile on pavement to a fork; take the left fork (gravel) and follow this road first west, then north, then east around the cove for 2.2 miles to the campground.

Facilities: 44 campsites with electrical hookups; sites are medium to large, with nominal to fair separation; parking pads are level, gravel, medium to long straight-ins; large tent areas; barbecue grills and fire rings; limited amount of firewood may be available for gathering in the surrounding area, b-y-o is recommended; water at several faucets; vault facilities; holding tank disposal station; gravel driveways; gas and limited groceries are available on the main highway and in Severy.

Activities & Attractions: Boating; boat launch; fishing.

Natural Features: Located in the Flint Hills on the west shore of Fall River Lake on the north edge of Rock Ridge Cove; campground vegetation consists of grass, and hardwoods which provide moderate shelter/shade for most campsites; elevation 1000'.

Season, Fees & Phone: April to October; $5.00 for standard camping, $7.00 with a hookup; 14 day limit; phone c/o Fall River SP (316) 637-2291.

Camp Notes: This is a pleasant enough, though apparently not heavily used campground. There's another small camping/picnicking loop just before you enter the main campground, on the right side of the road. It has 5 fairly large sites, no water, and apparently no fee. North Rock Ridge Cove might be a good alternative to campers seeking a little more seclusion and more rustic surroundings than at nearby Fall River State Park.

FALL RIVER
Fall River State Park

Location: Southeast Kansas east of Wichita.

Access: From Kansas State Highway 96 at milepost 361 +.9 (7 miles east of Severy, 27 miles northwest of Fredonia), turn north onto the paved park access road and proceed 1.7 miles to the park entrance; continue straight ahead to the hookup loops ("trailer courts") or turn left or right to the standard camping areas.

Facilities: 44 partial hookup campsites in 2 loops, plus scores of standard camping sites; sites are generally small with little separation; parking pads are level, gravel, medium+ straight-ins; large, grassy areas for tents; barbecue grills; b-y-o firewood; water at sites and at several faucets; rest-room with showers, plus auxiliary vault facilities; holding tank disposal station; gravel loop driveways; gas and camper supplies on the main highway and in Severy; adequate supplies and services are available in Fredonia.

Activities & Attractions: Fishing for white bass, crappie, and other warm water species (usually best in early spring, just after the ice is out); boating; boat launches and docks.

Natural Features: Located along the south shore of Fall River Lake; most sites are sheltered/shaded by large hardwoods; the lake is completely ringed by trees; elevation 1000'.

Season, Fees & Phone: Open all year, with limited services November to April; please see Appendix for standard Kansas state park fees and reservation information; 14 day limit; park office (316) 637-2291.

Camp Notes: There are a lot of really excellent campsites in this area (which is often referred to as "South Shore"). If you don't have to have an electrical hookup, check out the camping/picnicking spots on the ridge at the east edge of South Shore--the views are terrific. There are also lots of nice tent sites at Quarry Bay on the southeast corner of the lake. Autumn is a super time to camp in this park.

TORONTO POINT
Toronto State Park

Location: Southeast Kansas east of Wichita.

Access: From U.S. Highway 54 at milepost 302 +.3 (12 miles west of Yates Center, 19 miles east of Eureka), turn south onto Kansas State Highway 105 and drive 3.2 miles (taking the designated grand tour through the hamlet of Toronto) to the intersection of Main Street and Point Road on the east edge of town; turn south onto Point Road and proceed 1.3 miles to the park entrance station; continue down the hill for 0.1 mile, then turn left to the "trailer court" or proceed straight ahead or to the right to the standard camping loops.

Facilities: 43 campsites, including 29 with electrical hookups, and 14 with full hookups, plus standard camping, in 3 areas; sites are generally small+, with little to fair separation; parking pads are gravel, basically level, medium to long straight-ins or pull-throughs; space for a tent in most units; barbecue grills and/or fire rings; some firewood may be available for gathering in the area, b-y-o is recommended; water at sites and at central faucets; restrooms with showers; holding tank disposal station; paved or gravel driveways; gas and groceries in Toronto.

Activities & Attractions: Boating; sailing; fishing; hiking trail.

Natural Features: Located on a wooded hill on the north shore of Toronto Lake; full hookup units are less shaded/sheltered than the other spaces; most standard sites are in a grove of oak trees; elevation 1000'.

Season, Fees & Phone: Open all year, with limited services mid-October to April; please see Appendix for standard Kansas state park fees and reservation information; 14 day limit; phone c/o Fall River SP (316) 637-2291.

Camp Notes: Most spots have views of the lake through the trees. There are a few nice campsites near the tip of the point. Standard camping is also available at Manns Cove and Holiday Hill, on the east and south sides of the lake.

CRAWFORD
Crawford State Park

Location: Southeast corner of Kansas northwest of Pittsburg.

Access: From Kansas State Highway 7 at milepost 45 + .4 (9 miles north of Girard, 18 miles southwest of Fort Scott), turn east onto a paved access road and proceed 1 mile to the park entrance; continue straight, then left, across the dam, for 0.5 mile to the hookup area and the standard camping areas just beyond.

Facilities: 30 campsites with electrical hookups, plus numerous standard sites; hookup units are generally small and closely spaced; standard sites vary; most parking pads are level, short to medium-length, wide, gravel or grass straight-ins; very large, grassy tent areas; barbecue grills; b-y-o firewood; water at central faucets; restrooms with showers; holding tank disposal station near the park entrance; paved driveways; camper supplies at the marina; limited to adequate supplies and services are available in Girard.

Activities & Attractions: Fishing; limited boating; boat launch; marina; small swimming beach, bathhouse; playground.

Natural Features: Located along the east shore of Lake Crawford; campground vegetation consists of expansive grassy areas, and large hardwoods that provide good to excellent shelter/shade for most campsites; many of the better sites are along or near the edge of a long, narrow bay; woodlands and fields encircle the lake; elevation 900'.

Season, Fees & Phone: Mid-April to mid-October; please see Appendix for standard Kansas state park fees and reservation information; 14 day limit; park office (316) 362-3671.

Camp Notes: Park literature bills this spot as "a tiny piece of the Ozarks". Could be. Crawford is one of the smaller lakes associated with the state park system, and it is one of the prettier ones. The shoreline is unexplainably different from the shores of the big lakes. Simple and nice.

ELK CITY
Elk City State Park

Location: Southeast Kansas west of Independence.

Access: From U.S. Highways 160/75 at a point 3 miles west of Independence and 12 miles southeast of Elk City (at milepost 21 for Highway 75), turn north onto County Road 3325 (paved) and proceed 1.4 miles to a "T" intersection; turn west (left) onto County Road 4600 (paved) for 0.3 mile; turn right and follow this paved road around the west side of a dike for 1.4 miles; turn west (left) into the park entrance at Squaw Creek; at the "Y", turn left or right to the camping areas.

Facilities: 52 electrical hookup campsites, plus dozens of standard sites, in 3 areas; sites are smallish and closely spaced; parking pads are gravel, fairly level, straight-ins or pull-throughs; adequate space for a large tent in most sites; fire rings; b-y-o firewood; water at many hookup sites and at central faucets; restrooms with showers; holding tank disposal station; gravel loop driveways, paved roadways; virtually complete supplies and services are available in Independence.

Activities & Attractions: Boating; large boat launch; fishing; rock jetties; swimming beach; Table Mound hiking trail; Green Thumb nature trail.

Natural Features: Located on the gently sloping east shore of Elk City Lake; standard sites are well sheltered/shaded by large hardwoods; most hookup units are unsheltered to moderately sheltered; acres and acres of grass and woods surround the camping areas; elevation 900'.

Season, Fees & Phone: Open all year, with limited services mid-October to April; please see Appendix for standard Kansas state park fees and reservation information; 14 day limit; park office (316) 331-6295.

Camp Notes: Camping is also available at Corps of Engineers areas just north of Squaw Creek at Outlet Channel; and at Oak Ridge, 7 miles from here, on the west side of the lake.

TIMBER HILL
Big Hill Lake/Corps of Engineers Park

Location: Southeast Kansas east of Independence.

Access: From U.S. Highways 160/169 in midtown Cherryvale, drive east on Main Street to Olive Avenue, then south on Olive for 0.1 mile to County Road 5000; turn east (left) onto Road 5000 (paved) and proceed 1 mile to a "T" intersection; jog left across the railroad track, then immediately right, and continue east on a gravel road for 5 miles (past the Cherryvale and Mound Valley areas) to a gravel road; turn north (left) and proceed 2.3 miles; turn west (left) onto a gravel road and continue for 1.4 miles (after 1.2 miles the road is paved) to the campground.

Facilities: 20 campsites; sites are medium-sized, with nominal to very good separation; parking pads are paved, medium to long straight-ins, and some may require additional leveling; medium-sized tent areas, some leveled and framed; barbecue grills and fire rings; a limited amount of firewood is available for gathering in the area, b-y-o is suggested; water at several faucets; vault facilities; holding tank disposal station; paved driveways; limited supplies and services are available in Cherryvale.

Activities & Attractions: Fishing for crappie, walleye, largemouth and smallmouth bass; boating; paved boat launch; swimming beach near the Mound Valley area.

Natural Features: Located on a timbered hill on the east shore of Big Hill Lake; vegetation consists of varieties of oak and other hardwoods which provide good to excellent shelter/shade for most sites; the area is surrounded by low, heavily wooded hills; elevation 900'.

Season, Fees & Phone: April to October; no fee (subject to change); 14 day limit; Big Hill Lake CoE Project Office (316) 336-2741.

Camp Notes: They've got to be kidding. No place this nice is *free*. The lake views from here may not be the best, but the overall environment is really nice. Here's hoping that this pleasant spot continues to be one of the best bargains in Kansas camping.

MOUND VALLEY
Big Hill Lake/Corps of Engineers Park

Location: Southeast Kansas east of Independence.

Access: From U.S. Highways 160 & 169 in midtown Cherryvale, drive east on Main Street to Olive Avenue, then south on Olive for 0.1 mile to County Road 5000; turn east (left) onto Road 5000 (paved) and proceed 1 mile to a "T" intersection; jog left across the railroad track, then immediately right, and continue east on a gravel road for 3.6 miles (beyond the dam); turn north (left) onto a paved access road and proceed 0.1 mile to sites 1-8, or continue for another 0.5 mile to the remaining sites.

Facilities: 78 campsites, including many with electrical hookups, in 4 loops, plus a group area; sites are medium to large, with fair to excellent separation; most parking pads are paved, medium to long, straight-ins or pull-throughs; some pads may require additional leveling; medium-sized tent areas, some leveled and framed, others slightly sloped; many table areas are on concrete or leveled earth pads; barbecue grills and fire rings; a limited amount of firewood is available for gathering in the area, b-y-o is suggested; water at faucets throughout; restrooms with showers; holding tank disposal station; paved driveways; limited supplies and services are available in Cherryvale.

Activities & Attractions: Fishing for crappie, walleye, largemouth and smallmouth bass; boating; paved boat launch; swimming beach (with imported sand) nearby; short trail.

Natural Features: Located on a timbered hillside on the east shore of Big Hill Lake; vegetation consists of expansive areas of mown grass, and large hardwoods which provide excellent shelter/shade for most sites; elevation 900'.

Season, Fees & Phone: April to November; $5.00 for a standard site, $9.00 for an electrical hookup site; 14 day limit; Big Hill Lake CoE Project Office (316) 336-2741.

Camp Notes: Some of the campsites here are *huge*, with block-long parking pads to match. Good for tents, but great for rv's. Very attractive campground.

CHERRYVALE
Big Hill Lake/Corps of Engineers Park

Location: Southeast Kansas east of Independence.

Access: From U.S. Highways 160/169 in midtown Cherryvale, drive east on Main Street to Olive Avenue, then south on Olive for 0.1 mile to County Road 5000; turn east (left) onto Road 5000 (paved) and proceed 1 mile to a "T" intersection; jog left across the railroad track, then immediately right, and continue east on a gravel road for 2.6 miles; turn north (left) onto a paved access road and proceed 0.8 mile; turn east (right) into the campground.

Facilities: 30 campsites with electrical hookups, in 2 sections; sites are medium to large, with fair to excellent separation; most parking pads are paved, medium to long, straight-ins or pull-throughs; some pads may require a little additional leveling; medium-sized tent areas; barbecue grills and fire rings; a limited amount of firewood is available for gathering in the area, b-y-o is suggested; water at faucets throughout; restrooms with showers; holding tank disposal station; paved driveways; limited supplies and services are available in Cherryvale.

Activities & Attractions: Fishing for crappie, walleye, largemouth and smallmouth bass; boating; paved boat launch, swimming beach near the Mound Valley area; playground; softball field adjacent.

Natural Features: Located on a wooded bluff on the west shore of Big Hill Lake; vegetation consists of areas of mown grass, and large hardwoods which provide good to excellent shelter/shade for most sites; elevation 900'.

Season, Fees & Phone: Available all year, with limited services November to April; $9.00 for an electrical hookup site; 14 day limit; Big Hill Lake CoE Project Office (316) 336-2741.

Camp Notes: Big Hill Lake, with it's three very nice camping areas--Cherryvale, Mound Valley, and Timber Hill--wins the "Best Use of the Natural Environment" award for Kansas. Definitely recommended.

Jackcamping and Backpacking
in the West's Parks and Forests

In addition to camping in established campgrounds, as do the majority of visitors, thousands of campers opt for simpler places to spend a night or a week or more in the West's magnificent parks and forests.

Jackcamping

"Jackcamping", "roadsiding", "dispersed camping", or "siwashing" are several of the assorted terms describing the simplest type of camp there is: just pulling a vehicle a few yards off the main drag, or heading up a gravel or dirt forest road to an out-of-the-way spot which looks good to you. Sometimes, especially when the "Campground Full" plank is hung out to dry in front of all the nearby public campgrounds, or there *aren't* any nearby public campgrounds, it might be the only way to travel.

From what we can determine "jackcamping" is an extension of the Medieval English slang word "jacke", meaning "common", "serviceable" or "ordinary". The explanations of "roadsiding" and "dispersed camping" are self-evident. "Siwashing" is an old term from the Southwest. It apparently refers to the practice of cowboys and other travelers making a late camp by just hunkering-down in an *arroyo* or 'dry wash'. After hobbling your horse, the saddle is propped-up against the *side* of the *wash*, (hence *si'wash* or *siwash*), forming a leather 'recliner' of sorts in which to pass the night out of the wind and cold. It may not be the most comfortable way to spend the night, but by two or three a.m. you get used to the smell of the saddle anyway.

As a general rule-of-thumb, jackcamping isn't allowed in local, state and national parks. In those areas, you'll have to stay in established campgrounds or sign-up for a backcountry site.

However, jackcamping is *usually* permitted anywhere on the millions of road-accessible acres of national forest and BLM-managed federal public lands, subject to a few exceptions. In some high-traffic areas it's not allowed, and roadside signs are *usually* posted telling you so. ("Camp Only in Designated Campgrounds" signs are becoming more common with each passing year.) In certain high fire risk zones or during the general fire season it may not be permitted. For the majority of areas in which jackcamping is legal, small campfires, suitably sized and contained, are ordinarily OK. All of the rules of good manners, trash-removal, and hygiene which apply to camping anywhere, regardless of location, are enforced. (Would *you* want to camp where someone else had left their "sign"?) For off-highway travel, the "Shovel, Axe and Bucket" rule is usually in effect (see below).

Since you don't want the law coming down on you for an unintentional impropriety, it's highly advisable to stop in or call a local Forest Service ranger station or BLM office to determine the status of jackcamping in your region of choice, plus any special requirements (spark arrestors, the length of the shovel needed under the "Shovel, Axe and Bucket" rule, campfires, stay limit, etc.) Local ranchers who have leased grazing rights on federal lands are sensitive about their livestock sharing the meadows and rangelands with campers. So it's probably best to jackcamp in "open" areas, thus avoiding leaseholder vs taxpayer rights confrontations altogether. (Legalities notwithstanding, the barrel of a 12-gauge or an '06 looks especially awesome when it's poked inside your tent at midnight.) Be sure to get the name of the individual in the local public office who provided the information "just in case".

If you're reasonably self-sufficient or self-contained, jackcamping can save you *beaucoups* bucks--perhaps hundreds of dollars--over a lifetime of camping. (We know.)

Backpacking

Take all of the open acres readily available to jackcampers, then multiply that figure by a factor of 100,000 (or thereabouts) and you'll have some idea of the wilderness and near-wilderness camping opportunities that are only accessible to backpackers (or horsepackers).

Backpackers usually invest a lot of time, and usually a lot of money, into their preferred camping method, and perhaps rightfully so (timewise, anyway).

Planning an overnight or week-long foot trip into the boondocks is half the work (and half the fun too!). Hours, days, even *weeks*, can be spent pouring over highway maps, topographic maps, public lands/BLM maps, and forest maps looking for likely places to pack into. (We know!)

Backpacking in Western National Forests

To be editorially above-board about this: Of all the possible federal and state recreation areas, your best opportunities for backpack camping are in the national forest wilderness, primitive, and wild areas. Prime backpacking areas in most state parks and many national park units are measured in acres or perhaps square miles; but the back country in the national forests is measured in tens and hundreds and thousands of square miles. Here's where planning really becomes fun.

Backpacking in Western National and State Parks

Finding a backpack campsite in the West's *parks* is relatively straightforward: much of the work has been done for you by the park people. Many state and national parks which are large enough to provide opportunities for backcountry travel have established backcountry camps which are the *only* places to camp out in the toolies. Yes, that indeed restricts your overnight choices to a few small areas in many cases; but you can still enjoy walking through and looking at the rest of the back country.

Throughout this series, designated backpack campsites and other backpacking opportunities are occasionally mentioned in conjunction with nearby established campgrounds.

Backpacking in Northern Plains National Forests

Several thousand acres of beautiful national forest backcountry can be explored in the Northern Plains. They are found primarily in Black Hills National Forest in South Dakota, and in Nebraska National Forest and Samuel McKelvie National Forest in the Sandhills of Nebraska.

Backpacking in Northern Plains National Parks

Backpacking in the badlands of *Theodore Roosevelt* National Park can be a very satisfying adventure, even for 'mountain goats' who are used to the higher, more-vertical landscapes west of here. Hike-in or horse-in camps are available in both the North Unit and the South Unit of the park. In South Dakota, *Badlands National Park* and *Wind Cave National Park* both offer a limited number of hike-in backcountry camps. A permit is mandatory for backcountry camping in all the foregoing areas. (Neither Nebraska nor Kansas have national park areas with camping opportunities.)

Backcountry reservation information and other 'regs' are highly subject to change. We therefore suggest that you use the *Phone* information in the text to contact your selected park's headquarters and ask for the "backcountry office" or "backcountry ranger" to initialize your trip planning. In virtually every case, they'll be able to provide detailed information and maps--at no charge, or at most a couple of bucks for first-rate maps. The majority of the backcountry people are enthusiastic boondockers themselves, and they'll generally provide sound, albeit conservative, suggestions. Let's face it: they don't want to have to bail anybody out of a tough spot by extracting them on foot, in a dusty green government-issue jeep, a helicopter--or by what they call at Grand Canyon an "emergency mule drag-out". (Try living *that one* down when you get home, dude!)

At the risk of demagoguery: We can vouch that it really pays to start planning months in advance for a backcountry trip. Besides, planning *is* half the fun.

SPECIAL SECTION:

Creative Camping

In their most elementary forms, outdoor recreation in general, and camping in particular, require very little in the way of extensive planning or highly specialized and sophisticated equipment. A stout knife, some matches, a few blankets, a free road map, a water jug, and a big sack of p.b. & j. sandwiches, all tossed onto the seat of an old beater pickup, will get you started on the way to a lifetime of outdoor adventures.

Idyllic and nostalgic as that scenario may seem, most of the individuals reading this *Double Eagle*™ Guide (and those *writing* it) probably desire (and deserve) at least a few granules of comfort sprinkled over their tent or around their rv.

There are enough books already on the market or in libraries which will provide you with plenty of advice on *how* to camp. One of the oldest and best is the *Fieldbook*, published by the Boy Scouts of America.

Really. It is a widely accepted, profusely illustrated (not to mention comparatively inexpensive) outdoor reference which has few true rivals. It presents plenty of information on setting up camp, first aid, safety, woodlore, flora and fauna identification, weather, and a host of other items. Although recreational vehicle camping isn't specifically covered in detail, many of the general camping principles it does cover apply equally well to rv's.

So rather than re-invent the wheel, we've concentrated your hard-earned *dinero* into finding out *where* to camp. However, there are still a few items that aren't widely known which might be of interest to you, or which bear repeating, so we've included them in the following paragraphs.

Resourcefulness. When putting together your equipment, it's both challenging and a lot of fun to make the ordinary stuff you have around the house, especially in the kitchen, do double duty. Offer an "early retirement" to servicable utensils, pans, plastic cups, etc. to a "gear box".

Resource-fullness. Empty plastic peanut butter jars, pancake syrup and milk jugs, ketchup bottles, also aluminum pie plates and styrofoam trays, can be washed, re-labeled and used again. (The syrup jugs, with their handles and pop-up spouts, make terrific "canteens" for kids.) The lightweight, break-resistant plastic stuff is more practical on a camping trip than glass containers, anyway. *El Cheapo* plastic shopping bags, which have become *de rigueur* in supermarkets, can be saved and re-used to hold travel litter and campground trash. When they're full, tie them tightly closed using the "handles". In the words of a college-age camper from Holland while he was refilling a plastic, two-liter soft drink bottle at the single water faucet in a desert national park campground: "Why waste?".

(Re-labeling tip: After soaking-off a paper label in hot water, there's often an unsightly, sticky adhesive residue on the outside of the container. Use a 'general purpose adhesive cleaner', available from automotive paint outlets, and a paper towel to quickly wipe-off the old glue. A pint of cleaner will last many years. Make a new label with self-adhesive, plastic embossing tape and a label maker, available for a couple of bucks at discount stores. A wide strip of tough, clear plastic book-mending tape over the new plastic label will help ensure that it stays put.)

Redundancy. Whether you're camping in a tent, pickup, van, boat, motorhome or fifth-wheel trailer, it pays to think and plan like a backpacker. Can you make-do with fewer changes of clothes for a short weekend trip? How about getting-by with half as much diet cola, and drink more cool, campground spring water instead? Do you really *need* that third curling iron? Real backpackers (like the guy who trimmed the margins off his maps) are relentless in their quest for the light load.

Water. No matter where you travel, *always* carry a couple of gallons of drinking water. Campground water sources may be out of order (e.g., someone broke the handle off the hydrant or the well went dry), and you probably won't want to fool around with boiling lake or stream water. (Because of the possibility of encountering the widespread "beaver fever" (*Giardia*) parasite and other diseases in lakes and streams, if treated or tested H_2O isn't available, boil the surface water for a full five minutes.)

Juice. If you're a tent or small vehicle camper who normally doesn't need electrical hookups, carry a hotplate, coffee pot, or hair dryer when traveling in regions where hookup campsites are available. The trend in public campground management is toward charging the full rate for a hookup site whether or not you have an rv, even though there are no standard sites available for you to occupy. In many popular state parks and Corps of Engineers recreation areas, hookup sites far outnumber standard sites. At least you'll have some use for the juice.

Fire. Charcoal lighter fluid makes a good "starter" for campfires, and is especially handy if the wood is damp. In a pinch, that spare bottle of motor oil in the trunk can be pressed into service for the same purpose. Let two ounces soak in for several minutes. Practice the same safety precautions you would use in lighting a home barbecue so you can keep your curly locks and eyebrows from being scorched by the flames. Obviously use extreme caution--and don't even *think* about using gasoline. A really handy option to using wood is to carry a couple of synthetic "fire logs". The sawdust-and-paraffin logs are made from byproducts of the lumber and petroleum industries and burn about three hours in the outdoors. The fire logs can also be used to start and maintain a regular campfire if the locally gathered firewood is wet.

Styrofoam. This flimsy synthetic may not be environmentally acceptable, but it's a fact of modern life. After you stop for a fuel-up and a rest break along the highway, save the foam cups which contained your coffee, cocoa or soft drinks; then rinse them out at the next stop or when you arrive in camp. The cups can be used again for drinks, collecting specimens for nature study, or to hold nightcrawlers gathered from under a log for fishing bait. Cups weighted with a few stones occasionally can be seen holding a small collection of wildflowers and left on the picnic table as a centerpiece for the next campers.

Mosquitoes. The winged demons aren't usually mentioned in the text because you just have to *expect* them almost anywhere except perhaps in the dryest desert areas. Soggy times, like late spring and early summer, are the worst times. If you're one of us who's always the first to be strafed by the local mosquito squadron, keep plenty of anti-aircraft ammo on hand. The most versatile skin stuff is the spray-on variety. Spray it all over your clothes to keep the varmints from poking their proboscis through the seat of your jeans. A room spray comes in handy for blasting any bugs which might have infiltrated your tent or rv. Fortunately, in most areas the peak of the mosquito season lasts only a couple of weeks, and you can enjoy yourself the rest of the time. Autumn camping is great!

Plants. Poison ivy, oak and sumac can be found in many wooded regions throughout the West. Avoid off-trail brush-busting or brushing up against trailside vegetation with bare skin. Oleander, those beautifully flowering bushes planted in campgrounds all over the Western Sunbelt are toxic, so keep your pets and your kids from nibbling on them. Likewise, in the desert regions, steer plenty clear of cholla cactus. The Indians call it the "jumping cactus" with good reason.

Rattlers. Anywhere you go in the Desert Southwest, expect to find rattlesnakes, so place your hands and feet and other vital parts accordingly. (While preparing the *Double Eagle*™ series, one of the publishers inadvertently poked her zoom lens to within a yard of a coiled rattler's snout. The photographer's anxieties were vocally, albeit shakily, expressed; the level of stress which the incident induced on the snake is unknown.)

Creepy-crawlers. In arid Desert Southwest regions, watch for scorpions and other ground-based critters. In the Southwest Plains, tarantulas make their appearances in spring and fall, but the fuzzy arachnids will leave you alone if you reciprocate.

Bumps in the night. When you retire for the night, put all your valuables, especially your cooler, inside your vehicle to protect them against campground burglars and bruins. While camping at Canyon Campground in Yellowstone National Park more than two decades ago, a pair of young brothers unwittingly left their stocked cooler out on the picnic table so they had more room to sleep inside their ancient station wagon. Sometime after midnight, they were awakened by a clatter in the darkness behind the wagon. After they had groggily dressed and crept out to investigate, the sleepy siblings discovered that a bear had broken into their impenetrable ice chest. Taking inventory, the dauntless duo determined that the brazen backwoods *bandito* had wolfed-down three pounds of baked chicken breasts, a meatloaf, one pound of pineapple cottage cheese, four quarters of margarine, and had chomped through two cans of *Coors*--presumably to wash it all down. The soft drinks were untouched. (We dined sumptuously on Spam and pork 'n beans for the rest of the trip. Ed.)

Timing. Try staying an hour ahead of everyone else. While traveling in Pacific Time, set your clock to Mountain Time; when in the mountains, keep your timepiece ticking on Central Time. That way you'll naturally set up camp an hour earlier, and likewise break camp an hour prior to other travelers. You would be amazed at how much that 60 minutes will do for campsite availability in the late afternoon, or for restrooms, showers, uncrowded roads and sightseeing in the morning.

Horsepower. Your camping vehicle will lose about four percent of its power for each 1000' gain in altitude above sea level (unless it's turbocharged). Keep that in mind in relation to the "pack like a backpacker" item mentioned previously. You might also keep it in mind when you embark on a foot trip. The factory-original human machine loses about the same amount of efficiency at higher elevations.

Air. To estimate the temperature at a campground in the mountains while you're still down in the valley or on the plains, subtract about three degrees Fahrenheit for each 1000' difference in elevation between the valley and the campground. Use the same method to estimate nighttime lows in the mountains by using weather forecasts for valley cities.

Reptile repellant. Here's a sensitive subject. With the rise in crimes perpetrated against travelers and campers in the nation's parks and forests and on its highways and byways, it's become increasingly common for legitimate campers to pack a 'heater'--the type that's measured by caliber or gauge, not in volts and amps. To quote a respected Wyoming peace officer: "Half the pickups and campers in Wyoming and Montana have a .45 automatic under the seat or a 12-gauge pump behind the bunk". If personal safety is a concern to you, check all applicable laws, get competent instruction, practice a lot, and join the NRA.

Vaporhavens. Be skeptical when you scan highway and forest maps and see hundreds of little symbols which indicate the locations of alleged campsites; or when you glance through listings published by governmental agencies or promotional interests. A high percentage of those 'recreation areas' are as vaporous as the mist rising from a warm lake into chilled autumn air. Many, many of the listed spots are actually picnic areas, fishing access sites, and even highway rest stops; dozens of camps are ill-maintained remnants of their former greatness, located at the end of rocky jeep trails; many others no longer exist; still others *never* existed, but are merely a mapmaker's or planner's notion of where a campground *might* or *should* be. In summation: Make certain that a campground exists and what it offers before you embark on 20 miles of washboard gravel travel in the never-ending quest for your own personal Eden.

We hope the foregoing items, and information throughout this series, help you conserve your own valuable time, money, fuel and other irreplaceable resources. ***Good Camping !***

Appendix

State Maps

NORTHERN PLAINS STANDARD STATE PARK FEES

North Dakota

Primitive campsite	$5.00
Standard/developed campsite	$10.00
Electrical hookup campsite	$13.00
Daily park entry fee for most parks, per vehicle	$3.00

South Dakota

Basic campsite (drinking water, vaults)	$5.00
Semi-modern campsite (drinking water, restrooms)	$6.00
Modern campsite (drinking water, restrooms, showers)	$7.00
For Custer State Park campsites add $2.00-$3.00 to the above fees	
Add to the above campsite fees for Electrical hookup	$3.00
Daily park entry fee, most parks per person	$2.00
Daily park entry fee, Custer State Park per person or	$3.00
per vehicle	$8.00

Nebraska

Primitive campsite (Included with park entry fee)	No charge
Standard/developed campsite	$5.00-$7.00
Electrical hookup campsite	$8.00-$10.00
Daily park entry fee for most parks, per vehicle	$3.00

(Fees continued on the next page)

Standard State Park Fees (continued)

Kansas

Standard campsite	$3.00
Electrical hookup campsite	$5.00
Daily park entry fee for most parks, per vehicle	$3.00

A Rent-a-Camp program is available in several of the more popular Kansas state parks, including Cheney, Clinton, El Dorado, Pomona, Prairie Dog, Tuttle Creek, and Wilson. You get a basic equipment package consisting of a large tent, stove and fuel, cooler, four cots, etc. The $15.00 fee includes a campsite reservation. Park entry and regular campsites fees are additional.

Note: Annual park entry permits, offering substantial savings for frequent park users, are available in all states.

Please remember that all fees are subject to change without notice.

NORTHERN PLAINS CAMPSITE RESERVATIONS

Northern Plains State Parks

North Dakota

Campsite reservations may be made for several state park campgrounds in North Dakota. Reservation procedures are subject to change, so a telephone call to the state park department office will get you started with the latest information. (As a guideline, reservations must be obtained in person or by telephone directly from the individual park at least several days in advance. A reservation fee of $5.00 is charged.)

North Dakota State Parks and Recreation Department
1835 Bismarck Expressway
Bismarck, ND 58504
(800) 807-4723
(701) 221-5358

South Dakota

A reservation system has been implemented for approximately 30 selected state parks and recreation areas in South Dakota. Reservations may be made in person, by mail, or by telephone with a district office at least three days in advance. A reservation fee of $6.00 is charged. It is suggested that you contact the following office for a brochure detailing current reservation information.

South Dakota Department of Game, Fish & Parks
Parks & Recreation Division
Foss Building
523 East Capitol
Pierre, SD 57501-3182
(605) 773-3391

Nebraska

Reservations for up to a year in advance are accepted for designated campsites in Eugene T. Mahoney State Park. A $3.00 reservation fee is charged in addition to the regular entry and campsite fee. Most other campsites throughout the Nebraska state parks system are available only on a first-come, first-filled basis (subject to change).

The following office may also be helpful:

Nebraska Game & Parks Commission
2200 N. 33rd St.P.O. Box 30370
Lincoln NE 68503
(402) 471-0641

(Reservations, continued on the next page)

Campsite Reservations (continued)

Kansas

Campsites may be reserved in most Kansas state parks by directly contacting the selected state park. A reservation fee of $5.00 is charged for an individual campsite; a $10.00 fee is charged for a group campsite.

For more information, contact:

Kansas Department of Wildlife and Parks
State Office Building
900 Jackson St. Suite 502
Topeka KS 66612

(913) 296-2281 (phone)
(913) 296-6953 (fax)

Northern Plains
National Forests and National Parks

The *USDA Forest Service* and the *National Park Service* have also established reservation systems which affect hundreds of national forest campgrounds and certain national park areas nationwide. At present, national forest and national park campgrounds in the Northern Plains are not included in the reservation systems. However, continuous changes can be expected as campgrounds with reservable sites are added or removed from the lists. For additional information about campgrounds with reservable sites you may call (toll-free) the independent agents handling the reservation systems. (A touch-tone phone will speed the info/rez procedure):

For *national forest* campgrounds:

800-280-CAMP   (800-280-2267)

For *national park* campgrounds:

800-365-CAMP   (800-365-2267)

Reservations for certain other campgrounds in the Northern Plains *may* be obtainable directly from the public agency responsible for the camping area, as indicated in the text.

(Reservations are not available for any of the many campgrounds operated by the U.S. Army Corps of Engineers.)

For additional information about campsite reservations, availability, current conditions, or regulations about the use of campgrounds, we suggest that you directly contact the park office in charge of your selected campground, using the *Phone* information in the text.

Please remember that all reservation information is subject to change without notice.

INDEX

Important Note:

In the following listing, the number to the right of the campground name refers to the Key Number in the upper left corner of each campground description in the text.
(The number does *not* indicate the page number; page numbers are printed in the text as secondary reference sources only.)

* A thumbnail description of a campground marked with an asterisk is found in the *Camp Notes* section of the principal numbered campground.

NORTH DAKOTA

SOUTH DAKOTA

NEBRASKA

KANSAS

Time-and-money-saving *Double Eagle*™ Guides!:

The Double Eagle Guide to
WESTERN STATE PARKS

__Volume I Pacific Northwest   ISBN 0-929760-11-5
           Washington∗Oregon∗Idaho $11.95
           (Soft cover 6x9)

__Volume II Rocky Mountains   ISBN 0-929760-12-3
            Colorado∗Montana∗Wyoming $10.95
            (Soft cover 6x9)

__Volume III Far West   ISBN 0-929760-13-1
            California∗Nevada $12.95
            (Soft cover 6x9)

__Volume IV Desert Southwest   ISBN 0-929760-14-X
           Arizona∗New Mexico∗Utah $9.95
           (Soft cover 6x9)

__Volume V Northern Plains   ISBN 0-929760-15-8
           Kansas∗Nebraska∗North & South Dakota $16.95
           (Hard cover 8 1/2x11)

__Volume VI Southwest Plains   ISBN 0-929760-16-6
           Texas∗Oklahoma $17.95
           (Hard cover 8 1/2x11)

Available from:

Discovery Publishing

P.O. Box 50545   Billings, MT 59105   Phone 1-406-245-8292

Please add $2.75 for shipping the first volume, and $1.25 for each additional volume. Same-day shipping for most orders.

Please include your check/money order, or complete the VISA/MasterCard information in the indicated space below.

Name_____

Address_____

City_____ State_____ Zip_____

For credit card orders:

VISA/MC #_____ Exp.Date_____

Prices, shipping charges, and specifications subject to change.

Thank You Very Much For Your Order!

(A photocopy or other reproduction may be substituted for this original form.)

Other volumes in the *Camping* series:

The Double Eagle Guide to
CAMPING *in* WESTERN PARKS *and* FORESTS

__Volume I   Pacific Northwest   ISBN 0-929760-27-1
           Washington*Oregon*Idaho   Hardcover 8 1/2x11 $18.95^
           (Also in paper cover 6x9 (C) 1992 $12.95)

__Volume II   Rocky Mountains   ISBN 0-929760-22-0
            Colorado*Montana*Wyoming Hardcover 8 1/2x11 $17.95^

__Volume III Far West   ISBN 0-929760-23-9
            California*Nevada   Hardcover 8 1/2x11 $18.95^

__Volume IV Desert Southwest   ISBN 0-929760-29-8
           Arizona*New Mexico*Utah Hardcover 8 1/2x11 , $17.95^
           (Also in paper cover 6x9 (C) 1992 $12.95)

__Volume V   Northern Plains   ISBN 0-929760-25-5
           The Dakotas*Nebraska*Kansas Hardcover 8 1/2x11 $16.95^

__Volume VI Southwest Plains   ISBN 0-929760-26-3
           Texas*Oklahoma   Hard cover 8 1/2x11) $17.95^

^^^ Softcover, spiral-bound editions are also available. Recommended for light-duty, personal use only.
    Subtract $3.00 from standard hardcover price and specify "Special binding" when ordering.

Available exclusively from: *Double Eagle* camping guides are regularly updated.
Discovery Publishing
P.O. Box 50545   Billings, MT 59105   Phone 1-406-245-8292

Please add $3.00 for shipping the first volume, and $1.50 for each additional volume.
Same-day shipping for most orders.

Please include your check/money order, or complete the VISA/MasterCard
information in the indicated space below.

Name_____

Address_____

City_____ State_____ Zip_____
For credit card orders:

VISA/MC #_____ Exp.Date_____

Prices, shipping charges, and specifications subject to change.

Thank You Very Much For Your Order!

(A photocopy or other reproduction may be substituted for this original form.)